1977-78 EDITION OF

Arthur Frommer's Guide To

LOS ANGELES

by
STANLEY HAGGART
DARWIN PORTER
RENA BULKIN

Published by
THE FROMMER/PASMANTIER PUBLISHING CORPORATION
380 Madison Avenue
New York, New York 10017

Distributed by
SIMON AND SCHUSTER
A GULF+WESTERN COMPANY
1230 Avenue of the Americas
New York, New York 10020
671-22733-5

Distributed outside the U.S. and Canada by
FLEETBOOKS
c/o Feffer and Simons, Inc.
100 Park Avenue
New York, New York 10017

Distributed in Canada by
P J PAPERBACKS LTD.
330 Steelcase Road East
Markham, Ontario L3R2M1

Motif drawings by Erv Chips

NOTE: Although every effort was made to insure the accuracy of price information appearing in this book, it should be kept in mind that prices can and do fluctuate in the course of time.

CONTENTS

MAPS

Chapter I

LOS ANGELES

ONE VISITOR, and it could only have been an Easterner, wrote that the expression—"flying to the coast"—was the most romantic phrase in our language.

Unless you are actually from the "The Coast," Los Angeles remains the "Getaway" incarnate—a fantasyland of dreams and ambition, a sunny pleasure ground of movie and TV studios and Disneyland extravaganzas, a place where inhibitions are released and imagination given full rein—an entranceway to the real-life magic of Southern California.

Within the last few years, a new image of Los Angeles has emerged. One newspaper headlined this turn of events as "Lotus-land Is Changing." Up to now, Los Angeles has been the proto-type of the 20th-century supermetropolis.

But the phenomenal growth that characterized the city in the post-war era may have peaked. Although Southern California still symbolizes a "land of milk and honey" to millions, the time when a thousand or so people moved in every day of the week is over. Now they come to visit—some for the Promised-Land-like pleasures of sun and sea, some to verify the ever-changing images Los Angeles brings to mind, and some to ogle the so-called oddities.

One local politician said, "Back East, people think of us as running around dressed in chartreuse sequins and walking rasp-berry-dyed poodles. But," he added "we're just average, hard-working folks like everybody else."

That comment has much truth. Los Angeles is now more than ever in the mainstream of American life—not some zany, kooky, Western outpost espousing sexual freedom and fanatical causes. But the land has always been a haven for the eccentric and the offbeat, who somehow manage to coexist with what has been called "the most seriously dedicated conservative constituency in America."

The "L.A. Lifestyle," as it's called, has spread across the land. Freeways now crisscross most American cities. Orange Julius long ago invaded New York. Nudity on the beaches, once considered so shocking, has spread eastward. Shopping malls and sprawling suburbs ring most U.S. cities.

A visit to this changing and dynamic metropolis is more compelling than ever. Each year there are more things to see and do. Moreover, each year increasing numbers of visitors—whatever ilk—come to realize that Los Angeles is just the beginning. What lies beyond is an extraordinary stretch of land that is too simply termed "Southern California." For those two words comprise one of the greatest tourist attractions in the entire world. Your only problem may be that you didn't budget enough time to take it all in. "It," in the context of this guide, includes everything from ranch houses around Santa Barbara to the border of Mexico.

HISTORICAL BACKGROUND: Wherever we've roamed, we've sought to bring you the best of Southern California—in all price ranges, and for most tastes. But before we get to specifics, first a bit of history . . .

FROM PUEBLO TO METROPOLIS: The odds that Los Angeles would become one of the world's most important cities appeared slim when it was founded in the 18th century. The founding of Los Angeles dates from August 1, 1769, when a Spanish expedition party—led by Gaspar de Portolá, with Father Crespi taking notes—discovered an Indian village on the spot and named it "Pueblo del Rio de Nuestra Señora la Reina de los Angeles." The name was too much work for the ordinary tongue, and after a while even its masculine "Los" was feminized to "Las," though the original spelling stuck.

In those days, Spain was the power in Mexico. And the Iberians looked with increasing apprehension at the establishment of Russian trading posts on the North Pacific coast, and also at the growing power and potential of the American colonies in the East. Hence, Spain ordered a colonizing party of less than 50 souls to trek upward through the desert from Mexico to found a settlement on the site of the present city of Los Angeles. The rather unprepossessing and haggard group arrived on August 18, 1781, to begin what must have seemed like a fruitless venture.

By 1822, Mexico was free of Spain, and new rulers were in

control in California. In the following decade, Los Angeles was made the capital of California (an unpopular choice with many San Franciscans). Following the annexation of Texas to the Union in December, 1845, open conflict with Mexico seemed inevitable, though it was delayed temporarily by efforts of conciliation. War was declared the following spring. On August 13, 1846, Union troops—led by Commodore Stockton and Captain Frémont—moved into Los Angeles, and routed its south-of-the-border government. But the new ruling garrison met with such disfavor that it, too, was booted out. In January of the following year, the city was reclaimed for the United States by Commodore Stockton and General Stephen Kearny.

AN EPIDEMIC OF GOLD FEVER: California was ceded to the United States by Mexico in 1848, and on September 9, 1850, it was admitted to the Union as a free state. Its admission was greatly accelerated by a discovery on January 24, 1848: gold at Sutter's mill! The rush westward—one of the great sagas in the history of human migration—was on.

It seemed that few were spared from the gold fever sweeping the nation. What army could keep its soldiers? What ship its sailors? Even midwestern Babbitts were transformed into daring Forty-Niners, and set out to strike it rich.

Washington, D.C., bureaucrat J. Goldsborough Bruff typified many of the pioneers lured by the yellow dust. In his *Gold Rush*, written in 1849-51, he evoked the drama of the mining camps, the boom towns that sprang up in the wake of the discovery. Across the wide Missouri, through the Sierra Nevadas, he traveled with the fortune seekers. Disease, hostile Indians, eventual starvation, were the lot of many. As it turned out, Mr. Bruff got not one nugget, and eventually returned east—except this time by an easier route, via the Isthmus of Panama!

Of course, San Francisco was the queen of the Gold Rush. But all those miners and exploiters flocking north had to be fed. Los Angeles ranchers never had it so good. In the lawless decade preceding the Civil War—perhaps the most turbulent and violent in the city's history—it was not unusual for a "rancho" master to sell cattle at $435 a head, even more if he were a shrewd bargainer.

TO LOS ANGELES FOR $1: When the final tracks of the cross-country railroad were laid on May 10, 1869, by the Central

Pacific and the Union Pacific, a new era opened up for California, and the railroad was a major step in turning America into one nation. In 1885, the Southern Pacific and the Santa Fe rail companies—fierce competitors—dropped fares to only $1 from Mississippi junctions to Los Angeles. Another "rush" was on.

Of course, not everybody rode out on the rails. It is said that Charles F. Lummis (1859-1928), later to become a well-known writer, editor, and historian of the Southwest, walked from Cincinnati! Obviously, he was a man to take his own advice: he originated the slogan "See America First."

Long after the gold fever waned, California drew thousands of homesteaders in the post-Civil War era. Many men came seeking not gold—but orange. In Los Angeles and Southern California, citrus belts were planted to satisfy the ever-growing demand from such "back East" port cities as New York and Boston.

Actually, it was "black gold," or petroleum, that proved the most financially profitable for California, and Los Angeles in particular. Production began in the closing years of the 19th century, and it soared in the boom days of the 1920s, when derricks, such as those on Signal Hill, were silhouetted against the bright Western sky.

PIGTAILS, VAMPS, AND SHEIKS: The 20th century provided yet another lure, except this time the gold was flowing into the state instead of out.

The "flickers" were to spread the fame of Hollywood around the world, eventually making legends, or at least household words, out of a host of its star-kissed actors. In rebellion against Thomas Edison and his eight partners in the Motion Picture Patents Co., and their monopolistic stranglehold on the fledgling Eastern industry, independent filmmakers headed west. Many found the character and especially the sunny climate of Hollywood more suited for their camera work. By 1911, 16 motion picture companies were operating out of Hollywood. Films, such as *Birth of a Nation* in 1915, established Hollywood in the eyes of the world and earned for its director, D. W Griffith, a reputation as "the father of American cinema."

By World War I, the star system was established, and a triumvirate was formed by "Charlie, Doug, and Mary." William S. Hart rode into the hearts of Saturday-afternoon moviegoers as the first prototype of the American Western hero. Theodosia Goodman, the daughter of an Ohio haberdasher, vamped across the screen as Theda Bara.

In the '20s, salaries and box office receipts multiplied fantastically. An opulent spending spree was launched with each star or producer trying to outdo the other. Newly rich stars created an aura of luxury and glamor. His nostrils flaring, Valentino as *The Sheik* electrified women around the world. Mae Murray, the eternal *Merry Widow* with the patented "bee-stung" lips, was "self-enchanted." Clara Bow, with her red chow dogs to match her flaming hair, was the "It" girl. And Cecil B. de Mille saw to it that Gloria Swanson took a lot of baths!

HOLLYWOOD TALKS: On August 6, 1926, the Manhattan Opera House in New York screened Vitaphone's *Don Juan,* with John Barrymore. The great actor didn't talk, but there was background music. Warners released *The Jazz Singer,* with Al Jolson, in October of the following year. The Talkie Revolution was on. Garbo could talk, albeit with a Swedish accent; but her romantic leading man, John Gilbert, couldn't—at least not very well. The invasion of voice-trained Broadway stage stars began, including the likes of Tallulah Bankhead, who made a number of films of which she said later, "I'd rather forget about them."

Perhaps no invader was as formidable as the author of *Good-*

Hollywood and Vine

ness Had Nothing to Do With It. As Mae West herself relates, she wondered if she could "show my stuff" in a "land of palm trees, restaurants shaped like derby hats, goose-fleshed bathing beauties, and far-flung custard pies." She could and did! Her invitation to "Come up n' see me sometime" was accepted around the world, and she became a phenomenal success at the box office. Or to use her own modest summation: "More people had seen me than saw Napoleon, Lincoln, and Cleopatra. I was better known than Einstein, Shaw, or Picasso."

The '30s marked the rise of some of Hollywood's greatest stars: Bette Davis, Joan Crawford, Humphrey Bogart, Cary Grant, Jean Harlow, Clark Gable, James Cagney, Marlene Dietrich, Gary Cooper, Shirley Temple, James Stewart, Katherine Hepburn, Spencer Tracy, and Claudette Colbert. The decade was climaxed by the release of the money-making classic, *Gone With the Wind.*

Even during the low slump of the Depression, the magnetism of California continued—persuading poverty-stricken inhabitants of near-starvation areas to turn in the direction of the land of plenty. "Okies" from the Dust Bowl abandoned their grubby existence, packed their possessions, including the rocking chair and sewing machine, into broken-down cars, many of which would never make it west. This moving drama was compellingly portrayed in Steinbeck's *Grapes of Wrath.*

AIRPLANES, PIN-UPS, AND TV: In 1940, Dudley C. Gordon wrote: "Having survived a long, leisurely pioneering infancy, and an uncouth adolescence characterized by intensive exploitation, Los Angeles has now blossomed into one of the major cities of the nation." It was at the dawn of great change.

World War II brought even greater prosperity and growth. Pin-ups of Grable and Lamour were plastered in dugouts around the world. Hope and Crosby went on the road. West Coast defense plants, centered in Southern California, attracted workers in industry, marking the rise of Los Angeles as a leading manufacturer of aircraft, both military and civilian. The postwar era brought an even greater influx of residents.

After the war, the threat of television loomed over Hollywood. Though the movie colony valiantly hung on with three-dimension and earphones with stereophonic sound, the die was cast. A savvy redhead who had once been a bit player at RKO personified the change. Lucille Ball not only created her niche in the new medium, but ended up on the board of directors. The demands of television brought a fresh wave of life into Hollywood, as studios converted to make way for television serials and commercials. By the 1960s, the great day of the Hollywood cinema industry had passed. Studios now opened their doors to show visitors film sets, such as Ashley Wilkes's Twelve Oaks in *Gone With the Wind*, and Lana Turner's dressing room.

Indeed, as Los Angeles entered the 1970s, it appeared to some that the dream factory had become a near nightmare. One large studio reported a loss of $67 million; another, whose stars had once included Gary Cooper, Gloria Swanson, Frederic March, Betty Grable, Jean Arthur, Richard Arlen, Rudolph Valentino, and Mae West, announced that its 52-acre main lot was for sale. In the months to follow, MGM, which once boasted that it had "more stars than there are in heaven," was auctioning off Clark Gable's trench coat. The days of film glory were over, but few doubted that a more stable cinema industry would emerge and remain as one of Los Angeles' chief attractions and employers.

WHY GO TO LOS ANGELES?: Millions who have moved here have answered this question satisfactorily for themselves. But for the tourist who has only a few days or weeks at most to spend in L.A., the reasons are different, of course. The most compelling reason to go to Southern California is to have a good time. No place in America, perhaps the world, offers such a unique blend of man-made attractions and natural sights compressed into such a small area. In one hour you're out at Calico Ghost Town, then you're calling on Roy and Dale (and a stuffed and mounted Trigger!) at Apple Valley, or you're being serenaded by Mexicans in the Padua Hills. Or you're watching the swallows return to San Juan Capistrano thrilling to the attractions of Disneyland . . seeing the surfers at Laguna, the bikinis (or bare skin) at Malibu following in the footsteps of the stars along Hollywood Boulevard . enjoying a concert at the Music Center . . . driving around to see where the stars live in Beverly Hills . . . touring Universal Studios watching Johnny Carson tape a "Tonight Show." You're being served tea in a simulated Japanese garden, before going on to enjoy boysenberry pie at Knott's Berry Farm; then it's on to relive "The Loved One" as you tour Forest Lawn. Or you may even run down to Tijuana to watch a bullfight.

Finally, Greater Los Angeles has some of the finest restaurants in America, as well as some of its best hotel and motel bargains.

There seemingly is no end to Los Angeles. And although the events we've cited may sound frivolous, the city is increasingly taking itself more seriously. Los Angeles is perhaps the personification of American fulfillment, revealing both the country's shadow and its strength. If you come away from it with an increased understanding of the people who created and are creating Southern California, your trip will not have been wasted. At least you should give Los Angeles a chance to shake up your preconceptions.

MacArthur Park

Chapter II

SETTLING INTO LOS ANGELES

LOS ANGELES is an incongruous collection of communities, joined like a crazy patchwork quilt. Each town or district has been sewn onto the ever-expanding blanket, none more notably than **Hollywood**, eight miles northwest of "downtown L.A.," which was annexed in 1910. New areas in suburbia, as they emerged, were continuously tacked on.

However, there were holdouts, such as monied **Beverly Hills** —a separate municipality that is a virtual island inside Los Angeles. Similarly, the mile-long **Sunset Strip**, between Hollywood and Beverly Hills—long the refuge of nightclub operators and other businesses wanting to escape the restraining hand of the City of Los Angeles—is under the jurisdiction of the county.

Though some towns or cities are independently incorporated, their destiny is linked with Los Angeles. Examples include the sheep ranch that became "Beautiful Downtown **Burbank**" (NBC-TV, major aircraft industries, Warner Brothers); **Pasadena** (setting of the New Year's Tournament of Roses and the Rose Bowl Classic football game); **Culver City** (home of MGM); **Santa Monica** (known for its beaches).

Sprawled between sea and mountains, Los Angeles meets the Pacific at settlements such as **Venice,** while in the east it encompasses treeless foothills leading toward the **Mojave Desert** and **Palm Springs.** There are those who live in the hills, such as **Laurel Canyon,** and there are the "flatlanders." Generally, with notable exceptions, of course, the better homes are in the hills— built on shelves scooped out of granite, shrub-covered mountains. These are usually low and rambling houses—many occupied by movie stars of yesterday and today.

On the crest of the Santa Monica mountain chain from the north—forming part of Beverly Hills and Hollywood—is the

LOS ANGELES: WEST

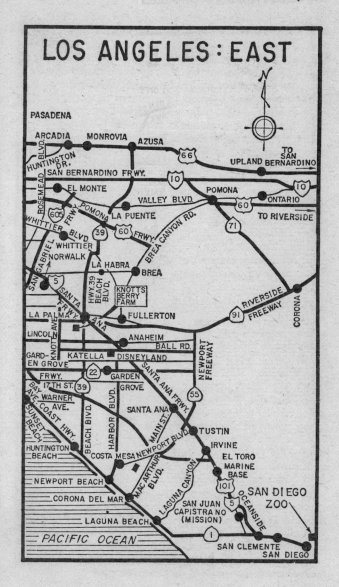

LOS ANGELES : EAST

"sky-high" **Mulholland Drive,** where tourists go for a bird's-eye view, and young and not-so-young natives park at night beneath the California stars. From here one can see a flatland called the **San Fernando Valley,** between the Hollywood Hills and the Mojave Desert mountains. Once all orange groves, it is now both residential and commercial. There are those who say that it—not Hollywood—is the movie and TV capital of the world, because of the location of such studios as **Universal City.** Many motion picture and television stars do in fact live in the Valley.

The more commercial areas of Los Angeles have remained in the flatlands, including **Wilshire Boulevard ("Miracle Mile"),** running from downtown to the sea. Beverly Hills and Hollywood are half flatland, half hilly. The highest point in Los Angeles is Mount Hollywood. **Sunset** and **Hollywood Boulevards**—the main thoroughfares—run along the foot of the mountains. Sunset Boulevard begins near the downtown Los Angeles Civic Center and stretches to the ocean.

Because of earthquake scares, no skyscrapers were allowed until recent times—which partially explains why the city is so spread out, encompassing more than 450 square miles.

DRESSING FOR SUN AND SMOG: A sense of humor is required to savor the special qualities of Los Angeles. The city provides a clear record of its waves of invasion, without ever becoming a monument to the past. Buildings come and go in Los Angeles like the changing of a movie set. Nazimova's residence on Sunset Boulevard (near Schwab's Drug Store) blossomed into the Garden of Allah Hotel (at which F. Scott Fitzgerald stayed in the '30s); nowadays, it's the parking lot of a bank!

The oddities of the people reveal the drama of a society willing to experiment and to take chances, to do whatever is necessary to make for a better or different way of life. Visitors may be surprised at the shopping center extravaganzas, where department stores, chic boutiques, grocery stores, beauty salons, and other businesses are set harmoniously around tree-filled courtyards with fountains (and lounge chairs for nonshopping spouses). Drive-ins provide armchair comfort for colorful and tasty meals. Perhaps the shopping center, more than any other post-war phenomenon, illustrates the supreme triumph of the automobile. Restaurants and other establishments, occupying prewar sites that didn't provide for adequate parking, are folding their doors or else watching declining receipts.

. The accent is breezy, scintillating, and experimental. You wear whatever you want in this town—as long as it's casual. And in some parts of town, like Beverly Hills, you might take care that it's chic. True, there are some staid restaurants, requiring that their male clients dress "formal"—that is, wear a jacket! And some Hollywood hotel owners have taken to posting signs in the lobby: "No bare feet allowed."

Be warned that when the sun goes down, the air is cooler. Night-owls may prefer light coats and woolen jackets, especially in late autumn, winter, and early spring. The citizens know how to dress lightly during the day, switching to warmer apparel for their nocturnal adventures. Everyone is an individualist, and Los Angeles has long accustomed itself to unusual costumes—be they the satin swathings of Gloria Swanson; the loincloth worn by Herman the Hermit on his daily pilgrimages to Hollywood Boulevard from his mountain tent; or the togas of self-exiled Midwesterners masquerading as East Indian cultists.

Because Los Angeles lies between a chain of coastal mountains and the ocean, there is a large pocket of morning mist. In former days, it was dissolved by the brilliant morning sun. Nowadays, the influx of industry, with its smokestacks, and the car-clogged freeways running in all directions, cause an emission of more carbon monoxide than can drift out to sea or over the Mojave Desert. The much-publicized smog—subject of many a comedian's friendly barb at Los Angeles and many a resident's irate letter to the mayor—comes and goes along no predictable lines. The local citizen has much to complain about, but the transient visitor may experience only a minimum of discomfort, as many days the sun and wind are powerful enough to drive the smog away.

WEATHER: Los Angeles enjoys a mild climate, or one of "little variability," as one expert put it. The rainy season usually begins in January and lasts sometimes until May. From then until October, there is little, if any, rainfall. The winter days are likely to be warm and sunny, although the temperature occasionally drops dramatically at night.

It's possible to sunbathe throughout the year, although only die-hard enthusiasts and the more adventurous surfers in wet suits venture into the water in winter. In spring, summer, and fall, however, you can swim and frolic in the surf with comfort.

Los Angeles Average Monthly Temperatures

January	55.8	July	73.0
February	57.1	August	73.1
March	59.4	September	71.9
April	61.8	October	67.4
May	64.8	November	62.7
June	68.0	December	58.2

GETTING AROUND L.A.: You need a car in Los Angeles like you
need your liver! The analogy is apt for many Angelenos, who
view their trusted automobile virtually as an organic part of their
bodies. In Los Angeles—to which automobile-manufacturing
Detroit pays homage, the two-car family is already passé. The
three- and even four-vehicle household is a fast-rising status
symbol.

Although there is a bus service, it is almost imperative that
you drive your own car—particularly if you have an ambitious
sightseeing agenda that includes more than just a trip down to
Disneyland in Anaheim.

To aid you in your auto touring, Los Angeles has the world's
most brilliantly designed freeway system—though there are others who suggest it is the work of a madman. At its best, it allows
experienced motorists to reach long distances in an astonishingly
short amount of time. For example, from a motel in Hollywood,
you can arrive at a restaurant in Chinatown in about 15 minutes.
At its worst, the freeway system evokes a futuristic, soulless city
of tomorrow, with streams of pollution-making traffic moving
into vague nothingness.

Car Rentals

Your adventure in Southern California can be enhanced tre-
mendously with a car—in fact, having or renting one is almost
a necessity. The sights and restaurants are so numerous and so
spread out you'll never make the rounds unless you have a car.

If you do a minimum of traveling, then you might consider the
usual rate—so many dollars per day and so many cents per mile,
including gasoline. But if you're really going to tour, then you'll
do better to seek an unlimited mileage arrangement or else

one that provides sufficient free mileage to make your trip economical. On the freeway those few "cents per mile" tend to mount rapidly into dollars.

When you select a car-rental firm, be sure to read the small print. Each company offers something another company might omit, ignore, or fail to mention. Small details might make a big difference to you. You should know if you're getting a new car, how much insurance, etc.

Hertz is as handy and reliable a car-rental firm as you are likely to find in Los Angeles. It has depots throughout Southern California and, of course, at the airport. Hertz offers all possible combinations, but we recommend the unlimited mileage rate. A Pinto costs $97.65 for seven days, a Gran Torino, $139.65. Basic insurance is included, and you pay for the gas. Full coverage for either car is $28 a week. Telephone toll free 800/654-3131.

Avis (800/331-1212) is also well represented in Southern California, having a desk and car space at Los Angeles International Airport, plus locations throughout the city.

Do check, too, with **Econo-Car** (tel. 776-6184 in L.A., 772-2164 in Anaheim; 800/228-1000), which offers excellent service and competitive prices.

Buses

If you don't have a car, you can reach most of the sightseeing centers in Greater Los Angeles by bus. The network of local and express buses is operated by the **Southern California Rapid Transit District (RTD)**.

The line's **Information Office** is at 425 South Main Street, where you can obtain maps and schedules on request, either by writing, calling in person, or telephoning 626-4455. You can also dial that number for detailed information on a given trip from point to point. The office provides a pamphlet—prepared in conjunction with the Southern California Visitors Council—outlining "20 Vest Pocket Tours," including visits to such places as Busch Gardens, Beverly Hills, the San Fernando Mission, and Disneyland.

The general bus fare is 35¢ for the first two zones in Los Angeles County; additional zones are 35¢ (transfers for another 10¢). Senior citizens pay only 10¢. Students with a valid ID can enjoy the same arrangement at 25¢.

RTD covers four counties—Los Angeles, San Bernardino,

Orange, and Riverside. Incidentally, the exact fare is required as no change is given on the bus. For $25 you can buy a pass for unlimited riding for an entire month ($4 for senior citizens).

A "mini-bus" runs every four to six minutes in the downtown area of Los Angeles, covering such places as Olvera Street, the Civic Center, Chinatown, Pershing Square, the Plaza arcade, and City Hall. It charges only 25¢ per ride (exact change, please) and operates from 7 a.m. to 7 p.m. Monday through Saturday (holidays excepted.) You can sight it easily with its wide orange-and-white canopied roof. Hop on, get off whenever you want to visit or shop, then catch another bus later, paying only another quarter. There are marked bus stops along the route.

Taxis

There are over 800 taxicabs serving Los Angeles and Beverly Hills, all of which start their meters at 90¢. For each additional quarter of a mile, it costs 20¢. There is no charge for extra passengers, and no charge for luggage or groceries. The main office of the **Yellow Cab Company** is at 1408 West Third Street, Los Angeles (tel. 481-2345).

Some 60 cabs are franchised to serve Sunset Strip, which is in the County of Los Angeles. You can go anywhere in the city on the straight fare, but you can't be picked up unless you are in the areas where specific taxis are franchised. This means that you may see a cab and hail it—and it might not stop. If a taxi driver isn't licensed for the area through which he is passing, he will most likely go on—and you can get furious to no avail. But, remember, if a cab not franchised stops and picks you up, the driver is running the risk of being fined.

A Central Information Bureau

The **Southern California Visitors Council,** 705 West Seventh Street in downtown Los Angeles (tel. 628-3101), has exceptionally comprehensive information for visitors. You can get a variety of maps, brochures on hotels, resorts, climate information, self-guided tours, a monthly calendar on entertainment and sports events, and advice on transportation problems, with timetables and prices. The hosts are informed, genuinely courteous—ready to help. The bureau is open Monday through Friday from 9 a.m. to 5 p.m.

Chapter III

FINDING "A PLACE IN THE SUN"

YOU'LL NEED a different concept of hotel living in greater Los Angeles. More than half of our hotel and motel recommendations are, in truth, miniature resorts, often with self-contained recreational facilities and swimming pools. Only a small selection are more conventional, chosen for the woman or man who is there strictly for business, wanting secretarial service and little to distract.

It's assumed you'll have a car with unlimited mileage (the bus system is difficult for visitors who select out-of-the-way places). The freeways can make it possible to choose a hotel in a spot you would have rejected years ago. You'll be amazed at how little time it takes to reach various points. Signs are well placed, and maps make it easy.

If you're with your family, combining business with holiday activities, there are many hotels to select to satisfy both needs. If you're interested in marinas, yachts, and the sea life, consider a chic hotel in Marina del Rey, just minutes from the airport. Or, if you want to "go suburban," what about Pasadena, 15 or 20 minutes from downtown Los Angeles? At a Bel Air hotel, you'll be only 20 minutes from the beach. Those travelers with children will want to consider the Greater Anaheim area, and may want to turn now to Chapter VIII, which previews Disneyland and all the many attractions of Orange County. Many motels there have supervised playgrounds.

Nearly all of our selections quote daily rates, though the budget-conscious will find weekly prices lower at most lodges and hotels.

Those who prefer the most elegant address in Southern California will seek rooms in Beverly Hills. The famous residential retreat of movie stars shelters some of the most expensive hotels in the West (the Beverly Hilton, the Beverly Wilshire, and the Beverly Hills).

The actual budget inns of Los Angeles are few and far between. Nevertheless, they do exist, and we've described them below—as well as a few offbeat places for those whose taste runs to the more unusual or atmospheric.

A word about how this chapter is organized. Since Greater Los Angeles is such a far-flung metropolis, encompassing many separate communities, we've thought it best to break the city down into areas, then to discuss the different kinds of accommodations—deluxe, first class, moderate, and budget, in that order —within each sector. We'll lead off in downtown Los Angeles with a good selection of hotels and motels.

Downtown Los Angeles

THE UPPER BRACKET: Los Angeles Hilton, 930 Wilshire Boulevard at Figueroa, Los Angeles (tel. 629-4321), is the third largest hotel in California, enjoying a prime position at the point where Wilshire Boulevard commences, near the entrances to major freeways. Personal service is paramount in this huge, 1,250-bed hotel staffed by 800. Shutting itself off from the busy traffic, it turns inward onto a subtropical garden with palm and banana trees. A grouping of outdoor tables for dining and drinking surrounds an oval-shaped swimming pool.

The room rates depend upon placement, size, and furnishings —the range wide enough to satisfy many purses. A single can be rented for as low as $33, graduating upward until it reaches a luxurious $45. Double- and twin-bedded rooms are in the $44 to $56 range.

The furnishings for so modern a building are conservatively traditional, with fine furniture styles, such as Queen Anne, Chippendale, and Hepplewhite. Every convenience and luxury is at hand, from laundry doors to in-house movies on your TV. The public rooms are plentiful, including four varied restaurants. The Veranda Rib Room converts from a poolside garden-style cafe for luncheons into a seductive candlelit room for dinner and dancing. At midday, king-sized sandwiches are featured; at night, guests enjoy a roast prime rib of beef from the open hearth at $6.75. Fashion shows are staged around noon.

In addition, the main dining room offers a complete buffet between 5 p.m. and 10 p.m. The Beef Barron lures with its Gay

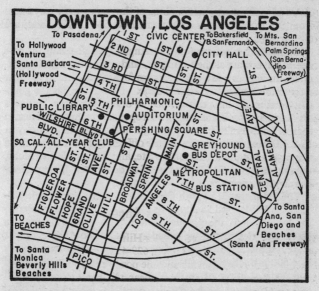

90s atmosphere, its mugs of cold draught beer at $1.25, and its sirloin steak for $8.90. At lunch guests are invited to build their own sandwiches. There's a piano bar weeknights. The Lobby Bar is a rendezvous for libations, and there's also Kiku of Tokyo, serving Japanese cuisine for dinner nightly and luncheon weekdays.

Hyatt Regency Los Angeles, Broadway Plaza, 711 South Hope Street, at 7th Street, Los Angeles (tel. 683-1234), is a dazzling jewel in the Hyatt crown. It's an integral part of the adjoining skyscraper, the Broadway Plaza business and shopping complex. The avant-garde tone is set by the two-story entrance lobby, glass covered, with a garden plaza, lounges, sidewalk cafe, and boutiques. In all, it's a world of harmonious design, with a bank of wide escalators taking you to the multi-leveled reception areas and poolside gardens. Everything is a melange of rich browns, reds, rusts, and golds. Informal banjo, mariachi, steel band, and organ concerts are presented during the day.

Conceived with the executive in mind, 487 ultra-contemporary rooms await you. All are oversized, with extra-large beds. Each room has an excellent view for a downtown hotel, color

TV, deep pile carpets, and bold textures. Singles go for anywhere from $46 to $60; doubles and twins from $54 to $70; suites are $75 to $160.

On the garden level is Joint Venture, where glistening mirrors reflect the shining plexiglass in a million prismatic images (nightly entertainment). More informal, the Nook & Cranny is right next to the lobby—a good place for drinks. Hugo's is the gourmet restaurant, the prestige place to dine, featuring hothouse service in an opulent atmosphere. Specialties include Indonesian rack of lamb at $20 for two, and boned duckling lingonberry at $9.25. Dining at the rooftop Angel's Flight is thrilling: you circle the city once an hour. Luncheon offerings begin as low as $3.50, though you'll pay $14.50 for the prime rib dinner. It's especially popular for cocktails.

The Biltmore, 515 South Olive Street, Los Angeles (tel. 624-1011), is self-labeled "a city of its own." And it is. Facing Pershing Square, it is the grande dame of L.A.'s deluxe hotels, a position rivaled by the Ambassador. The Biltmore shows proper respect for its architectural richness, though all its massive block of 1,500 attractive and spacious bedrooms has been renovated and updated in recent years. And new owners Phyllis Lambert and Gene Summers are currently giving the hotel a $13-million facelift.

Each accommodation is decorated in warm colors, with walk-in closets, air conditioning, direct-dial telephones, color TV, radios, message lights, and circulating ice water. One of the less expensive hotels in the deluxe bracket, it charges from $36 to $46 in a single, from $46 to $56 in a double.

Many visitors drop in to the Biltmore for drinks or dining, even if they aren't staying there. Its seemingly endless miles of corridors and public rooms are a virtual museum. For example, you enter the three-story Renaissance lobby, and you may think at first you're in a cathedral with a vaulted ceiling. From here you can stroll into the Castilian Lounge, a reproduction of the royal hall in which Queen Isabella learned about America from Columbus. Up the twin staircases, and you're in a large hallway, The Galeria, taking its name from the famous place in Naples. Spanning the length of the Biltmore, it was painstakingly decorated by the artist Giovanni B. Smeraldi.

Lancers Inn is like an English pub. The day begins, however, at the Ranchero, probably the world's largest coffeeshop, with booths and counter space for 550 guests.

Incidentally, you might want to stop in at the Biltmore Importation Shop, a liquor and wine store known for the quality of the Biltmore's private label stock. Finally, an underground garage on Pershing Square holds 2,000 cars.

The Bonaventure, 350 South Figueroa Street (tel. 624-1000), is the newest and most spectacular addition to the downtown hotel scene. The creation of world-famous architect John Portman, its five gleaming gold cylindrical towers not only revise the L.A. skyline, but contain what is probably the world's most innovative hotel.

Right in the six-story lobby is a one-acre lake surrounded by trees which grow upward to a skylight roof. Twelve glass-enclosed elevators leave from the lobby transporting guests to the 1,500 rooms.

In all, the hotel has 12 places to eat and drink, including a revolving rooftop restaurant on the 35th floor. Above the lobby is a shopping gallery with five levels of shops and boutiques. A huge game deck (40,000 square feet) contains an Olympic-size swimming pool, men's and women's health clubs, a putting green, a poolside restaurant, and tennis courts.

And, of course, the rooms are ultra-modern with every amenity from color TV to electric blankets—to keep you warm in your fully air-conditioned room.

Underneath the Bonaventure is parking space for 10,000 cars.

The rates for singles are $39 to $54; doubles and twins, $49 to $64.

New Otani, 120 South Los Angeles Street, adjacent to the Music Center (tel. 629-1200), will soon replace the Bonaventure as the *newest* downtown hotel. Scheduled for completion in September, 1977, it will also rival the above for uniqueness, though on very different grounds. The New Otani will be the city's first Japanese hotel, with such novelties as a Japanese health club offering sauna, traditional Japanese baths and shiatsu massage, as well as a classical 16,000-square-foot Japanese garden.

Facilities will include four underground parking levels, lots of service desks, a shopping arcade, and a choice of several eating and drinking places.

At the Black Ship, named for Commodore Perry's famous ship that forced Japan to trade with the West, gourmet French fare will be featured.

The Canary Garden will serve three meals daily in a garden setting, with rare birds enhancing the ambience.

Of course, there's a Japanese restaurant, A Thousand Cranes, for traditional Japanese lunches and dinners.

And there'll be live jazz in the Genji Bar (open for lunch, hors d'ouevres, and cocktails), designed in the style of a Japanese feudal-age country villa.

The rooms are Western rather than Oriental in style, with all imaginable luxuries, including refrigerators, phone and radio in the bathroom, message-alert lights, and alarm clocks; hotel information channels on the radio are in Japanese and English, and the tubs in the bath are extra deep, Japanese-style.

Those with enough "yen" for Japanese accommodations can opt for a tatami suite—$120 per night. Regular accommodations cost $48 to $56 for singles, $58 to $66 for doubles.

THE MODERATE RANGE: Mayflower, 535 South Grand Avenue, Los Angeles (tel. 624-1331), overlooking Library Park, has been given a new lease on life, in keeping with the upward trend in the downtown area. It's left over from the days of grandiose decor in the '20s, now brightened and made more cheerful. Those who prefer a traditional ambience should like its precincts, with 350 tastefully appointed bedrooms, all with color TV, radio, and individually controlled air conditioning. Strong colors in fabrics and upholstery are used. Singles cost from $23 to $33; doubles or twins, from $26 to $39; and triples, from $33 to $43.

The Mayflower's coffeeshop and room service operate around the clock. For more festive dining, try the Chart Room, a nautical nook with navigational charts and maritime mementos.

East Wilshire

THE UPPER BRACKET: The **Ambassador Hotel, Tennis and Health Club,** 3400 Wilshire Boulevard (tel. 387-7011), has undergone a $4-million face-lifting. For half a century it has been a Los Angeles landmark; it is surrounded by 23 acres of park-like grounds, appropriately dubbed "a city-within-a-city." Well-seasoned, but fresh appearing, it still preserves the plush atmosphere it had in the 1920s, though with a decidedly modern accent.

Set back protectively from ever-growing Wilshire Boulevard, it is one of the leading hotels for luxury living in California, complete with swank boutiques, palms, sweeping lawns, a lanai-styled swimming pool, and a new Tennis and Health Club with ten lighted courts.

Back to the Good Old Days

Alexandria, Spring at Fifth Street, Los Angeles (tel. 626-7484). At the turn of the century the Alexandria was one of the great downtown hotels, and guests included Presidents Wilson, Taft, and Theodore Roosevelt, as well as Churchill, Caruso, Bernhardt, and Paderewski. Usually hotels of this period are allowed to fade away in Los Angeles; but the present owner of the Alexandria has fully restored it with imagination and taste. He searched far and wide for good reproductions of the period, and now the main lounge is lush again, with frosted globe chandeliers, red tufted circular banquettes, Victorian sofas, and potted ferns.

The hotel is earning its present renewed fame particularly for its Victorian rooms and suites, named after the stars who once frequented the Alexandria—Valentino, Francis X. Bushman, Mary Pickford, Gloria Swanson, Mae West. Victorian singles are $26; doubles and twins, $29 to $32; suites, $65 and up. There are also Mediterranean-style rooms—considerably cheaper but much plainer—at $19 to $25 for singles, $22 to $31 for doubles and twins.

Several spots here are available for drinking and dining, including Charley O's, an 1890s-style Irish pub with entertainment; and the Coffee Mill, linked to the past by its stained-glass windows and oak-paneled walls. Lunch and dinner are served daily.

Throughout its existence, hundreds of the celebrated have arrived in every means of transport—from the Pierce Arrow to the helicopter that brought astronaut Neil Armstrong to its grounds. It was chosen as the hotel for Nikita Khrushchev during his infamous pilgrimage to California. Presidents Truman, Eisenhower, Kennedy, and Johnson, as well as Nehru and everybody else from Charles Lindbergh to D. W. Griffith and Clara Bow, have checked in. As an historical footnote, the Ambassador was the setting for one of the tragic events in American political annals, the assassination of Senator Robert F. Kennedy.

The rooms are priced according to size and view. In the main building, singles with bath go for $28 to $37; doubles, $34 to $43. In the garden villas, singles cost $31 to $40; doubles, $37 to $46. All the rooms have color TV and air conditioning; decor and furnishings are in the Southern California tradition of casual elegance. Extras include the "His & Her Hacienda," a tiny honeymoon cottage retreat, sumptuously designed, with its own private pool for skinny-dipping.

On our latest rounds, the hotel's world-famous Cocoanut Grove was a dim and faded memory. Its once-plush auditorium had been booked by a convention for a sales meeting. In its heyday, it was a showcase for such "unknown crooners" as Bing Crosby. The last Academy Award dinner at "The Grove" was in 1943, when Greer Garson won the Oscar as best actress for *Mrs. Miniver,* and James Cagney won as best actor for *Yankee Doodle Dandy.*

Le Restaurant Lautrec, the elegant old-world European restaurant off the Ambassador lobby, is undergoing renovation. The hotel management plans to have a new restaurant open in February, 1977. Meanwhile, the popular Winetasters Buffet Luncheon has been moved to the Celebrity. This buffet is still served Monday through Friday and for $4.25 features a nonskimpy selection of colorful and tasty California salads and assorted relishes, plus hot dishes and vegetables, followed by dessert. The Celebrity also is open daily for dinner with entrees starting at $5.95.

Wilshire Hyatt House, 3515 Wilshire Boulevard, Los Angeles (tel. 381-7411). In the heart of Wilshire Center, the hostelry is a contemporary palace of glass. It's geared to the traveling businessman and visitor who wants push-button comfort in a convenient location.

Its ten floors of bedrooms—each with an all-glass wall—are set back from the busy boulevard by a raised terrace deck, where luncheon guests enjoy an hour of sunshine while dining. The rooms, 400 in all, each with all the creature comforts, are finely decorated, the furniture a combination of traditional and modern. Single rooms are in the $34 to $38 bracket; double- and twin-bedded rooms are $39 to $47.

As expected of a first-class hotel, there are many added services on the premises, including boutiques, beauty salons and barbershops, a car-rental agency, a heated swimming pool, and a piano bar with nightly entertainment.

An innovation is the staff imported from Switzerland for the Hugo Restaurant, including the maître d'hôtel (Tony Bachman), the chef de cuisine, and the food manager. For $8.95 you can order a steak Diane. The tab also includes soup, a fresh salad, and vegetables. Hugo's serves luncheon as well. The hotel's Café Carnival opens for lunch, but entertainment—a singer—begins at 5 p.m. At 9 p.m., there's usually a comedian and a combo plays for dancing.

Hollywood

THE LEADERS: Hollywood Roosevelt, 7000 Hollywood Boulevard, Hollywood (tel. 469-2442), is one of Hollywood's most prestigious hotels, chalking up many successful years. Across the street from Mann's Chinese Theatre, the older portion was built in the '30s when 13 floors were the legal limit; in recent years a group of two-story Hawaiian-style lanai (a Hawaiian word meaning porch or veranda) rooms have been erected in the rear garden, offering luxury suites around an Olympic swimming pool, set against a lush, tropical background of flowering shrubs and towering date palms. Though the rear seems like a tropical resort setting, the front of the hotel is "down to business."

To stay at the Roosevelt, you have a choice of many price categories. The least expensive rooms are in the main building, with doubles or twin-bedded rooms in the $23 to $27 range. The more modern and elaborate doubles in the lanai section go for $30 to $35 The air-conditioned rooms have small foyers, built-in wardrobes, gleaming tiled baths with tub and shower, and color television sets. Colors are coordinated in a sophisticated way—the newer rooms with Spanish lamps and leather headboards. The Roosevelt contains excellent facilities: a valet service, a hairdresser, a barber, a theater agency, shops, a covered garage. It's the major air terminal limousine stop for Hollywood. In the glamor nook, the Cinegrill, there's dancing nightly from 9 p.m. till 2 a.m. in a clublike atmosphere. The room also features a "TV Wall of Fame."

Continental Hyatt House, 8401 Sunset Boulevard, Hollywood (tel. 656-4101), is one of the most prestigious hotels along the famed "strip," with 14 stories encasing 300 bedrooms. Half of them overlook the Los Angeles skyline; the other half, the mountains. This link in a chain is close to Restaurant Row and, naturally, the nightlife along Sunset Strip. Rooms, done in autumnal color schemes, have modern furnishings, all amenities, and for the most part contain private balconies. Singles cost from $28 to $34, doubles from $33 to $41. Facilities include a heated rooftop swimming pool, valet parking, a coffeeshop open from 7 a.m. to midnight, and a Red Roulette room for cocktails and entertainment, open Monday through Saturday from 11 a.m. to 2 a.m. At night there's a singer and a combo for dancing; a big plus is that celebs who stay at the Hyatt occasionally get up and entertain—people like Stevie Wonder, Gordon Lightfoot, and Redd Foxx.

Holiday Inn, 1755 N Highland Avenue, at Hollywood Boulevard in Hollywood (tel. 462-7181), is a 23-story "miniskyscraper" in the heart of Old Hollywood. It features a circular rooftop restaurant called Oscar's with a revolving bar, and on the second floor guests may lounge around a swimming pool, surrounded by a sundeck. There's also a coffeeshop open for breakfast, lunch, and dinner.

It is, in reality, a glorified motor lodge (there's a garage on the premises with free parking). The accent is on the comfortable and well-equipped bedrooms, 462 in all, complete with air conditioning, color television, and wall-to-wall carpeting. Singles are $26 to $32; doubles, $30 to $36. An extra bed in the room goes for $4.

BUDGET TO MODERATE: The Saharan Motor Hotel, 7212 Sunset Boulevard, Hollywood (tel. 874-6700), provides splashy, comfortable accommodations at low prices. It's convenient to Hollywood Boulevard, Mann's Chinese Theatre, and the Hollywood Freeway, the latter providing easy connections to the major attractions of Los Angeles. Built in the "California modern" style, all the rooms overlook a central flagstone patio and swimming pool enclosed by a protective ornamental screen. Rooms for one or two persons are $16 with black-and-white TV, $17 with color. These accommodations contain queen-sized beds. Twin-bedded rooms with black-and-white TV go for $18. A room with two double beds and color TV is $22 for two, three, or four persons. Suites with kitchenettes begin at $26 for two, three, or four persons.

The large units are tastefully decorated with contemporary pieces; each has hi-fi music and air conditioning. There's a 24-hour switchboard service, and bonus offerings include dry cleaning and laundry service, free parking, complimentary coffee, and free tickets to popular TV shows. Families with small children will welcome the babysitting service.

Aladdins Highlander Motor Inn, 2051 North Highland Avenue, Hollywood (tel. 851-3000), is the kind of lushly planted hillside motel, near the Hollywood Bowl and the Hollywood Freeway, which a budgeteer might reject on sight as being too expensive. Not so! The hacienda-style motel, with two courtyards and a garden with palm trees and subtropical plants—even a filtered and heated swimming pool—is happily within the budget of the average traveler. Built in the Western ranch style,

"Privacy for the Harassed"

Château Marmont, 8221 Sunset Boulevard, Hollywood (tel. 656-1010), is a chateau-style apartment hotel, lodged on a cliff just above Sunset Strip. Recently remodeled, and in the process of expanding its facilities, it still is the home center for many a visiting film celebrity. There isn't enough space to list some of the famed who have lived here (and still do on occasions). Carol Channing met her mate here; Howard Hughes once maintained a suite; Boris Karloff stayed here for many years; Dustin Hoffman once made it his home; Greta Garbo has checked in using the name of Harriet Brown; John and Yoko have maintained a suite here, as have Sophia Loren and Sidney Poitier. And it once sheltered Marilyn Monroe, not to mention Valentino.

Actors, producers, and writers often gather in the great baronial living room furnished with grandiose Hollywood antiques. Otherwise you'll find them lounging around the egg-shaped swimming pool, edged with semitropical trees and shrubbery. You can get almost any kind of accommodation here, including an expensive lanai-style bungalow out back. However, the regular rooms cost $25 for a single, $30 for a double; the studio apartments are $40 a day for two persons. The latter are "living roomettes," with a recessed bed, a kitchen, dressing room, and bath. One-bedroom suites are available for $50; two-bedroom suites are $60. There's even a three-bedroom penthouse suite for $80. In all the rooms, the furnishings are tasteful, the rooms spacious, the kitchens fully equipped. There is daily maid service, plus a 24-hour switchboard and garage. Hopefully, you'll be assigned one of the higher apartments with a penthouse balcony, affording a view of Los Angeles—especially beguiling at night.

One British guest wrote, "The Château offers tolerance for the eccentric and privacy for the harassed."

with picture windows, it provides privacy for each unit with shafts of roof-high stone walls. Singles range in price from $16 to $24. Two persons, with double or twin beds, pay from $19 to $27, increasing to $22 to $25 with king-size beds. Apartments go for from $29 to $38. Bonuses include a complimentary continental breakfast, 24-hour free coffee, air conditioning, free ice, direct-dial phones in rooms, free parking, and use of the extra-large pool.

El Centro and La Mirada Weekly Apartments, 1225 North El Centro, Hollywood (tel. 464-0948), is a bargain hideaway of refurbished, stylish apartments, just off famed Vine Street. While

Hollywood's Super Bargain!

Cine Lodge (also known as **Howard's Weekly Apartments**), 1738 North Whitley Street, Hollywood (tel. 466-6943), is our featured wonder bargain! You can rent a bachelor apartment with a counter bar, refrigerator, and a private bath, all recently built and harmoniously decorated with studio couches that convert into beds at night. Yet the cost is only $44.95 weekly. If you take a double, with two studio beds, it's only $54.95, averaging out to less than $3.95 per person per day.

New for 1977 are a limited number of kitchenette apartments for weekly rental. These units offer a newly designed bar and kitchenette area with refrigerator and two-burner gas stove, together with all necessary utensils. Rates for the kitchenette apartments are $64.95 per week for two-person occupancy. A deposit of $25 is requested to confirm all mail reservations.

Also a new "Mini-Week Special" is now being offered as a package of three days and three nights (subject to availability). We suggest you call on arrival or up to 24 hours in advance for last-minute availability. Three-day mini-rates range from $30 (one person in an efficiency apartment) to $45 (two persons in a new kitchenette apartment).

This surprisingly good offer is the brainchild of Gordon Howard. Cine Lodge was his pilot venture—a highrise building, with a two-story lobby with tall glass panels. Since, he has taken over a number of buildings with hundreds of apartments, operating them on a do-it-yourself basis, with a minimum of staff—and passing the savings on to his guests. The shortcut service means you make your own bed, although fresh, clean linens are provided with the regular weekly cleaning service. There is no telephone in the rooms, though there is a message service, with a hookup on every landing. In addition, there's a laundromat on the premises. In the basement is a garage where you can park your car for $5 weekly. Another asset is the convenience: half a block from Hollywood Boulevard, about four blocks from the Hollywood Freeway. Apartments are rented (except for the abovementioned special) for a minimum of seven days; if you give a week's notice that you're leaving, any portion of the second or third week will be computed on a daily basis—whichever arrangement is cheaper for you. If the Lodge has no space, the manager may offer to secure you an apartment at associated establishments, such as the one near Vine Street in Hollywood, and an exceptionally fine one near NBC, the Burbank Studios, Warner's, and the Columbia Movie Ranch, as well as Universal Studios.

half of them are used permanently by TV and film employees, the other half are available at startlingly low rates to tourists. Again, visitors get this break because of the genius of Gordon R. Howard (see our Cine Lodge recommendation), who has worked it out so his apartments can cut your living costs.

Over the years he has acquired these apartments which touch shoulders with Hollywood's Ranch Market (where seemingly every other customer is a candidate for a profile on "the most unforgettable character"). Rental charges begin at a low of $29.95 per week in the older building on La Mirada. These apartments are small and not suitable for two. They contain private baths and a refrigerator and bar with some kind of countertop. The apartments in the newer building on El Centro rent for $39.95 weekly, accommodating two for an additional fee of $10 weekly. The decor is attractive, contemporary, and utilitarian. Preferred are guests who like to stay for a few weeks. When available, weekly parking for your car is $2.50 ($5 in a covered carport, and $10 in a locked garage).

Beverly Hills

THE DELUXE CHOICES: The **Beverly Hilton,** 9876 Wilshire Boulevard, Beverly Hills (tel. 274-7777), is a world unto itself. Lodged in a wedge-shaped area in the heart of Beverly Hills, it offers glassed-in rooms, many opening onto a swimming-pool terrace. In all, there are 634 air-conditioned rooms, with the latest comforts, color TV sets, and "in-room" movies. The different rates depend on size and placement, with the stiffer tabs assessed for the rooms overlooking the Olympic-size pool or those on a higher level. Singles range from $38 to $52; doubles from $50 to $64. For the poolside room with lanais, the rate for two people is $64. A plus is that there is no charge for children occupying the same room as their parents.

At the Hilton's L'Escoffier restaurant, you dine with a view, seated in Louis XVI-style chairs. A portrait of the famous chef sets the aura for the French-inspired meals. The restaurant is a winner of many awards for its quality food and service. Entrees, such as medallions of veal Bohemienne or pepper steak, average around $13. A full prix-fixe dinner is $17. There is dinner dancing and a delightful "living room" style lounge for cocktails until 2 a.m. (except Sundays). The Mr. H. Restaurant offers international cuisine in a traditional setting, with Jacobean chairs, crystal chandeliers, and paneled damask walls. Most popular of all

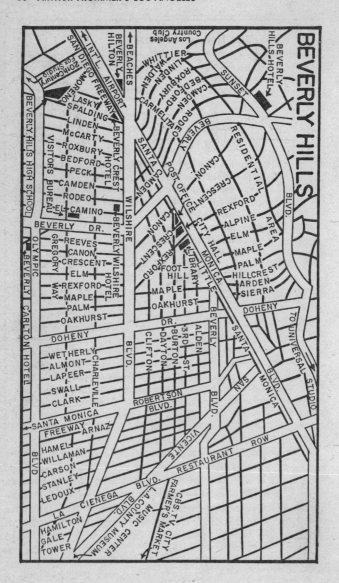

"The World's Finest Little Hotel"

Royal Palace Apartment Hotel, 2528 South Sepulveda Boulevard, West Los Angeles (tel. 477-9066). Only individualists like Jack Hamner and his wife, Kay, would invest more than a million and a half dollars in a miniature Shangri-La in such an unfashionable commercial area, on the fringe of Westwood. But he set out to fulfill his dream of creating "the world's finest little hotel" in this spot, and that he did. This compound is near the junction of two important freeways —San Diego and Santa Monica—in the direction of International Airport.

Mr. Hamner has crammed a tremendous amount of luxury living into so small a place. The three-story contemporary structure has glamorous corridors—one side all mirrored, the other imported marble. You pass lily ponds and fountains along the way to the rooms. Singles range from $24 to $36; doubles, from $28 to $40; and suites, from $32 to $75. The furnishings and trappings are excellent, tasteful, and color coordinated, and include crystal chandeliers and original oil paintings. Most rooms have either a pint-sized private patio or balcony. Four-channel stereo is wired to all suites, which are also furnished with three telephones and two color TV sets! Many also have oversized beds. Each kitchen offers Meissen china and Rogers flatware. There's even a little meditation room for those who want to practice their yoga, plus an exercise room, a Finnish sauna (complete with wood dipper, hot coals, and slatted benches), a tropical garden with rare and beautiful plants, a small free-form swimming pool, a game room, and a restaurant. Luxurious extras include: free liveried chauffeur service for guests (in a new white Cadillac limo) to and from the airport, as well as Century City, Beverly Hills, and Westwood; a paging system to all public areas; and daily newspaper delivery each morning.

is its prime rib buffet nightly between 6 p.m. and 10 p.m., costing $9 per person. You can go back for seconds and thirds of the succulent ribs (no one counts here). Sunday brunch, by the way, is a Beverly Hills tradition here, and is served for $7.50; you can also order à la carte meals at Mr. H. The Red Lion is a well-styled replica of an English pub, complete with a genuine room-wide fireplace with a cast-iron stove. Drinks average around $1.50 and are served until 2 a.m. There is also the Library Bar, with its book-lined shelves. One of the most famous of all Beverly Hills restaurants, Trader Vic's, is described in the chapter to follow.

Beverly Wilshire Hotel, 9500 Wilshire Boulevard, Beverly Hills (tel. 275-4282), is a prestigiously elegant city hotel, with a touch of Park Avenue and Paris. In the heart of Beverly Hills, it is two buildings joined by a swank driveway entrance with liveried attendants. The owner, Hernando Courtright, a noted wine connoisseur, sets the tone of the hotel, utilizing much crystal, French paneling, and fine furniture.

In the older building, where many a film star has booked a suite, singles start at $51, ascending to $85 for more luxurious accommodations. Doubles range from $63 to $97. Furnishings are traditional, baths are marble, and naturally all the necessities and luxuries are included. In the newer Beverly Wing, living is even more lavish and individualized. Singles are $61 to $89 here; doubles, $73 to $101. Rooms overlook a tropical garden, and on the rooftop is a swimming pool.

On the premises, the dining room La Bella Fontana is acclaimed. It has a formal French touch, with Pompeian fluted columns, velvet-covered walls, half a dozen shimmering chandeliers, and a bubbling fountain. In the evenings you can try such dishes as chateaubriand bouquetière ($25.25 for two). At the Sunday champagne brunch, you can often star gaze. El Padrino (the godfather) is more informal. At lunch it offers a $6.25 to $7.25 buffet, a rather unusual choice, with original and tasty salads. Dinner is also served, featuring selections from the rôtisserie. The newest dining facility here is Don Hernandos, a lovely Mexican restaurant serving a daily luncheon buffet at $4.55 or $5.95, depending on the entree chosen. A la carte lunches and dinners are also served. And, finally, for cocktails, there's the exotic Zindabad Pub, with an East Indian motif.

The **Beverly Hills Hotel**, 9641 Sunset Boulevard, Beverly Hills (tel. 276-2551), has a history intertwined with that of the power and glory of the film colony. Its present owner, Ben Silberstein, has run the show since 1955, and he loves Hollywood stars and their folklore. The hotel has been homebase or else a home away from home for everybody from kings, queens, and presidents of vast economic empires, to John Wayne, Barbra Streisand, Vanessa Redgrave, Elizabeth Taylor, Richard Burton, Art Carney, Paul Newman, Sidney Poitier, Groucho Marx, and Johnny Carson. Many of these personages have selected one of the hotel's exclusive bungalows, set in lush, semitropical gardens.

Keyed to luxury living, the hotel enjoys a site on a 16-acre parkland. No wonder the Rockefellers, the du Ponts, the Whitneys, the Astors, the Vanderbilts, plus the more "average" well-heeled American, have preferred its charms. You'll know why when you see the iridescent turquoise pool of the Pool and Cabana Club; the patio offering al fresco dining; a set of championship tennis courts; the coffee room; the cocktails and celebrities of the Polo Lounge; the Lanai Restaurant, with its provincial decor, continental food, and excellent wine cellar.

Each of the 325 rooms is custom-designed in the Hollywood traditional style, with tropical overtones. Of course, there is everything: television sets, telephones, room service, and, in many cases, patios or terraces and even wood-burning fireplaces. The rates are determined by the size of the room, its view, and furnishings. Single rooms range in price from $37 to $82; doubles, from $49 to $82.

THE MEDIUM-PRICED RANGE: Beverly Rodeo, 360 North Rodeo Drive, Beverly Drive, Beverly Hills (tel. 273-0300), was conceived by Max Baril as "a smart little European hotel." It's his personal pride, and he's crammed a lot of glamor into this intimate 100-room hotel in the heart of the Beverly Hills shopping area, near such prestigious stores as Gucci, Van Cleef & Arpels, Saks, and I. Magnin. A liveried attendant opens the door, and you're ushered into a lobby that is both provincial French and Californian, although the ceramic stove will remind you of Austria. The bedrooms are individualized and stylized in the continental fashion, with provincial furnishings. Rates for singles range from $30 to $36; for doubles, from $36 to $42; the more expensive tariffs charged for courtside accommodations with balconies. Of course, more opulent suites are available as well, including a Presidential Suite. Opening onto a charming inner courtyard is the Cafe Rodeo, with banquettes, red velvet, and glittering crystal chandeliers. A dinner in this luxurious setting averages around $8, though you can get the twilight dinner at $5.50. Adjoining is a piano bar with entertainment from 5 p.m. till 1:30 a.m.

Beverly Hillcrest, Beverwil Drive at Pico Boulevard, Beverly Hills (tel. 277-2800), is a luxuriously styled establishment at the edge of Beverly Hills, close to the San Diego and Santa Monica Freeways. The hotel is dramatic and sumptuous, a multimillion-dollar plaza structure, with bedrooms boasting roomy lanai balconies. Part of the drama is the 12-story ascent via a blue steel and glass outside express elevator to the Top of the Hillcrest for the view, cocktails, dining, and dancing. The guest accommodations are unusually spacious, each with its remote-control color TV, air conditioning, plus genuine marble (and a phone) in the bathroom. A decorator has definitely been at work, giving each room style and flourish. Some rooms have half-canopied beds, and the furnishings are a mixture of French and Italian pieces. Five levels of rates are presented to dazzle you: they range from $40 to $49 in a double, from $34 to $41 in a single. For a spectacular view, visit the cocktail lounge and dining room. On the lower level is Portofino, a plush, candlelit restaurant with dark-paneled woods and high-backed armchairs. Off one of the plazas, the swimming pool is surrounded by sun-bathing areas, palm trees, and a terrace for refreshments.

Beverly Crest Hotel, 125 South Spalding Drive, Beverly Hills (tel. 274-6801), lives up to its illustrious address. Here are exceptionally well-planned bedrooms, many encircling a courtyard, and in the patio is a swimming pool surrounded by towering banana and palm trees. Sundeck chairs in clusters around the terrace make for a favorite spot for sun-bathing and a shady place for cool drinks. The impressive glass-door entry is decorated with subtropical planting.

Single rooms are $24 to $27; doubles are $30 to $33. All of the units have plenty of closet space, color television, room service from 7 a.m. till 11 p.m., self-controlled air conditioning and heating, and a bath with a tub-shower combination. The decorating themes of the bedrooms are highly professional, with a sense of what is fitting and harmonious. There is adequate living space, simple, yet fine, modern furnishings and fabrics. You can park your car at an undercover garage at no extra charge.

Adjoining the pool patio is the Venetian Room Restaurant and Bar, serving three meals a day in a tasteful atmosphere. The hotel is within walking distance of some of the high-quality department stores of Beverly Hills.

A BUDGET CHOICE: Beverly Vista, 120 South Reeves, Beverly Hills (tel. 276-1031), is a modest, three-floor hotel at a secret address zealously guarded by those wanting to live economically in high-priced Beverly Hills. The hotel has a large European clientele, probably because Europeans are quite used to rooms containing only hot and cold running water. For these bathless accommodations, the management charges only $5 a day, just

$25 a week. Super economy! Singles with full bath are $8 nightly, $45 weekly; doubles with bath or shower, $10 to $12 nightly, $50 to $60 weekly. Much effort has been expended to refurbish the little hostelry. The work of painters, upholsterers, and carpet layers is clearly visible. A courteous receptionist in the small lounge will take care of phone messages between 8 a.m. and 10 p.m.

Century City—Deluxe

Century Plaza Hotel, Avenue of the Stars, Century City (tel. 277-2000), is a super-star, built in 1966 on a corner once occupied by Twentieth Century Fox Studios. In the center of Alcoa's new skyscraper city, it was designed by the celebrated architect Minoru Yamasaki. Everything seemingly is larger than life, built for tomorrow. Occupying a commanding position adjoining Beverly Hills, the hotel contains 20 floors (5½ miles of corridors!), spread out like an overscaled Japanese fan, with a dramatic formal entrance.

Slightly reminiscent of Rockefeller Plaza in Manhattan, it offers a number of restaurants opening onto a sunken forecourt. The rear courtyard is like a world's fair exposition, with islands of sundecks placed in a wide lily pond with bridges. Off this garden, suspended in air, is the swimming pool lanai. The main lobby is cathedral high, with sunken lounge areas, and a wall of glass overlooking the front plaza with its fountains and theaters.

Throughout the structure, 1,800 oil paintings are hung. The bedrooms are generously endowed with space and comfort—800 in all, including 67 "palatial" and penthouse suites. The design is modern and traditional, with one wall of glass, a balcony of your own, color television, air conditioning, oversized beds, and sometimes a sitting area as well.

The rooms are priced according to their size, view (some of the rooms overlook Fox Studio), and furnishings. The singles range in price from $46 to $58. Standard- and medium-priced doubles are in the $56 to $62 range, the deluxe ones priced at $62 to $68. Of course, more expensive suites are available.

In addition to the lobby court, there are six major places at which to drink and dine. Decorated in Andalusian style, the Granada Restaurant serves a continental cuisine—the average lunch costing $4; dinner, $9.50. The Cafe Plaza, open from 6 a.m. to 2 a.m., features inside dining overflowing onto the front plaza, in the tradition of a French sidewalk cafe. A typical lunch here averages around $3.50. A dinner costs around $4.95. In the Garden Room, a restaurant lounge, a three-piece combo plays on Friday and Saturday nights. A lunch here costs as little as $3.75; dinner, $7.50. The Hong Kong Room and the Yamato Japanese Restaurant are also on the premises.

The **ABC Entertainment Center** has opened directly across the street from the hotel. The complex features an 1,850-seat Shubert Legitimate Theater and two ultra-modern cinema theaters.

West Wilshire—Suites Only

Beverly Comstock, 10300 Wilshire Boulevard, Los Angeles (tel. 274-8211), caters to the carriage trade. It only offers suites, and interestingly decorated ones at that. Most of the suites open onto the courtyard pool area, and contain either private balconies or patios. The pleasantly styled rooms are quite large. It's easy to settle in and enjoy such facilities as a fully equipped kitchen, color TV, valet and laundry service. Under new ownership since April, 1975, the Comstock has undergone extensive renovation and is looking better than ever. You'll pay from $45 daily for a one-bedroom suite (for two), or $90 for a two-bedroom suite (for three or four persons). Monthly rates are available. A restaurant and cocktail lounge are on the premises.

Westwood—First Class

Tiverton Terrace, 1052 Tiverton Avenue, Westwood (tel. 473-0995), is small and elegant, revealing the impeccable taste of its owner, Jack Hamner and his wife, Kay. Right in the heart of Westwood Village, it resides in the newly emerging restaurant and cinema section of Los Angeles, near the U.C.L.A. campus. Mr. Hamner is a perfectionist concerning deluxe details—even the telephone booth has a marble counter and a crystal chandelier! Each accommodation is thoughtfully decorated, many with original oil paintings. Several of the little kitchens are equipped with Meissen china and Rogers flatware, and the bathrooms contain marble vanities. You get color TV and piped music in all rooms. Doubles range between $28 and $40; singles, between $24 and $36. Suites range from $32 to $75. There's a homey lounge and gameroom; a liveried chauffeur service takes guests to and from the airport, to Century City and Beverly Hills.

Century Wilshire Hotel, 10776 Wilshire Boulevard, Westwood (tel. 474-4506), is a continental-type hotel with an inner courtyard and swimming pool. It's become so popular that many studios book some of the suites for their stars "doing shows on the coast." Each of the rooms has individuality, tasteful furnishings, good color coordination, and paintings, color television, radio, direct-dial telephones, and 24-hour switchboard service. They're extremely charming and homey. Single rooms are $28 to $34; doubles are $28 to $40. A single with a fully equipped kitchen costs $34. Suites are more expensive, of course, ranging from $34 to $65. Most pleasant is the inner courtyard, with its splashing fountain and garden furniture. The ambience is further enhanced by potted plants strategically placed. At this writing a continental restaurant is being built on the premises. Westwood Village is a five-minute walk from the hotel. There guests can enjoy 15 movie theaters, more than 200 specialty shops, and more than 80 restaurants.

Cavalier Hotel, 10724 Wilshire Boulevard, Westwood (tel. 474-4561). Appropriately self-appraised as a "resort garden hotel," the Cavalier provides the most imaginative architectural setting of the "swimming pool hotels" in Wilshire West. Set back from the glamorous boulevard by a group of palm trees and a forecourt for parking, its facade is enticing, and inside it opens onto a courtyard. There are two floors of bedrooms, some with wide balconies, others overlooking the pool-patio area. Gabled windows and beamed ceilings create interesting bedrooms, and afford an indoor-outdoor concept of living. A rather dashing clientele frequents the hotel—everybody from entire theater casts from the Cafe La Mama in New York to ballet companies to Joshua Logan to Wayne Newton. Many of the 120 bedrooms are suites, complete with air conditioning, color television, a fully equipped kitchen or a kitchenette bar. The larger suites have a definite *House Beautiful* character.

For the lone traveler, the rates are $20 to $24 in a bedroom, $25 to $30 in a junior suite. For two, the bedrooms range in price from $24 to $40. Guests congregate at the pool for their morning dip and free continental breakfast.

Holiday Inn, 10740 Wilshire Boulevard (tel. 475-8711). For standard, reliable accommodations—or, as they say of themselves, "no surprises"—you can always count on a Holiday Inn. This one has 300 attractively furnished rooms, each with two double beds, bath with tub and shower, direct-dial phone, and color TV. Furnishings are quite attractive—somewhat antiquey-looking with green or gold shag rugs and hunting prints on the walls. Many offer a nice view. Facilities include a swimming pool and whirlpool on a sundeck lined with chaise lounges. There's also a restaurant, Sir Lance's, offering continental cuisine from 6:30 a.m. to 10:30 p.m. in—as the name implies—an English Tudor ambience. A cocktail lounge adjoins.

Single rooms are $30 to $35; doubles, $35 to $40. Kids 18 or under can stay free in a room with parents.

West Los Angeles—Moderate

Los Angeles West TraveLodge, 10740 Santa Monica Blvd. (tel. 474-4576), is within easy access of U.C.L.A., Beverly Hills, and Century City, and offers a small swimming pool, morning coffee, plus color TV. And rooms, of course, which are large, modern, and moderately priced: $18 to $22, single; $22 to $26, double. Plenty of free parking.

Bel-Air—Deluxe

Hotel Bel-Air, 701 Stone Canyon Road, Bel-Air (tel. 472-1211), is the country club of the deluxe hotels in the Greater Los Angeles area. Removed from all commercialization, it lies in the foothills of the exclusive residential Bel-Air section above Sunset Boulevard, surrounded by the rising Santa Monica mountains and some of the most prestigious estates of Southern California. In fact, staying here is like a visit to a private estate where Spanish architecture prevails, and there are covered arcades leading from one building to the other. Everything seems surrounded by semitropical planting, such as banana, orange, and lemon trees, bamboo, and palm.

A large oval-shaped swimming pool is set in the midst of the gardens and is surrounded by a flagstone terrace. In a stone- and flower-edged pond, the now-famous white swans glide by (best viewed from an arched stone bridge).

The public rooms are richly traditional, with a lavish use of fine antiques. A fire is kept burning in the entrance lounge, especially nice on nippy evenings. There are 70 individually decorated bedrooms and garden suites, some with patios and a terrace overlooking "swan lake." The tariffs vary according to the size, furnishings, and location. All have the *Vanity Fair*, lushly decorated look. You may, for example, have a room with a wood-paneled wall, a fireplace, and a generous stack of "burn-all-you-want" logs outside your door. Picture windows, coordinated fabrics and colors, as well as French and English antiques, complete the elegant picture. Single rooms are $46;

twin-bedded rooms range in price between $50 and $58. Bed-and-sitting rooms with private patios are priced between $58 and $70. More expensive suites are offered as well.

In the wood-paneled drinking lounge, you can relax in comfortable armchairs, and listen to piano music. Have at least one luncheon in the flower-scented bougainvillea court, where daily specials—such as cold poached salmon, with sliced cucumber— are featured at $6.25. In the more traditional interior dining room, the entrees average between $7.75 and $11 in the evening, and include such delights as broiled breast of capon, Hawaiian-style, with grilled pineapple and ham.

Bel-Air and Brentwood—First Class

Bel-Air Sands Motor Hotel, 11461 Sunset Boulevard, West Los Angeles (tel. 476-6571), is a spreading, hacienda-style hotel, nestled at the base of the hilly Bel-Air-Westwood luxury estate area. The inn has a country club look to it, and is set on eight and a half acres landscaped with towering palms, spacious lawns, banana trees, and brilliant flower borders. In addition, there are two swimming pools, three tennis courts, a large view terrace, underground parking, and a Spanish-style drinking lounge. On the premises is an attractive restaurant, overlooking the pool and serving three meals daily. Entrees range from filet of sole meunière ($4.75) to chateaubriand bouquetière ($21 for two). The air-conditioned bedrooms—all with picture-window walls—are large and smartly outfitted with modern appointments. One person pays anywhere from $27 to $34; two persons, from $32 to $38. Also available are rooms with two double beds (or with twin studio beds), plus kitchenettes. Near the foot of the U.C.L.A. campus, the hotel stands at the crossroads of the San Diego Freeway (at Sepulveda) and Sunset Boulevard.

Sherman Oaks—First Class

Valley Hilton, 15433 Ventura Boulevard, Sherman Oaks (tel. 981-5400), is wisely situated in the heart of the valley, at the crossroads of two major freeways, San Diego and Ventura. It boasts a rooftop swimming pool, sauna, and sundeck, plus the use of the nearby golf course, tennis, and other facilities at the Braemar Country Club. Some 200 spacious, balconied, and well-decorated rooms await guests who pay from $27 to $33 in a single, from $33 to $39 in a double. Accommodations are equipped with color TV, direct-dial telephones, and air conditioning. Excellent food is served at the Ground Floor Dining Room & Lounge. Especially popular are the daily buffet and the Sunday brunch. The Valley Hilton is near NBC, Universal Studios, Busch Gardens, and Magic Mountain.

Universal City—First Class

Sheraton Universal, 30 Universal City Plaza, Universal City (tel. 980-1212), could only happen in the film world. Set on a studio lot, it is drenched in the extravaganza of Hollywood magic, thus becoming one of Southern California's most glamorous hotels. It's lodged high on a hill on Cahuenga Pass on a corner of the Universal lot—a spot where Indians once chased covered wagons over the rough terrain.

The hotel is almost a skyscraper (20 floors), all glass outside, allowing unblocked views from every bedroom. The formal entrance is reached via a winding avenue of olive trees. Most inspired of all is the extensive courtyard, with its overscaled swimming pool. It's almost a tropical isle. Wide, flagstoned terraces encircle the pool, and garden and sunning furniture is set in the shade of the semitropical trees and vines.

For dining, there's the unique Four Stages Restaurant (about which more in Chapter IV), and the Portuguese Lounge is one of our favorite L.A. spots for cocktails.

From the simplest accommodation to the most lavish suite, the bedrooms reflect the experience, the taste, and imagination of some of the best set designers and decorators at Universal. They have used their movie know-how to produce charm and individuality, appropriately combining the streamlined contemporary look with fine antiques. For one person, the tariffs range from $25 for a "minimum" room to $36 for a luxury one. For two persons, the rate is in the $31 to $44 bracket.

Van Nuys—Moderate

Carriage Inn, 5525 Sepulveda Boulevard, Van Nuys (tel. 787-2300), is on "motel row," near the San Diego Freeway at Burbank Boulevard. It's a super structure, with a seemingly endless maze of two-story accommodations. Somewhere in the middle is a small swimming pool, plus a coffeeshop as well as a dining room and cocktail bar, the latter featuring nightly entertainment. The air-conditioned rooms are spacious, designed skillfully in a contemporary fashion, with color TV, many built-in units, and a small sitting area. Singles are priced at $21; doubles, $25.

Toluca Lake—Burbank

BUDGET APARTMENTS: Howard's Weekly Apartments, 322 North Pass Avenue, Burbank (tel. 843-9283), provides one of your best bargains in the Toluca Lake district. Its location is extremely practical—next to the two major freeways, Hollywood and Ventura, both allowing for zippy 20-minute rides to downtown Los Angeles. It's also adjacent to Toluca Lake's Restaurant Row, the Burbank Studios, Warner Bros., the Columbia Movie Ranch, NBC Studios, Universal Studios, and Hollywood. The rates are low because of the remarkable and efficient planning of owner Gordon Howard. The charge is $49.50 weekly for one person in a bedroomette; $69.50 weekly for two in a one-bedroom garden apartment. In addition, a group of garden apartments is available, accommodating four persons each. A bonus is the charge of only $9.50 weekly for each additional person. The garden apartments come complete with a separate bedroom, a full kitchen including cooking utensils, and dining area. Nothing is neglected here, and you get clean linens with the regular weekly maid service. Make reservation as soon as possible.

A new "Mini-Week Special" is being offered as a package of three days and three nights (subject to availability). Call on arrival or up to 24 hours in advance for last-minute availability. Three-day mini-rates range from $34.50 (for one person in an efficiency apartment) to $49.50 (for two persons in a kitchen-garden apartment). A deposit of $25 is asked when making reservations. Howard's offers more apartments at its annex at 115 North Pass Avenue.

Studio City

MODERATELY PRICED: Sportmen's Lodge, 12825 Ventura Boulevard, Studio City (tel. 769-4700). If you're a movie or TV star, you probably already know about the Sportsmen's Lodge. Perhaps you live there. Out in the Valley, it is so near to so many of the studios that actors often make it their second home. Except when Ethel Merman gets eggs intended for Joan Blondell, it's a peaceful lodge. A major asset is its adjoining restaurant, one of the finest in the San Fernando Valley. The rooms are set back from the busy highway, and many of them open onto a central playland-garden center. A bridge, a pond, rock gardens, a waterfall, lush semitropical planting, a swimming pool —everything makes for a romantic setting. Although built and furnished some years ago, the rooms have good standards, and most of them have private lanai balconies or patios. Each has direct-dial telephones, radio and color TV, and many contain refrigerators. Singles are $23 to $25; $29 for an "executive studio." Doubles are $26 to $30; $34 for a studio. Airport limousines connect the hotel with terminal points.

Pasadena

THE UPPER BRACKET: The Pasadena Hilton, 150 South Los Robles Avenue, Pasadena (tel. 577-1000), is a 13-story hostelry crowned by a rooftop restaurant. Fifteen minutes from downtown Los Angeles, it's only a block and a half south of Colorado Boulevard, famed for its Rose Parade. Although the hotel is only six years old, all guest rooms have recently been completely redecorated, with ladderback chairs, brightly colored spreads and draperies, and many of the beds have elaborate high headboards. All rooms have color TVs and spacious bathrooms.

Singles range in price from $28 to $37; doubles, from $35 to $44. The higher figures are for accommodations with king-sized beds and balconies. You can dine in the Top of the Hilton Restaurant, overlooking the entire San Gabriel Valley, or dance and enjoy live entertainment in the adjoining Lounge. Breakfast is served on the ground-level French-style coffeeshop, and a recently added lobby bar called Fanny's is a favorite rendezvous during Happy Hour.

Huntington-Sheraton, 1401 South Oak Knoll, Pasadena (tel. 792-0266), has reigned supreme with conservative dignity since 1909 as one of the great old hotels of Southern California. Families from the East used to come out for the winter in their private railway cars. There are 24 landscaped acres which include the Japanese and horseshoe gardens. The hotel was built by General Marshall Wentworth who wanted "a dream" (he closed it one year because it rained!). Henry E. Huntington, the Pacific Electric Railway tycoon, acquired it in 1914 and renamed it "The Huntington." Finally, it was acquired in 1954 by Sheraton, becoming the first West Coast hotel in that international chain.

Staying here is like being in the country. Guests can enjoy the covered "picture bridge" spanning the pool and garden area, with 42 paintings by Frank Moore illustrating California scenes.

Room prices depend on location, view, and size. Accommodations are attractively furnished and built to have good light, space, and a fine view. In the main building, singles range from $24 to $40; doubles, $31 to $47. A newer lanai building, surrounding the grass-edged pool, charges from $36 to $40 for singles, from $43 to $47 for doubles.

There are many dining areas, including the Crystal Terrace, overlooking the pool and open for breakfast, lunch, and dinner. In summer you can dine and dance on "The Deck Under the Stars," though the Ship Room is a year-round choice.

FOR THE BUDGET: Pasadena Motor Hotel, 2131 East Colorado, Pasadena (tel. 796-3121), is an attractive new motel at the eastern edge of Pasadena, right on the path of the annual Rose Parade. All its units have good style, are nicely decorated, and are equipped with telephones, central air conditioning, television (half black-and-white, half color), and balconies or patios. Some Pullman-type kitchenettes are available as well. The bungalow rates (around the pool) are $9.50 in a single, increasing to $10.50 for doubles. In the main building, with studio beds and balconies, singles cost $12.50; doubles, $14.

Marina del Rey—First Class

This emerging resort represents a new way to live in Greater Los Angeles. Those who want a relaxing resort atmosphere will anchor here minutes away from California's famed beaches. The Los Angeles International Airport is only ten miles away, and you're two minutes from the freeway system which will take you to most of the attractions of Southern California.

Marina International Hotel, 4200 Admiralty Way, Marina del Rey (tel. 822-1010). The core of this top-notch hotel is a three-story-high courtyard, with a mansard-style glass roof, giving it a greenhouse look. On one side a fire burns in a baronial fireplace. Rooms have low-key, luxurious furnishings, with *House & Garden* colors, sitting areas, and color TV. Singles range from $34 to $48; twin or doubles, $44 to $58. The hotel's Flagship Restaurant offers continental cuisine with flambé specialties, and in the lounge entertainment and dancing are featured. You have a choice of swimming in the pool, or else going to the public beach across the street. Tempting bonuses include free limousine and Mercedes Benz bus service to and from the airport and a free Sunday cruise through Marina del Rey, where you sip complimentary champagne on the high seas.

Marina del Rey Hotel, 13534 Bali Way, Marina del Rey (tel. 822-1010), is under the same ownership as the International. Your room here will have color TV, oversized beds, furnishings both harmonious and dramatic, and harbor-view windows. Many have private balconies, so you can breakfast in the sun, inspecting the yachts moored nearby. Singles cost from $34 to $38; doubles, $44 to $48. There's free limousine service to the airport 24 hours a day. Guests are also invited to join in the Sunday champagne cruise already mentioned. Those who don't want to go to the beach can enjoy a large, landscaped pool in the hotel's backyard. A branch of the famed Don the Beachcomber, where you can order those exotic drinks and Polynesian dinners, is on the premises.

An Airport Hotel

Los Angeles Marriott, Century and Airport Boulevards, Los Angeles (tel. 228-9290), is the plushest and most dramatic of the airport hotels. Its accommodations and facilities are quite luxurious. Adjacent to the International Airport, it offers more than 1,000 guestrooms, each with color television, AM-FM radio, climate control, and oversized beds. Accommodations display a warm use of textiles and colors, and most of them are commodious enough to have sitting areas. Many have private balconies. Singles go from $38 to $46; doubles, $46 to $54. Extra guests sharing the room are charged $4. The Marriott has a Miami Beach-type atmosphere, with a gigantic free-form pool, plus a "swim-up bar" and cabana for refreshments.

Dining is an event. There are seven restaurants and lounges from which to choose. The rooftop lounge, the Hangar, is for drinks and the view, and the Fairfield is for convenience (open 6 a.m. to 2 a.m.). Off the sunken lobby, you can have buffet meals (three a day) around the fountain in La Plaza. Served from 11:30 a.m. to 2 p.m. Monday through Saturdays, a buffet lunch here costs $3.50. On Sundays you get a champagne brunch from 10 a.m. to 2:30 p.m. for $4.25. Capriccio serves Italian dishes in a Mediterranean restaurant, and the King's Wharf Lounge is for dancing and entertainment. The Lobby Bar is good for a quiet drink and a rendezvous.

Chapter IV

RESTAURANTS OF LOS ANGELES

THE CHOICES ARE ENDLESS. You can have almost a totally different meal for every day of your visit to L.A. The ethnic dishes reflect this city's varied population—Japanese, Chinese, Mexican, Hawaiian, Viennese, Hungarian, Scandinavian, French, and Spanish.

In Greater Los Angeles, you can order mile-high hamburgers, served in more than a dozen different ways (even with ground peanuts!); milkshakes large enough for three and so thick you'll need a spoon; Japanese dinners for which you sit on a mat while a kimono-clad waitress prepares your sukiyaki in front of you; Polynesian restaurants offering exotic drinks of the South Seas; Wild West "chuck wagon" barbecues, featuring smoky, tender, and succulent plates of spare ribs or charcoal-broiled steaks; and seemingly endless Mexican specialties such as tacos and enchiladas. And then there are salads and juices, combining both fruit and vegetables (try the fresh papaya and coconut—two heralded California specialties). Pancake and waffle houses abound, as do imaginatively decorated ice cream parlors. Fish houses with seafood from the Pacific are plentiful, not to mention top-notch health-food restaurants featuring organically grown produce.

Portions are generally large in Los Angeles, so try not to overorder. With a car, you can play hop, skip, and jump through your visit, giving wide scope to your dining choices.

Note: For other restaurant recommendations, see the following chapters where occasional dining suggestions are combined with sightseeing attractions, such as on your visit to the beaches or Disneyland.

An explosion has brought many new restaurants into the culinary foreground in the last few years, and a new concept has been emerging. In some cases, a creative chef has joined forces with someone who has artistic flair (often a scenic designer from some major motion picture or TV studio). Together they have made dining an adventure.

The general trend is away from Los Angeles, La Cienega, or Beverly Hills. Restaurants at places like Marina del Rey, Malibu, Redondo Beach, Dana Point, or Costa Mesa in Orange County are being opened in increasing numbers, and a 1970s cuisine is often featured, combining organically grown foods with the cuisines of America and Europe. Whole grains, unusual vegetables, and exotic fruits are utilized to bring an original approach to traditional cooking.

We've surveyed the restaurants of Los Angeles in nearly every price range. But the bulk of our selections fall within the moderately priced category, and a really fine meal can cost as little as $6 or $7. Other good dining places in the budget category will offer you a complete dinner, including your beverage and dessert, for $4.50. And there are some for even less.

The Top Restaurants

The yardstick was demanding, but the following restaurants qualified as some of the finest in Greater Los Angeles. They're expensive—but worth it! Expect to pay at least $20 for a complete meal, though your tab could run much higher. Not only do they offer some of the best food available in the city, but some of the most charming and/or spectacular settings as well. Let a meal at one of these restaurants be a night on the town. And don't necessarily plan to do anything else that evening, as you may want to linger a while.

Le Restaurant, 8475 Melrose Place (corner of La Cienega and Melrose Place), West Hollywood (tel. 651-5553), is placed just behind the more opulent Restaurant Row of La Cienega in a stylish remake of an old-fashioned stucco bungalow. Robert Lawrence Balzer, gourmet and wine editor of *Holiday,* who awards honorary plaques to outstanding restaurants, pulls out all stops: he writes that it's "as chic as its memories of Lilyan Tashman, as suave and soigné as its ghosts of Ouida and Basil Rathbone, as glamorous as Gloria Swanson when she triumphantly returned to Hollywood from Paris in the '20s, the bride of Henri, le Marquis de la Falaise!"

Though owned by Bruce Vanderhoff, the star is the youthful chef Jean Bonnardot, who has that magic flair which has given many a culinary artist not only stature, but a devoted following. The front garden is enclosed by terra-cotta walls, and you enter through a black iron gate, passing peach trees on either side. Inside there are several intimate dining rooms often occupied by such stars as Kirk Douglas, Zsa Zsa Gabor, or Yul Brynner. Even a former star, Ronald Reagan!

The furnishings are eclectic: bentwood chairs with pink-covered tables, as well as individual bouquets of asters, carnations, roses, and cornflowers in cut-glass vases. Tables are divided from one another by etched-glass panels.

The menu is classically French, almost haute cuisine, without pretensions or "freakiness." If you want to dine here, and your purse is slim, go for lunch. Main dishes then start as low as $4, ascending to $5.50. Dinner entrees range between $11 and $14. You have 17 scrumptious hors d'oeuvres from which to choose. Perhaps le bisque de crab for $4, or foie gras de Strasbourg at $9. Main dishes include such delights as les grenadines de veau au cidre at $13; le carré d'agneau persillé at $12; and grilled sole au beurre Nantais at $12. For desserts, les pâtisseries du chef at $2.50 is most recommendable. Lunch is served from 11:30 a.m. to 2 p.m.; dinner, 6 to 10:45 p.m. Closed Sundays and no lunch on Saturdays. Reservations are imperative!

Perino's, 4101 Wilshire Boulevard, Los Angeles (tel. 383-1221), is one of the finest restaurants in the West. A winner of many awards, it is solidly entrenched on the local scene and well patronized by the "old families." It has attracted a lot of visitors, too, including the Roosevelts, the Kennedys, the Johnsons, and the Nixons (Mr. Perino once confided to a reporter that Barry Goldwater knew more about food and wine than any of the political families cited). George Christy of *Los Angeles* magazine wrote, "Perino's recalls a cruise ship out of a pre-war past, a dazzling Ziegfeld queen in her dotage, a civilized cosmos where the soft pop of a champagne cork is the loudest noise you hear—or, rather, it should be." The Empire setting of the oval-shaped dining salon is luxurious, with its faded peach damask walls, its tufted banquettes a dusty rose, its glittering crystal chandeliers reflected in the wall mirrors.

If you go for lunch, try one of the soups, especially the cream of fresh peas at $2.50 (a pale mint color and made with that rarity, fresh peas). On our most recent luncheon visit, the specialty of the day, at $5.75, was the carbonnade of beef—braised in beer with onions and tomatoes and served with the most delicate gnocchi this side of northern Italy. At dinner, a well-recommended main dish is calf's sweetbreads Mascotte ($11.75), but anything you order will be good. Finish up with one of the heavenly desserts—perhaps a chocolate mousse ($1.90), or, a real splurge, Mandarin, chocolate, or vanilla soufflé ($10 for two). Open from noon to 11 p.m. Monday through Friday, and from 5:30 p.m. to 11 p.m. on Saturday. Closed Sunday.

Scandia, 9040 Sunset Boulevard (tel. 278-3555), is one of the most acclaimed restaurants in Los Angeles (some say the United States)—and at lunch its prices are quite reasonable. As it's on Sunset Strip, it continues to capture a clientele from nearby Beverly Hills and Bel-Air bent on a rendezvous with haute cuisine. It's appropriately Scandinavian in design, with three major rooms serving fine food. Reservations are a necessity, but if you arrive early, you can head for a popular nook, Hansen's Vin Stue, inspired by the wine shops of Copenhagen. A retreat of businessmen and entertainment stars is the Skaal Room, its tables and oversized leather armchairs set within view of a raised fireplace. But the happiest place in which to dine is the Belle Terrace; the sun pours in during lunch, the city lights at night.

Luncheons at $5.25—the specials are posted on a blackboard —include a choice of soup (vichyssoise, gazpacho, soup du jour) or salad, followed by a list of entrees such as London broil, salmon with sweet-and-sour aspic, cracked fresh crab with mustard sauce, or bouillabaisse. You'll pay extra for your beverage and dessert. As an alternative, try at least two of the famous Danish sandwiches, smorrebrod, inspired by Oskar Davidsen's in Copenhagen. Two of our favorites include roast beef with béarnaise sauce ($4), and breast of duckling with apples and prunes ($3.75).

The fare is more expensive at dinner, at which time Hansen, the chef, pulls out all the stops—especially with his pièce de résistance, Danish sole cooked in chablis and stuffed with coral pink shrimps, all in a lobster sauce, for $9.75. You can order the "cold cabaret" (delicacies of the Scandinavian smörgasbord), costing $10.50 per person. Lunch, beginning at 11:30 a.m., lasts all afternoon; dinner is from 6 p.m. to 1 a.m. A Sunday brunch is served from 11 a.m. till 2:30 p.m., featuring eight entrees, all for $5. There is no menu then, only a blackboard, but offerings include eggs Benedict, steak and eggs, and crêpes with chicken and mushrooms.

The Windsor, 3198 W. Seventh Street, Los Angeles (tel. 382-1261). This is the restaurant that—deservedly so—is always winning *Holiday* magazine awards. At night, the area surrounding it is relatively dead, but it's well worth the trek downtown. Upon entering you step down into a sunken restaurant, the domain of owner Ben Dimsdale's continental cuisine. The atmosphere is sort of clubby English, a red glow lighting the coats-of-arms and the oil paintings. At your table you'll be presented with the lavish menu (it'll take at least an hour to read it, perhaps longer to make up your mind). Whatever you select, however, will be excellent. Offerings include frog legs sauté at $10.75, and breast of pheasant at $12.75. Recommendable are the snails bourguignon at $5.25, and the broiled calf's sweetbreads at $10.25. To begin your meal, why not a delicious wilted lettuce salad at $3? For dessert, it's crêpes suzette for two at $7, and Irish coffee as the perfect finish. Also try the Windsor for lunch and partake of the daily special at $6.75. Open daily from 11:30 a.m. (Saturday and Sunday from 4:30 p.m.).

Chasen's, 9039 Beverly Boulevard, Los Angeles (tel. 271-2168). According to Pauline Kael, Orson Welles threw a temper tantrum at Chasen's and "inspired" Herman Manckiewicz to write *Citizen Kane.* This is but one of the legends spinning around this long-enduring favorite, which began as a chili parlor, then went on to become a theatrical tradition. Movie stars *still* dine here, which is why you'll often see a line of photographers near the door.

The warm personal style of Maude Chasen, widow of the restaurant's founder, has created a pleasant atmosphere. You may dine in one of two areas: the main Dining Room, with its soft lighting, plush channel-tufted red booths; or the Green Room where white tables are set under umbrellas. Many a star comes here for big bowls of chili. Elizabeth Taylor has TWA fly it to her anywhere in the world. If you want to ascend the culinary scale, ask for chicken Kiev with saffron rice ($8.75), or Lake Superior whitefish ($9.75). Equally tasty is the filet mignon, at $12.75. The spinach salad ($2.75) originated here, and is a meal in itself. Top off your meal with the banana shortcake ($1.75). Open for dinner only, till 1 a.m. nightly, except Mondays. Reservations are essential.

The Bistro, 246 North Canon Drive, Beverly Hills (tel. 273-5633), is one of the current "in" places for private parties, as well as for the movie and society colony. The restaurant is like a stylized version of Grand Vefour in Paris, evoking memories of Colette and Jean Cocteau. The manager here runs a tight ship, and the service is top-notch. If you don't reserve at dinner, you haven't much of a chance. And if your table isn't ready, you can always attract attention by occupying a bar stool near the entrance. An upstairs room takes the overflow.

The menu is continental. At lunch, for around $2, you'll find some of the finest soups in town—not only the better-known ones such as vichyssoise and gazpacho, but some other interesting concoctions as well (for example, cream of broccoli). Most main dishes are priced from $5 to $10; at dinner, entrees are in the $8 to $12 range. The produce is invariably good, and the portions aren't large, so you don't leave feeling bloated.

Lunch is served from noon to 3 p.m., Monday through Friday; dinner nightly until 11 p.m.

La Chaumière, 207 South Beverly Drive, Beverly Hills (tel. 276-0239), is one of the finest French restaurants in Southern California. The "Thatched Cottage" is decorated in the French-inn style with a warm, inviting ambience (exposed beams, a stone fireplace, lots of copper and brass, candlelight, and country-style chairs). Chef Georges E. Peyré, who was born in the Pyrenees village of Pau, returns to France often looking for new ideas and recipes to surprise and delight his loyal customers. While he is a skilled pâtissier (his tarte tatin, an upside-down apple tart topped with crème caramel, $1.75, is proof of his skill), he prepares with equal flair the dishes of Normandy. In that part of France, apples are often mixed with meat dishes—a culinary custom reflected in the excellent loin of veal sauté with apples and cream sauce at $11.25. Every day there's a fresh fish special, priced at $8.25 to $8.75; also recommended is the carré d'agneau (rack of lamb) persillé, at $11.25. Included in the price of each meal are homemade soup and romaine salad. Each day the soup is an event—crab bisque, cucumber, avocado, New Zealand spinach, or pumpkin. La Chaumière is open daily, except Sunday, for dinner only, from 6 p.m. Reservations are imperative.

Jean Leon's La Scala, 9455 Santa Monica Boulevard, Beverly Hills (tel. 275-0579). The people who go here are just as interesting as the cuisine. The owner, Jean Leon, is the darling of the movie set. Originally from the Basque country, he arrived in Hollywood and began working as a busboy. His rise, though, was meteoric. Soon he was teaching John Kennedy how to distinguish good caviar from bad. And ever since 1956, he has run La Scala like a personal club devoted to good food and wine. By now he's used to the whims of the famous—knowing full well that Greta Garbo wants that "little table" in the kitchen, etc.

You make your entrance into the bar. There, perched on the

bar stools, you are likely to find some of the tallest, blondest, and most beautiful girls in Beverly Hills or Hollywood. Make your way to the dining room. Wine bottles are everywhere (the cellar below is one of the best in the world), and you sit in comfortable tufted red banquettes.

What to eat? You might begin with an appetizer of the aforementioned "good" caviar ($15 per ounce), or, less extravagantly, with Italian salami ($2.95). Pasta dishes are featured. The house specialty is fettuccine verdi at $7.95. Excellently prepared main courses include calf's livers alla Veneziana, $9.95, and the New York cut sirloin at $13.50. A soothing end to the meal is zabaglione, $5 for two persons, although many simply have the cappuccino at $2.25. Dinner nightly until midnight; closed Sundays. Lunch is served Monday through Friday, 11:30 a.m. to 2:30 p.m., at which time you can sample such entrees as chicken La Scala at $5.95, and lasagne verdi al forno, also $5.95.

The Palm, 9001 Santa Monica Boulevard, Beverly Hills (tel. 550-8811). Though a newcomer to Los Angeles, the Palm has a half-century tradition as a chic gathering place in New York. And in Beverly Hills, there's always room for one more in spot. Walter Ganzi's new West Coast Palm is already a huge success. In case anyone should miss the connection to the restaurant's New York counterpart, the entire wall of the entranceway is lined with reviews praising that establishment. Within, the walls are plastered with colorful caricatures (by well-known cartoonists) of the famous ranging from Flip Wilson to J. Edgar Hoover. As for the decor, it's speakeasy-casual with sawdust on the floor, bentwood chairs and roomy wooden booths, big fans overhead, and green-and-white checkered tablecloths.

At lunch, served weekdays only, and very popular, a simple menu lists about 15 items, all of which are served with hash browns or cottage fries. They range from steak tartare ($5) to corned beef hash ($4.50).

Dinner entrees are starkly phrased with no mouthwatering adjectives or clues as to preparation or garnishment: steak, $12; roast beef, $10.50; duck, $8; etc. Fear not—it's all delicious. A limited, but well-chosen wine list is offered. The traditional dessert is New York cheesecake ($2.50). Dinner is served nightly. Reservations suggested.

Hollywood

The Brown Derby, 1628 North Vine Street, Hollywood (tel. 469-5151). Remember the scene from *The Legend of Lylah Clare* where Kim Novak, playing a sort of combination Jean Harlow and Marilyn Monroe, meets the producer? The Brown Derby was the setting, as it has been in so many other films about Hollywood. With an exception here and there, movie stars no longer flock to the Brown Derby, and businessmen at lunch are in heavy attendance. However, the Derby persists as one of the finest dining places in the faded movie colony. The old custom of the plug-in telephones at the individual tables is also observed. The decor has always consisted of 400 autographed caricatures of the stars adorning the walls. The food is reliable and well-presented. "Specialties of the hat" include prime ribs of beef au jus, with a creamy horseradish sauce ($7.85 or $8.85, depending on the cut), and broiled Nova Scotia salmon ($8.50). The price of the main dish includes potatoes, salad, and bread and butter. A good dessert is the grapefruit cake at $2. This Hollywood institution is open daily from 11 a.m. for luncheon, from 4:30 p.m. for dinner. It's across the street from the Huntington Hartford Theatre.

The **Musso & Frank Grill,** 6667 Hollywood Boulevard, Hollywood (tel. 467-7788), is the granddaddy of all Hollywood restaurants, launched in 1919, and now run by Edith Garissimi, Rose Keegel, and Jesus Chavez. In the heart of Hollywood, it attracts with its friendly, well-heeled atmosphere, graced by old oak beams. The chef, Jean Rue, has set the high culinary pace for half a century, insisting on the use of fresh produce, such as eggs, vegetables, fish, meats, and poultry.

Daily specials are posted, and a good choice are the braised short ribs of beef with vegetables served on Saturday night for $5.75. Typical entrees include half a spring chicken sauté, $6.25; roast spring lamb, $7.25; and baked ham with a sherry sauce, $5.75. The dessert menu features the chef's well-known bread-and-butter pudding for $1.

You can park your car in the rear for two hours for 35¢ with the proper validation. An extensive liquor list is offered, plus a fine selection of wines from California vineyards. Closed Sundays, the restaurant is open from 11 a.m. till 11 p.m. Join the old-timers, the producers and stars who enjoy the well-cooked food.

Don the Beachcomber, 1727 North McCadden Place, Hollywood (tel. 469-3968). On this unprepossessing street were born such drinks as "The Zombie" and "Missionary's Downfall." Created in Hollywood in 1934, Don the Beachcomber not only launched the first of a chain, but sparked a host of imitators. The South Seas decor is what you've come to expect. However, this Hollywood branch points out its former famous patrons, such as Charlie Chaplin, on sticks of bamboo. It's customary to begin your repast with rumaki—bacon-wrapped chicken liver and water chestnuts ($2.95), which was created here. The best bet is to order the "Bahala Na Dinner" at $8.95, which begins with a choice of egg flower soup or crisp green salad. To follow, you're given an excellently prepared Mandarin duck, as well as king crab Chungking and chicken manuu. Many à la carte entrees are priced at $4.95 and up. Most of the exotic drinks are in the $1.50 to $2.75 category. Open for lunch weekdays and dinner nightly. A good bargain are the sumptuous luau buffets (a kind of Polynesian smörgasbord) for $3.50 at lunch, $4.95 at dinner (Sunday through Thursday only).

Dar Maghreb, 7651 Sunset Boulevard (tel. 876-7651). Save this one for a special occasion—it's not just a meal, it's a ritual Moroccan feast. The magic begins the moment you step foot in Dar Maghreb and find yourself transported from the prosaic world of Sunset Boulevard to a marble-floored patio with an exquisite fountain under an open sky. A kaftaned hostess leads you to the Rabat or Berber Room. The former has high ceilings, painted traditionally in geometric designs with much use of gold leaf. The floors are covered with handmade Rabat carpets upon which silk cushions are strewn. Low sofas line the walls.

The Berber Room is more rustic, done in earth tones, with raw wood-beamed ceilings and Berber rugs on the floor. Both rooms are lovely and authentic to the most minute detail; Berber and Andalousian music play in the background. Your waiter, attired in a costume made in Rabat, can answer any of your questions about the decor, furnishings, or food.

The meal is a multi-course feast, eaten entirely with the hands (no silverware is given). Everyone in your party partakes from the same dish, and lest you feel squeamish, a server comes and washes everyone's hands before the meal begins. There are five dinners offered, priced at $11.50 or $12.50 per person.

A typical dinner—the Marrakchi Feast—begins with Moroccan salads of cold raw and cooked vegetables: tomatoes, green pepper, and, eggplant; carrots, oranges, and cucumbers, in delicious dressings. You scoop up the salads with hunks of fresh-baked bread, and it's so good that you'll be tempted to fill up on

Dinner in an Oriental Temple

Yamashiro Skyroom, 1999 North Sycamore Avenue (entrance at Orange Drive and Franklin Avenue; tel. 466-5125), in Hollywood is a stunning Japanese palace, perhaps the finest and most authentic in the Western hemisphere. Placed at the top of a winding road, on the crest of a hill, the Oriental temple is in the midst of exquisite gardens. Even if you don't stay for dinner (in the 600-year-old pagoda by the pool) at least you can have a drink on the front-view terrace, enjoying the twinkling lights of Greater Los Angeles. The drinks are exotic concoctions such as a "Zombie" for $2.25 or a Tahitian (fruit juices and rum) for $1.50.

If you're a movie fan, you may already have been introduced to Yamashiro, as it was used for background shots in Brando's *Sayonara*, as well as for such TV shows as "I Spy," "Route 66," and one of the "Perry Mason" episodes. The late Ian Fleming, creator of James Bond, recommended a visit here in his travel saga *Thrilling Cities.*

Built as a private estate (once the home of the "Hollywood 400"), it now operates as a restaurant seven days a week, and is open between 5 p.m. and either 1 a.m. or 2 a.m.

A Japanese dinner (sushi, salad, teriyaki, tempura, and yakitori) is offered for $8.50. The teriyaki steak is the specialty of the house, at $6.95. But essentially the cuisine is American with well-recommended dishes like the filet mignon at $7.95 and the mountain brook trout amandine at $5.50.

it. Resist this impulse—more good things are on the way.

Next comes bstilla, a chicken- and almond-filled pastry topped with powdered sugar and cinnamon. This is followed by couscous with lamb and vegetables. Portions are huge, and it's best to eat slowly, lingering over each course. A bottle of wine helps slow things down, and has an enhancing effect generally. Dessert is fresh fruit and Moroccan pastries and cookies.

At this juncture, the server comes and washes your hands again, using hot towels perfumed with orange-blossom water. Dessert is accompanied by mint tea, the pouring of which is quite a performance. We're always in a state of blissful relaxation after a meal at Dar Maghreb, and like to relax on the cushions with an after-dinner drink and enjoy leisurely conversation. Dinner is served nightly from 6 p.m. Reservations are suggested.

Emilio's, 6602 Melrose Avenue (tel. 935-4922), is an award-winning Italian restaurant with a celebrity clientele that includes, among others, Frank Sinatra. There's an abundance of atmosphere, what with a central fountain bathed in colored lights, Italian music in the background, brick archways, marble columns, and stained-glass windows. Somehow, it all combines to create a romantic ambience, enhanced by very good food and very Italian waiters. We particularly like to sit in the balcony area, overlooking the scene below.

You might begin your meal with an appetizer of scampi ($3.25) or mussels al vino ($3.50). Complete dinners, including soup, salad, and tea or coffee, feature entrees like manicotti ($7), spaghetti with oil and garlic ($6), and calamari della casa ($8.50). A la carte, you have a choice of seven veal dishes priced between $7 and $9.50, as well as seafood—including a terrific cioppino ($9)—pasta, and chicken specialties. For dessert we definitely recommend the zabaglione for two ($3).

Emilio's is open nightly except Monday for dinner from 5 p.m. to midnight (till 12:30 Friday and Saturday nights). Reservations are suggested.

Chianti, 7383 Melrose Avenue (tel. 653-8333), is another very popular Hollywood Italian restaurant. It was founded in 1936 by the well-known New York restauranteur, Romeo Salta. Like Emilio's, it has a romantic Mediterranean ambience—Italian music, painted murals of Italy, gilt-framed paintings, fresh flowers, and candlelight—and an award-winning cuisine. We like both restaurants equally, and suggest that you try them both.

A dinner at Chianti might begin with an assorted antipasto or a Caesar salad, either of which costs $2.75. For an entree we're partial to the scampi risotto ($8.75). Other house specialties are veal Milanese ($7.25) and chicken cacciatore ($6.75). An order of spinach with oil and garlic ($1.50) on the side might change your mind about this much-maligned vegetable.

For dessert you can choose from a selection of rich goodies like cannoli ($1.75) and crêpes suzette ($5.50 for two), or order a plate of assorted cheeses and fruit $2.75).

Chianti is open Monday through Saturday from 5:30 to 11:30.

Cristianis Restaurant, 7066 Santa Monica Boulevard (tel. 464-8635), specializes in Italian fare and song—arias, light opera, and show music. Full dinners—including relish tray, homemade soup, salad, and garlic toast—are priced according to the entree you select: $4.95 for chicken parmigiana, $6.95 for scampi marinara, etc. Open weekdays for lunch, and Tuesday through Saturday for dinner.

Studio Grill, 7321 Santa Monica Boulevard (tel. 874-9202), is the rather individualistic creation of owner Ardison Phillips, whose paintings adorn the walls. Lest you have trouble finding the place, you should know that there is little to herald its entranceway, and even that is obscured by an illuminated Pepsi-Cola sign. But within all is elegance: classical or jazz music is played in the background, plum-colored walls make for a richly intimate ambience, plants are suspended from a skylight ceiling, and diners sit in comfortable brown-leather booths or bentwood chairs.

Not only has Phillips created a uniquely tasteful atmosphere, he has also had an experimental hand in the rather unusual and eclectic menu. It lists items as varied as game hen with cherry-plum sauce ($6.95), eggplant parmesan ($4.95), and an Oriental-influenced beef in black mushroom sauce ($6.95). Any of these might be prefaced by an appetizer of caviar aspic ($2.80). The wine list offers a good, reasonably priced selection. For dessert, you might try the raspberry walnut torte à la mode ($1.80).

Dinner is served nightly except Sunday. The Studio Grill also has a large lunchtime (Monday through Friday only) following. Lunch fare is a bit simpler, with items like sirloin steak ($6.95), cheeseburgers ($4.25), and omelets ($3.50 to $4.95) on the menu. Reservations advised at dinner.

Tom Bergin's Tavern, 840 South Fairfax Avenue (tel. 936-7151), has been L.A.'s Irish headquarters since 1936. But it's more than just an Irish bar, it's a haven for sports (particularly football) enthusiasts, athletes, and a sprinkling of actors, including, at times, Marlon Brando, Bing Crosby, and Cary Grant.

This was the first restaurant in town to charter buses to pro football games, and they still hold 104 seats to the games reserved five years in advance. Needless to say, it's a lively place. The ambience is pubby, with photos and paintings of Bergin's friends adorning the wood-paneled walls, and, most notably, about 1,000 cardboard shamrocks plastered all over the ceiling above the bar. The shamrocks were the idea of Bergin's general manager emeritis, Jake Ohlsen. It started as a Saint Patrick's Day gag (March 17 is, of course, a big deal here). Ohlsen made some cardboard shamrocks and inscribed them with the names of customers. It became a custom, and many favorite regulars have since been so honored. The shamrocks are hung on Monday nights.

But we digress. Primarily we're recommending Bergin's as a congenial restaurant. Meals are served in a rather charming room with a fireplace, away from the "fighting Irish" at the bar. Irish specialties, served with soup or salad and garlic cheese toast, include corned beef and cabbage with steamed potato ($5.50); prawns Hibernia, wrapped in bacon and deep-fried in Harp beer batter, with rice pilaf ($6.50); and chicken simmered in cream and cider sauce with bacon, leeks, and mushrooms, served with rice pilaf ($6). For dessert, the carrot cake with butter frosting is delicious ($1.15).

Luncheon fare is in the $2.50 to $5 range, with items like Irish pot roast ($3.75).

Bergin's serves lunch from 11 a.m. weekdays, dinner from 5 p.m. nightly, and late supper until 12:30 a.m. At this writing, a **Bergin's West** is opening at 11600 San Vicente Boulevard, Brentwood.

Cafe Figaro, 9010 Melrose Avenue, at Santa Monica Boulevard (tel. 274-7664). In the early '60s the Cafe Figaro in New York's Greenwich Village was the number-one hangout of the beat generation. But high rent finally drove the old Figaro out of town—all the way to the other coast. (Since, the New York Figaro, originally replaced by a Blimpie Base, has been restored, once again, at its old Village location.) For New Yorkers who knew the old Figaro, walking into this West Hollywood replica (complete with an authentic Macdougal Street sign at the cash register) provides a bit of a "pinch me, I'm dreaming" experience. It's the old funky hangout of yore—a meandering series of rooms eclecticly furnished, classical music in the background, shellacked copies of the French newspaper Le Figaro used as wallpaper, and Tiffany lamps overhead. Even the waitresses look the same—slimmer and hipper than thou—and so does the crowd that is hanging out, playing chess (or, these days, backgammon), engaging in earnest discussion, and doodling on the napkins.

The menu is printed on a French newspaper, complete with ads for chic Parisian shops and automobile classifieds. Fancy coffees like capuccino (90¢) and cafe mocha (90¢) are featured on the first page. The fare varies from snacks—perhaps onion soup gratinée with wheat bread ($2.85 the tureen)—to regular hot entrees like beef with mushrooms in ragout sauce, served with fresh vegetables, potatoes, wheat bread, and fruit ($3.75). There's also a choice of omelets, our favorite being the "omelette l'impossible" which is filled with green peppers, raisins, almonds, shredded coconuts, and spiced with curry ($3). Desserts are in the gooey caloric category: a hot-fudge sundae is $1.50; a banana split, $1.75.

The Figaro is open Monday through Thursday from 11:30 a.m. to 2 a.m. (Friday and Saturday till 3 a.m.); Sundays from 4 p.m. to 2 a.m.

Lucy's El Adobe, 5536 Melrose Avenue (tel. 462-9421), is a very in place for good Mexican food. One of the reasons, in addition to very good food, is that Governor Jerry Brown is a good pal of owners Frank and Lucy Casado; during the presidential primary the restaurant was a veritable campaign base. It has become a great favorite of other politicians, Hubert Humphrey among them, and also boasts a star clientele that includes Louise Lasser, Orson Welles, and Richard Thomas. In honor of the governor, there's a Jerry Brown special on the menu (it's actually arroz con pollo, or chicken with rice), modestly priced at $4.

The ambience is cozy and comfortable, but unpretentious; there are two small, stucco-walled rooms with leather booths and gaslight-style lamps on every table.

The chef's special combination—taco, enchilada, chile relleno, soup, salad, rice, beans, and tortillas and butter ($3.75) is highly recommended. For "leetle people" the menu has complete dinners priced at $2.25.

Lucy's is open Monday through Saturday from 11:30 a.m. to 11:30 p.m.

Hollywood—Budget

Kinder to wallets are the following restaurants, ranging from a world-famous drugstore to an "all-you-can-eat" establishment.

Tick Tock, 1716 North Cahuenga Boulevard, Hollywood (tel. 463-7576), provides the best "tearoomy," wholesome American food for the money of all of our recommendations in Los Angeles. A holdout against the more exotic California cuisine, it all began after the Wall Street crash, when Helen and Arthur Johnson packed their belongings in Minnesota in the backseat of a Model A—along with an heirloom clock—and set out for California to seek their fortune. They opened a restaurant, put their clock on the wall, and went into the kitchen to produce good old-fashioned meals. Their sons have joined them, and their success story is material for *Readers' Digest.* The waitresses have caught the friendly spirit, and enjoy bringing extra hot sweet rolls and lots of coffee.

The furnishings are Early American, the walls covered with

an intriguing collection of time pieces. All the clocks work, and dining here on the hour is an extraordinary experience. A special dish is offered for each day of the week, but the regular dinner menu provides a varied choice. With all meals, you are given a soup, such as beef noodle or clam chowder (or a shrimp cocktail), as a first course, followed by a good-sized salad, such as Waldorf or aspic. The entree selection determines the price of your meal. For example, a $4.95 dinner might consist of the roast loin of pork with gravy and dressing, apple sauce, plus a choice of potatoes and vegetables. There are about a dozen desserts from which to chose, ranging from deep-dish apple pie with a cascade of whipped cream, to a light and moist banana nut cake. Beverages, such as coffee or milk, are included.

Luncheons offer one course less; otherwise, complete meals are featured. The creamed turkey in a patty shell at lunch costs $3.10; the roast turkey with dressing, $3.50. Closed Monday and Tuesday, the restaurant otherwise ticks from 11:30 a.m. to 2 p.m. and from 4 to 8 p.m. (Sundays and holidays open noon to 8 p.m.). Also closed Christmas Day and the last two weeks in July.

Hamburger Hamlet, 6914 Hollywood Boulevard, Hollywood (tel. 467-6106), is indeed the "prince" of this restaurant chain which has lifted the lowly hamburger to glorious heights. The chain has come a long way from its pioneer sidewalk version on Sunset Strip to this plushy dining room in the ultra-modern Max Factor building, opposite Mann's Chinese Theatre. In addition to counter service, you can dine in harem-soft comfort in springy, tufted red-leather booth-chairs, with peacock-fan backs. On the walls are movie-star photographs, but the real star is the menu and the choice offered.

Your hosts are Harry (the "most patient man in the world") and Marilyn Lewis. Mrs. Lewis, "with a little bit of help from Shakespeare," even wrote an ode warning "balloon-pated chefs" against cooking a burger to "tatters." The restaurant offers hamburgers in about 20 different varieties. From the quarter-pound $1.75 grouping to the $3.75 half-pound, the hamburger gets more elaborate, served with chili, onions, and grated cheese, or with other concoctions such as guacomole, or sauteed mushrooms and a scoop of sour cream. The desserts are sumptuous as well, including hot apple pie with rum sauce and ice cream for $1.35.

Open daily for lunch and dinner till 9 p.m. (11:30 p.m. Friday and Saturday nights), the chain is a big family with 14 locations in Los Angeles and Palm Springs.

The World's Most Famous Drugstore

Schwab's, 8024 Sunset Boulevard, corner of Laurel Canyon Boulevard, Hollywood (tel. 656-1212), owes its celebrated status primarily to one disputed legend. Allegedly, Lana Turner was discovered while sitting on a soda-fountain stool at Schwab's, and this story has appeared as fact in numerous books documenting the history of the movies. However, Mervyn Leroy, who cast her (wearing a tight sweater) in a bit part in the 1937 *They Won't Forget,* denied the claim in a 1969 nation-wide television interview. The man who really publicized Schwab's around the world was Sidney Skolsky, who (to quote Ezra Goodman) is "the only reporter on record who operates out of a drugstore," and Goodman added, "Schwab's several years ago underwent an expensive facade-lifting and emerged looking like a Taj Mahal with pills."

Nowadays, you're likely to encounter some of the prettiest girls and handsomest guys in Hollywood there, along with such actors as Maximilian Schell or George Maharis.

"Schwab's (to quote a sales girl) just grew." It's one of the most popular spots in town for breakfast, including its ultra-fancy ones, such as the $3.50 special—eggs Benedict, covered with hollandaise sauce and served with grilled Danish ham and an English muffin. Only freshly squeezed orange juice is offered, and there's an ample selection of jams and jellies, and cinnamon-flavored apple butter. Of course, most starlets know Schwab's for its three-decker club sandwich at lunch, $2.75 to $3. It is open every day from 8 a.m. till 10 p.m.

2 Dollar Bills, 5931 Franklin Avenue, Hollywood, is one health-food restaurant where you really can get your fill for $2. It's an indoor garden and "front-porch" restaurant with shingled walls, cafe curtains, handpainted and stained windows, and potted trees and plants. It operates on a serve-yourself basis. You mix your own salad with many kinds of crisp lettuce. The price is according to what you choose. Breads are whole grained; cookies and cakes melt in your mouth, and soups are nutritious. Fare ranges from eggplant parmigiana to pita burgers. There's music nightly from 9 p.m.—jazz bands Thursday through Sunday ($1 admission); a variety the rest of the week. Open 11:30 a.m. to midnight Monday through Thursday; till 2 a.m. Friday through Sunday.

Sunset Strip

With its boutiques, swank nightclubs, colony of film agents, and plush apartments, Sunset Strip (Sunset Boulevard) provides all the extremes of everything from drop-in hamburger joints to some of the finest restaurants in Los Angeles—such as the Scandia, previewed earlier. Here is a selection of Strip restaurants in the moderate range.

A Temple of Organic Food

The **Aware Inn**, 8828 Sunset Boulevard, West Hollywood (tel. 652-2555), is the gourmet temple of organic foods. It is owned by Elaine Baker, who was way ahead of the times when she opened her restaurant in 1957 (it's now managed by her son, Bart). The inn is ideal for those who want the vitamin-packed foodstuffs grown under 100% natural conditions, then cooked and served almost with reverence.

There are two rooms in this Sunset Boulevard restaurant, but preferred is the little upstairs area, which has a large window opening onto a nice view. The restaurant is homebase for any number of knowing diners, including Jon Voight, Carol Burnett, Julie Christie, Mike Nichols, Warren Beatty, and Gloria Swanson.

The menu is enormous. You might start off with a wilted spinach salad ($1.75) or homemade split-pea soup ($1.50). For the main course there's an eclectic selection ranging from Rumanian stuffed cabbage ($5.50) to chicken curry with homemade chutney and assorted condiments ($6.95). Main dishes are served with a tossed salad, the vegetable of the day, whole-wheat rolls, and brown rice or baked potato. The inn is especially known for its desserts, such as "banana mañana" (made with a ripe banana and banana liqueur), topped with freshly whipped cream and toasted almonds, $2.50. Your host, Bart Baker, will help you in selecting these skillfully cooked organic dishes.

The Aware opens for dinner only (at 6 p.m.), the last orders being taken at 11:30 p.m. Closed Mondays.

Sneeky Pete's, 8907 Sunset Boulevard, West Hollywood (tel. 657-5070). It looks like a Hollywood version of a speakeasy, and serves some of the best steaks and chops in town. Right on the fabled Strip, Sneeky Pete's has a valet to park your car and a pretty waitress in a fringed 1920s dress to show you to your table. The meats are prime, and the portions are gargantuan. The small New York cut goes for $9.75. Try also the filet mignon at the same price, or the pork chops (three huge ones) at $8.75. While you're enjoying Pete's Italian salad ($2.25), you can guess the photos of the famous, and the speakeasy-era newspaper items, covering the walls. As a surprise, a complimentary dish of iced fresh fruit is served. Entertainment is offered (a piano bar trio) and the restaurant is open nightly, from 6 p.m. to 2 a.m. Reservations recommended.

Cock 'n Bull, 9170 Sunset Boulevard, at the end of the Strip, West Hollywood (tel. 273-0081). One magazine writer called it "unsinkable" and "unchangeable." If the Sunset Strip has an official pub, then this is it! The soft lighting, the regulars who hang out at the bar, the plaid carpeting, the oak tables, the copper lanterns—all combine to make the Cock 'n Bull a Hollywood tradition. *Everybody* has been there, at least one time or another, even the *real* Howard Hughes, probably Clifford Irving, certainly Dick and Liz before they fell out. The waitresses are friendly and motherly, providing your mother likes to hand you Scotch. Typical conversation—SHE: "He's a sweet guy, really." HE: "I don't want to hear it, baby. If ever I've seen a monster . . ." And so on. You can order an $8.50 dinner from "the board," a tasty buffet supper containing such delights as rare roast beef, roast turkey, roast duckling, roast lamb, steak-and-kidney pie, even a curry dish. The luncheon is reduced, but still heartily generous, for only $3.75. The $5.50 Sunday brunch is a tradition, complete with everything from kippered herring to finnan haddie. Incidentally, if you're collecting bar lore, "the Moscow Mule" was invented here.

Butterfield's Restaurant, 8426 Sunset Boulevard, West Hollywood (tel. 656-3055), is the delight of many an out-door-loving Angeleno, who heads for this patio-garden restaurant just below busy Sunset Strip. It's housed in John Barrymore's former guest house and garden. Tables are invitingly set out under the trees on a brick patio in the midst of flowering shrubbery and banks of ivy. Equally engaging is the health-culture cuisine, where whole grains are emphasized, and the nutrients are not cooked out of foods. A large selection of wines adds an extra glow of health.

In the evenings, meals are served inside, where Mr. Barrymore's living room has been given a turn-of-the-century decor, with lots of stained glass. Owner-host Rudy Butterfield plays recorded classical or other high-quality music as a background for his cuisine. At lunch, entrees are priced between $3.25 and $5.50, including soup or salad, french-fried parsley, and the vegetable of the day. A good starter is a bowl of fresh mushroom bisque at $1.75. An ending "not to be believed" is a homemade chestnut mousse. On the dinner menu, with entrees averaging around $7.50, a daily fish specialty is featured, plus giant stuffed pork chops with pears and pecans in a lemon, honey, and sherry sauce. It's chic-casual, with youthful waiters in jeans. Open daily from 11:30 a.m. to 3 p.m. for lunch; dinner from 6 p.m. to 10:30 p.m. Monday through Saturday.

The Brotherhood of "The Source"

The Source, 8301 Sunset Boulevard, West Hollywood (tel. 656-6388), is a low-budget Sunset Strip establishment where natural foods are enhanced by ingenious simple spicing. Everything served is organic and vegetarian—the philosophy of the place is not to serve anything that could have walked, swum, or flown away! And every dish served seems brimming over with vitamins and vitality.

Organic egg omelets and whole-grain cereals with lots of fruit are served for breakfast ($2.65). Soups, salads, and sandwiches are available from lunch on; dinners cost $4.25 and include soup or salad, a basket of whole-wheat rolls and butter, and an entree—perhaps cheese walnut loaf. Homemade date-nut cheesecake is a lovely dessert at $1.25. Open weekdays for lunch and dinner, Saturday and Sunday from 9 a.m. to 1 p.m.

Restaurant Row

La Cienega Boulevard is "Restaurant Row," and the Boulevard runs down the hill from Sunset Boulevard to Wilshire. Actually, the Row is in West Hollywood, near the boundaries of Beverly Hills. For some reason, it houses some of the finest restaurants in the Greater Los Angeles area. Nearly all of them are expensive, but not unreasonably so.

Both sides of the fabled street contain California-European-style restaurant extravaganzas, in which the atmosphere and background compete with the cuisine.

Perhaps the granddaddy of all the Restaurant Row establishments is **Lawry's The Prime Rib,** 55 N. La Cienega (tel. 652-2827). Here, in a simulated atmosphere of an old English inn, you'll be served some of the finest beef in Los Angeles. You can ask for a predinner drink at a pewter-topped, wood-paneled bar.

In all, the restaurant suggests a furnished country home, the dining room imbued with murals and fine decorative touches. Some Angelenos think of Lawry's as their private club.

Several chefs, imported from abroad, at a handful of Los Angeles restaurants, have dismissed Lawry's as having "no cuisine." The charge is ridiculous. The restaurant does one thing—roast prime ribs of beef—and it does it fantastically well! The management doesn't dissipate its energies trying to offer a variety of dishes.

There are three beef cuts, each super-delicious: the "English" cut and the "Lawry" cut, both $8.95, and the "Diamond Jim Brady" cut, $10.95. The ribs are served with Yorkshire pudding, mashed potatoes, and whipped, creamed horseradish. Served with each dinner is the house salad on its iced "spinning bowl," with a French sherry dressing. There is, in addition, a good wine list, featuring imports from Germany and France. For dessert, chocolate pecan pie is $1. The restaurant is open daily from 5 p.m. till midnight (on Sundays, from 3 p.m. till 11 p.m.).

Downtown L.A.

Downtown Los Angeles has a seemingly incongruous group of restaurants. Some are suitable for music and theater buffs. However, most Angelenos head downtown to sample Chinese and Japanese food in an ethnic setting. A few of the choices that follow are for nostalgia fans, holdovers from Los Angeles of yesteryear.

Music Center Restaurants, 135 North Grand Avenue, Los Angeles (tel. 972-7333), are in the Dorothy Chandler Pavilion at the Los Angeles Music Center. You can dine here either on the fifth floor, in the elegant **Pavilion,** or else at the more informal **Curtain Call,** on the Grand Avenue level. In addition, there is an adjoining coffeeshop with an enclosed sidewalk cafe for those desiring only a light snack.

The **Pavilion** (tel. 972-7333) is a chic place to dine if you're attending concerts or just visiting the downtown area. This establishment has gone a long way in recreating the glamor of Paris, with swagged and tasseled gold draperies, crystal chandeliers, Louis XV-style chairs, and most important, a key staff from Europe, not to mention the view five stories up.

German chef Hugo Fressler takes pride in an impressive à la carte menu, but the prize is the buffet luncheon or dinner, combining French specialties with dishes from Scandinavia as well

A Budgeteer's Haven

The Original Pantry Cafe, 877 South Figueroa (tel. 972-9279), Los Angeles. Those who remember living on a lean and hard budget in the 1920s and 1930s will feel right at home here. The Original Pantry—"we never close"—dates from those days. Its prices have gone up a bit, but its warm informality and good food—and truly bountiful portions—have remained the same. It still serves the best (not the fanciest) breakfast in Los Angeles, and the lines outside attest to its continuing popularity.

For $2.35 you'll get a plate of eggs any way you like them, plus two slabs of sweet cured ham, along with home fries and plenty of fried sourdough bread, and endless cups of freshly made coffee. In their long flowing aprons, the waiters are the friendliest anywhere, and if they weren't waiters they could easily go on the vaudeville circuit as stand-up comedians. Drop in for lunch or dinner and partake of a huge T-bone at $5.40 or good-tasting home-fried pork chops at $4.15. You'll be given plenty of cole slaw and hash brown potatoes as well. Sepia paintings hang on the walls; water is served in stainless steel pitchers; the floors are tile; and the menu hangs on the wall. May Old Los Angeles live forever!

as many California salads. The $3.95 luncheon buffet is a stunner, including such fare as pâté, marinated herring, apricot mousse, guacamole, fish and meat salads, plus a bowl of fresh fruit. Seconds are encouraged. You can also order à la carte.

At night this spread costs $8.95 and is more elaborate, with poached salmon, poultry, and a carver slicing off choice roasts as you desire them. Waiters have scheduled everything to serve you in time to make the curtain. Luncheon hours are from 11:30 to 2:30; dinner, 5 to 9:30. The restaurant is open on Sundays only when there is a performance at the center. Reservations are advised.

The **Curtain Call** (tel. 972-7322) is a bistro-style restaurant on the ground-floor entrance to the center. The decor is reminiscent of show-biz days of yore, with bentwood chairs set in a recreated stage with stylized scenery, bits of theater boxes, and blow-ups of two of the older Los Angeles theaters. Usually it's jampacked with pre- or post-theater diners, and reservations are always recommended.

The à la carte menu includes shish kebab ($6.25), roast prime ribs of beef with a baked potato and vegetable ($7.95), as well as many fish, poultry, and veal dishes. Excellent appetizers include a velvety smooth vichyssoise at 75¢. The chef's dessert specialty is cheesecake with a strawberry sauce, 95¢. Open for lunch from 11 to 1; dinner, 5 to 8; late supper, 9 to 1.

Adjoining is the **Patio Cafe,** all fresh white and green, with white iron chairs and lattice walls. It features the same menu as Curtain Call.

The New Moon, 912 South San Pedro Street (tel. 622-1091), is a landmark in the downtown garment district and a great local favorite for Cantonese fare. Like many Chinese restaurants that serve a very good and authentic cuisine, the New Moon is a little short on atmosphere. However, it is pleasant and spacious, and at night, when tables are clothed in black and there are fresh flowers on every table, it almost approaches elegance.

The main concern here is good eating. Many businesspeople come at lunch for items like glazed crystal shrimp ($4.80), New Moon chicken salad—a crunchy mix of shredded chicken, rice noodles, and greens ($3.10)—and sweet-and-sour almond duck ($3.10). Chinese food aficionados often opt for a selection of Chinese teacakes (30¢ each), a unique treat.

At dinner, those with adventurous palates can have the chef plan a meal for them, priced at $4.20 to $7.20 per person, the latter for a fairly elaborate feast. A la carte, you might order Westlake duck, cooked to an incredible tenderness and covered with a sauce containing black flower mushrooms, bamboo shoots, and Chinese parsley ($3.50). Another excellent dish is chicken walnut ($3.55). For dessert, ginger ice cream (55¢) is enthusiastically recommended.

For those who know Chinese food, the New Moon is a real find. For neophytes, it's a great place to experiment and break out of the eggroll and fried rice syndrome.

Open daily for lunch from 11 to 3, dinner from 3 to 10.

Little Joe's, 900 North Broadway, Los Angeles (tel. 489-4900), is a happy success story. It started the same year that Jolson's *Jazz Singer* was released: 1927. Like the flicks, it grew until it now occupies an entire brick-built, converted warehouse, and offers a grocery store, a collection of bars (including one in the cellar), and at least four dining rooms. With many out-of-towners, it's become a tradition to have at least one "real" Italian meal at Little Joe's.

The portions served are wholesome and large, the flavors aromatic. For those who are famished, the lead-off recommendation is a six-course dinner ranging in price from $3.60 to $6.95 and including antipasto, followed by the soup of the day, a choice of spaghetti or ravioli, then an entree with vegetables and potatoes, topped off with dessert and coffee.

There's an extensive list of salads, seafood, broiled meats, and cheese, such as gorgonzola. On the à la carte listings, you'll find such items as lasagne, $3.60, and osso buco with risotto, $4.95. Dinners are served from 2:30 p.m. to 9 p.m., though you can order lunch from 11:30 a.m., with daily specials costing $2.45. Closed Sundays.

New Chinatown

New Chinatown is a miniature Oriental community, just a few blocks from Olvera Street, three blocks north of Sunset Boulevard. A small slice of Hong Kong, it replaced the former Chinese section, where Union Station now stands. In many ways, it's far superior to the old. Between North Broadway and North Hill Street, it centers on a colorful open plaza, with narrow, traffic-free lanes, lined with shops and restaurants.

A Chinaman's Chinatown

In an offbeat section of Los Angeles, near the city market and in an unprepossessing warehouse district, sits **Man Fook Low,** 962 San Pedro, Los Angeles (tel. 972-9467), in business for half a century. Actually, it is but one of a cluster of Chinese restaurants, all of which put total emphasis on food. You'll often encounter an out-of-towner or the slumming chic from Beverly Hills here, enjoying a seemingly endless array of good-tasting wares ranging from sea bass with flaky almonds to succulent and tender barbecued spareribs. For $3.75 you can have not only a large, but a superb, repast. No chef's secrets here: the kitchen's out in the open. If you arrive at the right time, you may see the cooks patiently stuffing those delicious little pasta tidbits, known as "dim sum," or Chinese teacakes. Dim sum is served from 10 a.m. to 2 p.m. daily, and each plate of goodies costs between 25¢ and 40¢. Hard to find, but make the effort if you want a truly memorable dinner at a forgettable cost.

Grand Star, 943 Sun Mun Way, Los Angeles (tel. 626-2285), is owned by Frank and Wally Quon and their mother, Yiu Hai Quon, who, at the age of 77, still oversees the kitchen. Age and experience are still revered here. Madame Quon prepares three complete meals priced at $3.95, $4.95, and $7.95 per person. The latter is the gourmet selection, and with it you get several choices, including water-chestnut rolls, wonton soup, lobster Cantonese, rice, tea, and dessert. With a party of six, you get a bonus of barbecued duck. Meals are served from 11:30 a.m. till midnight. On the street level, in a room appropriately hung with ornate lanterns and panels of silk with brocaded tassels, entertainment, usually a Chinese woman singing with piano accompaniment, is featured at cocktail time and on most evenings.

Hong Kong Low, 425 Gin Ling Way, Los Angeles (tel. 628-6217), is a pagoda-style restaurant in the heart of New China-town, opening onto the central plaza. The dining room on the second floor is preferred (note the exceptionally fine staircase lantern), because of the views of the ornate rooftops and square.

Family-style meals are available for two or more. For example, for $5 per person, you can order the lobster dinner, including a chef's soup, papered chicken, siu gow, butterfly shrimp, Hong Kong Low special, rumaki, Cantonese lobster, pineapple chicken stick, barbecued spareribs, and fried rice. Less elaborate dinners go for $3 and $3.50 per person. Cantonese specialties include beef with oyster sauce, $2.75, and sweet-and-sour chicken, $2.50. A child's combination plate (soup and mixed appetizers) costs $1.75. The list of apéritifs features such exotic drinks as "Singapore Sling." On our latest rounds, a five-piece combo from Hong Kong was featured.

Grandview Gardens, 951 Mei Ling Way, Los Angeles (tel. 624-6048), just off the plaza of New Chinatown, is for those who like an Oriental repast in a modern setting. The spacious dining room is refreshing and colorful, though the skillfully prepared meals dominate the scene. You can order drinks first in the cocktail lounge, named after a large Buddha who greets you at the door. Family-style luncheons are served from 10 a.m. till 3 p.m. daily. The least expensive family-style dinners—at $4.50 per person—include wonton soup, fried shrimp, fried chicken toast, fried rice, chicken chow mein, almond chicken roll, as well as a choice of barbecued spareribs or almond duck. A minimum of two is required, and with each additional person another dish is included.

Little Tokyo

Little Tokyo is a portion of downtown Los Angeles, close to City Hall, between Alameda and Los Angeles Streets. Here you can find restaurants providing authentic Japanese meals. Roughly, the area is confined to about three blocks, with gift shops and restaurants interspersed with banks and clothing stores.

Angelenos are expressing great interest in Japanese cooking in the wake of more and more reports revealing the relatively fat-free cuisine to be good for the health and heart. The presentation is also striking. Nina Froud, an authority on Japanese cooking, wrote: "Japanese cooks are dedicated artists, sculpting fantastically beautiful shapes out of vegetables and transforming prosaic turnips into chrysanthemums and carrots into cherry blossoms."

Tokyo Kaikan, 225 South San Pedro Street (tel. 489-1333), is the most raved-about Japanese restaurant in Little Tokyo, and many devoted patrons feel that it's the best in L.A. It's certainly among the most attractive. The interior is designed like a Japanese country inn, with much use of raw woods, rattan and bamboo, enhanced by straw baskets and other traditional artifacts. Overhead are brightly colored globe lights. In addition to the regular menu, there are four different food bars specializing in tempura, steak, shabu-shabu, and sushi.

Japanese cocktails are offered along with the American martinis and whiskey sours. For $2.20 you can order a drink described as "delicately smooth as silver satin shimmering forever in Oriental moonlight." Who could resist?

Appetizers are equally tempting: for $2.50 you might order a kushi kebab—cubed fruits or beef skewered and fried with chicken and scallops. Entrees include beef sukiyaki ($5.50), beef teriyaki ($5.90), and Kaikan nabe—steamed vegetables and assorted seafood ($5.90). All are served with soup, salted vegetables, and rice. For dessert the green-tea sherbet (50¢) is delicious and refreshing.

At lunch entrees range from about $3 to $5.

Tokyo Kaikan is open Monday through Saturday from 11:30 a.m. to 2 p.m. and 6 to 10:30 p.m. There's another branch nearby at 337 East First Street, off San Pedro, open the same hours, but closed Monday instead of Sunday. Reservations recommended.

East Wilshire

From downtown Los Angeles along Wilshire Boulevard and the section known as "Miracle Mile" a string of varied restaurants of fine quality is found.

Pacific Dining Car, 1310 West 6th Street (tel. 483-6000), is

Dining in a Derby Hat

The **Brown Derby Restaurant**, 3377 Wilshire Boulevard, Los Angeles (tel. 384-4147), lays claim to being "the original" of this famous restaurant name. It traces its origins back to 1926, to a hot-dog stand owned by Gloria Swanson's second husband. Larry Anderson, the grandson of the great silent screen actress, is now the manager. The original Brown Derby is not to be confused with the more expensive one on North Vine Street, with its caricatures of show-biz folk.

The main dining room of the Wilshire Boulevard Brown Derby is the interior of a large derby. Adjoining it are intimate dining rooms, built hacienda-style, with sloping ceilings and thick arches. The decor —rich in the early California sense—invites with soft leather booths. You enjoy your meal by flickering candlelight. Mondays through Fridays, live music intensifies the mood.

Lunch is served from 11:30 a.m. to 4 p.m., dinner from 4 p.m. to 10:30 p.m. (Sunday to 10 p.m.). For lunch, you can try the Cobb Salad for $4.75, including avocado, egg, turkey, bacon, blue cheese, and tomato resting on a nest of chopped salad greens, and topped with a special old-fashioned dressing. A gourmet seafood salad at $4.95 consists of chilled shrimp, lobster, crab, mushrooms, artichoke hearts, and mixed greens. At dinner you might order veal piccata ($6.50) or prime rib of beef au jus ($7.25); both come with plenty of trimmings. The dessert specialty is the Derby chocolate mousse at 85¢, and standard beverages go for 50¢.

actually housed in a luxury, wood-paneled Pacific dining car. The Idol family, who still run the place, started serving diner food in 1921; since, they have added on a few rooms and become a venerated Los Angeles tradition. The P.D.C. even boasts a celebrity clientele that includes Glenn Ford, Liza Minnelli, and Richard Thomas.

Only prime meats and fresh vegetables are served (charcoal-broiled items are the specialty). At lunch, a steak sandwich costs $4.95; an eight-ounce charcoal-broiled cheeseburger with cole slaw is $3.25. Salads with homemade dressings are excellent, and homemade desserts like the apple pie ($1.15) and cheesecake ($1.45) are most satisfying.

At dinner, huge charcoal-broiled steaks begin at $9.45; another favorite entree is half a broiled chicken ($6.50). But anything you order will be high quality and prepared with care.

The Pacific Dining Car is open Monday through Friday from 7 a.m. to 11 p.m., Saturday from 5 p.m. to 11 p.m., and Sunday from 4 p.m. to 10 p.m.

Eggs and Crafts

The Egg and The Eye, 5814 Wilshire Boulevard, Los Angeles (tel. 933-5596). At first, the name seems merely a pun on the old Claudette Colbert movie, *The Egg and I.* But, in actuality, The Egg and The Eye is the finest omelet house in Los Angeles. Across from the La Brea Tar Pits, it is housed on the second floor of an exhibition center for arts and crafts. Either before or after dinner, you can enjoy the gallery collection. The omelets are expensive, but well worth the money, considering their quality. You're faced with a choice of 54, ranging in price from about $3 to $6 and filled with everything from peanut butter to caviar and champagne. With all meals comes a basket of black raisin bread. The restaurant serves a Sunday brunch from 11 a.m. to 6 p.m.; otherwise it's open Tuesday through Friday, 11 a.m. to 3:30 p.m. and 5 to 10 p.m.; Saturday, 10 a.m. to 11 p.m. Reservations are a must.

West Los Angeles

Geographically an impossible area, West Los Angeles embraces such dining choices as the Farmers Market, going north to the edge of Sunset Strip at the edge of Beverly Hills.

Antonio's, 7472 Melrose Avenue, Los Angeles (tel. 655-0480). One food critic called it "the most innovative Mexican restaurant to be found anywhere today in the U.S.A.!" Burdened by that declaration, Antonio's has a lot to live up to. In its own simple and unpretentious way, it does. The location's in an unchic neighborhood, and the decor is ethnic, with paper flowers in foil-wrapped beer bottles on each table, plus overscaled paper flowers hanging from ceiling baskets. It's small and crowded, but from there on, it's heaven. First-timers often select Antonio's special combination, including an enchilada, taco, and New York steak with refried beans for $5.95. For a dollar less, you can order the Yolanda special: chili relleno, taco, and enchilada, with rice and beans. Or you might begin with a plate of assorted appetizers ($1.50). A most recommendable main course is chicken mole ($4.25); ditto the shrimp in garlic sauce ($5.95). Fried bananas at $1 are the featured dessert. Lunch is served Monday through Friday from noon to 2:30 p.m. Dinner is Monday through Thursday, 5 p.m. to 11 p.m. (Friday and Saturday, until midnight). On Sundays, the hours are from 5 p.m. to 11 p.m. Wine and beer are served (try Carta Blanca dark beer at $1) as well as cocktails.

The Great American Food & Beverage Co., 8500 Santa Monica Boulevard, West Hollywood (tel. 652-9594), is a hip eatery with indoor and terrace dining, at the corner of Santa Monica Boulevard and La Cienega, the beginning point for the famous Monday night stroll through the art galleries. Architecturally, it's crazy California, a pseudo-Norman cottage combined with a cuckoo-clock design. Each waiter or waitress (the former attired in knickers, suspenders, and a variety of hats; the latter in long dresses) hangs his or her guitar on a central rack. One by one, they stop serving to play and sing ballads, do mime, juggling, or comedy. The interior is Victorian, with gas-style chandeliers, big slow whirling fans overhead, Tiffany lamps, an oil portrait of Queen Victoria, many trailing plants, bentwood chairs, old photographs, and 19th-century inn and shop signs. The menu reflects the health-food outlook, with natural vegetables and fruits served in ingenious ways. Featured is the "hi-pocket," a meal in itself with fresh fruit, corn on the cob, and an unusual choice of yogurt or barbecued rib. Priced anywhere from $2.95 to $3.95, "hi-pockets" range from a mixture of raw, chopped vegetables to hot sliced Polish sausage. The less serious diner can enjoy an ice cream "orgy," priced anywhere from $5 to $40, the latter serving guaranteed to do you in. There's an elaborate coffee list, including a Titian, orange-flavored espresso, $1.15. Hours are Monday through Thursdays and Sundays, 11:30 a.m. until midnight (till 2 a.m. on Friday and Saturday).

Budapest, 432 North Fairfax Avenue, West Los Angeles (tel. 655-0111), is where old-time Eastern Europeans, many of them retired screen writers, give their palates a nostalgic reminder of cooking from "the old country." Many authorities consider the Budapest the most genuine Hungarian restaurant in the West. The dining room is plain but comfortable, in the family-style. The price of the entree includes the cost of a complete meal, which is almost unbelievably filling.

For just $5.75, you can begin with stuffed cabbage, a bowl of relishes, potato soup, then continue on to Hungarian goulash with peas, egg barley, and a boiled potato, and end with dessert (the strudel's light and flaky), and a beverage. For the same price, you can substitute an entree of chicken paprikash; roast young goose is $6.95; blintzes with all the above trimmings, $4.95. Children under 12 may order a complete dinner for $3.95. The restaurant is open from 4 p.m. to 10 p.m. (Sundays from 1 p.m. to 10 p.m.) No luncheon is served. Closed Mondays.

El Coyote, 7312 Beverly Boulevard, West Los Angeles (tel. 939-2255), is a Mexican cafe that has settled most comfortably into its well-earned fame, enjoying a steady stream of habitués from stars to camera grips. Many an Angeleno will agree that this is one of the finest and least expensive places for top-notch south-of-the-border viands. Started during the Depression, it was the brainchild of Mrs. Blanche March and her late husband. Their original postage-stamp location didn't fit with their increasing popularity, so they eventually moved to their present expanded quarters, near La Brea and CBS. With a keen artistic eye, Mrs. March selected Mexican decorations to make for a warm and inviting ambience. The favorite spot for dining is the outdoor patio, though you may want to stop off first in the Cantina de La Paz to sample the tequila Margarita, the house cocktail special at 80¢.

In food, the house specialty is a "Mexican pizza" (an assortment of hors d'oeuvres), for $1.40. The best bargains are the combination dinners, such as the one for $2.75, which includes albondigas (Mexican meatball soup), chili relleno, with fried rice and beans, plus corn tortillas and coffee. Other favorites include green corn tamales for $1.75; beef enchilada, with rice and beans, $2.75; two beef tacos with rice and beans, plus a choice of soup, $2.55. A bottle of Mexicali beer goes for 75¢. The restaurant is open daily from 11 a.m. to 10 p.m.

Beverly Hills

In Beverly Hills, restaurants put their best foot forward. All this splash produces some high tabs.

La Scala Boutique, 9455 Santa Monica Boulevard, Beverly Hills (tel. 550-8288). On the whim of a moment, Jean Leon created this "gourmet boutique/delicatessen" in Beverly Hills. It's now become one of the two or three truly chic luncheon spots in Greater Los Angeles. Natalie Wood's likely to drop in for a quick meal—she likes the spaghetti; or perhaps Suzanne Pleshette will show up here, too, and order the smoked fish. There are just a few booths and even fewer tables; and if you arrive anytime after noon (it opens at 11:30 a.m.), you must wait in line, as reservations are accepted only for dinner.

The Farmers Market

At Fairfax and Third Avenue, in West Hollywood, the **Farmers Market** is the world's most glorified "cafeteria" and grocery store. It is jampacked with produce—not only the homegrown California stuff (those sun-ripened oranges, grapefruits, and dates), but those foreign oddities as well (pickled Georgia freestone peaches, Norwegian cod roe, even beef blood pudding, and, of course, Japanese pin head gunpowder, a type of green tea, each leaf rolled into a pellet). Wheeling around wooden carts along with Beverly Hills matrons is only part of the adventure. (For shopping recommendations, see Chapter VI.)

There's no better way to introduce yourself to California fare than by heading to the major **Juice & Salad Bar** (pavilion 334), where for 45¢ or 60¢ you can drink pomegranate and cherry juice, papaya and pineapple, strawberry and coconut, and most certainly, passion fruit. The bar's specialty is "green drink," a strange combination of pineapple, celery, watercress, spinach, and parsley. Those luscious Hawaiian salads—made with fresh fruit—can be yours at $2.85 a plate.

The stalls offer a mixed bag of food. Personally recommended are: **Magee's Kitchen,** dispensing corned beef, cabbage, and parsley potatoes since the end of World War I—except the price is higher than ever: $3. At the **Fish & Oyster Bar,** you can select crab Louie at $3.60, or Bay shrimp Louie, $2.45. **Michael's** is known for his blintzes, with an order of two with sour cream and preserves costing $1.60. **Castillo's Spanish Kitchen** takes diners back to the early California style of cooking. Its Mexican dishes are duplicated in many places, but its tacos (75¢, beef or bean) rate an ole! **Bryan's Pit Barbecue** keeps the focus on Texas and its "real" chili is 94¢ a bowl; its barbecued beef, pork, and ham dinner, $3.55; and a tasty Texas salad goes for $1.74. If you're still walking, head for **Le Mart,** where gourmands can order an entire pie such as gooseberry at $3.75 or pecan at $4.25.

Something simpler? At one of the kiosk-type stalls, you'll find *fresh* peach, banana, or strawberry ice cream. On the premises is a most substantial dining room, **Du-par's,** the family restaurant, open till 1:30 a.m.

The market dates from 1934, when 18 farmers, some of them right out of *Grapes of Wrath,* started hauling in fresh produce on the spot and selling it from the backs of their trucks. Who knows when the first Jane Darwell predecessor decided to fry a chicken, bake some raisin bread, and whip up an old-fashioned potato salad the way the folks back home in Oklahoma like it? Eventually, tables were set up under olive trees, at which customers could consume the prepared food.

The walls are decorated with caricatures by Gerald Price, but if you look at them, you'll be branded a foreigner. Deluxe sandwiches are in the $2.95 to $4.25 range. Two good main dishes are the cannelloni "Gigi" at $4.45 and the shrimps marinara at $6.95. A pitcher of the house wine costs $2.95. A piece of cheesecake at $1.25 rounds out the meal. You can also dine here in the evening, until 9 p.m. Closed Sundays. On the way out, you can always buy some Iranian caviar to take with you.

The Magic Pan, 9601 Brighton Way at Camden, between Santa Monica Boulevard and Wilshire, Beverly Hills (tel. 274-5222). When a movie star wants luscious lace-thin French crêpes or Hungarian palacsintas, chances are he or she will head for The Magic Pan. This charming restaurant, much like an idealized version of a European country inn, deserves its special fame. The crêpes—made on a wheel rotating over a gas flame—are in the $2.20 to $4.95 range, the latter made with crab. Fresh-fruit crêpes go for $2.10 (try the one with strawberries). A bowl of soup at 95¢ makes the best beginning. If you can possibly manage it, finish with a crêpe à la mode, a delightful chocolate specialty, at $1.85. Open daily from 11 a.m. to midnight (Friday and Saturday till 1 a.m.). The weekend brunch is especially popular. No reservations.

Trader Vic's, 9876 Wilshire Boulevard, Beverly Hills (tel. 274-7777), is one of the country's most imaginative restaurants with foods inspired by the cuisines of the world. In addition to the Trader's own interpretation of the South Sea island cuisine, the restaurant features meats and fish from Chinese ovens (Trader Vic's own specialties), and Chinese food as well as an impressive selection of curries.

The restaurant is in the Beverly Hilton Hotel, with its own entrance and parking and is, as would be expected, decorated with tropical artifacts. While Trader Vic's is a large restaurant, the various areas for seating are intimate and are placed on different levels. The restaurant faces on a small Oriental garden spanned by a red lacquered bridge.

The menu has so many tempting possibilities that choosing your food and drink is difficult. Diners may select any one of a number of exotic tropical drinks along with perhaps the "Cosmo Tidbits" which features a large assortment of the restaurant's most popular appetizers, including fried shrimp, spareribs, crab Rangoon, and sliced pork at $4.25.

A rich chicken broth with diced potatoes, sliced green onions, and shredded egg called "Trader Vic's Own Soup" is a good suggestion for the first course at $1.35.

The Indonesian lamb roast at $10 is succulent and one of the Trader's specialties. Paper-thin filets of beef prepared at the table with a flaming mustard sauce at $10 is also a favorite. The mild or "susu" curry with a cream sauce at $8.25 with lobster or the stronger "Calcutta curries" are both good bets as well. A baked peach flambé with rum ice cream at $3.25 is for the non-counter of calories, but those who do count may want the fresh fruit compote when in season. Open every day from 4:30 p.m. till 1 a.m.

Nate 'n Al Delicatessen, 414 North Beverly Drive (tel. 274-0101), offers an alternative to chic and expensive dining in the heart of this posh shopping area. It's a bustling Jewish kosher-style deli that has been an institution in Beverly Hills for over 30 years. Attesting to the quality of the food is the fact that it's always mobbed. Some of the crowd is waiting to take out food from an appetite-whetting glass counter up front stocked with chopped liver, stuffed cabbage, creamed herring, and every kind of deli meat, but there's usually a line for tables, too.

All the bread is fresh-baked. The extensive menu lists a wide variety of hot entrees: cheese blintzes with sour cream and apple sauce are $2.75; roast turkey with dressing and a vegetable is $3.75; sweet-and-sour boiled beef with potato and a vegetable, $4.95. Those with hearty appetites might want to start with an appetizer of chopped liver ($1.95), or gefilte fish ($1.75). Sandwich offerings encompass everything from pastrami on rye ($2.35) to French-dip roast brisket of beef on an onion roll dipped in natural gravy ($2.50). If you're looking for a new taste treat you might try matzo brie ($2). Like everything else, desserts are numerous; we suggest the blueberry cheesecake (85¢).

The decor is unpretentious, with bright lighting and seating in comfortable leather booths. Open daily from 7:30 a.m. to 9 p.m.

Konditori, 362 North Camden Drive (tel. 550-9950), is an unpretentious but pleasant little restaurant, very popular with Beverly Hills shoppers. It looks like an especially attractive coffeeshop, with seating in red-and-blue booths, old-fashioned wallpaper, some wood-paneled walls, and beamed ceilings. The Scandinavian cuisine is first rate.

At lunch, cold open-faced sandwiches are featured—Swedish marinated herring, Swedish meatloaf with cucumbers, and homemade liver pâté are all priced at $2.65. Also on the menu are crêpes with lingonberries and sour cream ($2.10) and avocado filled with salmon salad ($3.25).

At dinner, you might begin your meal with Swedish pea soup ($1.25). Entrees include a very good poached salmon, sauce mousseline ($6.95), and Swedish meatballs served with lingonberries and vegetables ($4.95). Diners can also opt for a full Swedish smörgasbord ($7.50) laden with three kinds of homemade herring, egg with shrimps, cured salmon, poached salmon with dill sauce, roast beef, ham, liver pâté, Waldorf salad, potato salad, cucumber salad, and cheeses, plus a hot entree. There's a wine list on the back of the menu, including a selection of akavits ($1.50). Konditori is famous for desserts—try one of the homemade cakes ($1.50).

Open Monday through Saturday for lunch and dinner.

Century City

UPPER BRACKET: Yamato, Century Plaza Hotel, Century City (tel. 277-1840), is the finest Japanese restaurant in Los Angeles. In a lavish setting, adjacent to Beverly Hills, you can enjoy authentic regional food, prepared and served with immaculate care—truly an art! Much attention was given to recreating this mini version of Japan, and decorative objects were collected from all parts of that country. Two massive carved Buddhist temple dogs—at least four centuries old—grace the foyer. They stand as "guardians against evil." The elaborately carved overhead beams, 350 years old, are from Kyoto, and the fusumas—made into decorative panels—are 250 years old.

You have a choice of dining in the Occidental style, at tables with bamboo chairs, or you can enter the tatami rooms, where you eat on traditional floor mats, surrounded by sliding screens. The latter is like your own private dining room, its decor enhanced by a Japanese flower arrangement, painting, or scroll, and soft light filtering in through the shoji screens. Your shoes are checked. You have your own Japanese waitress in a classic kimono who kneels to prepare your food.

Under the thatched and beamed roof of the main dining area is a sushi bar, where you can order exotic appetizers adapted to Western palates. A five-course gourmet dinner—"planned with the emperor in mind"—goes for $9.95 and includes shrimp tempura and beef teriyaki. A combination family-style dinner for two or more costs $8.75 per person. From the hibachi, you can order such delights as a charcoal-grilled, basted sirloin steak teriyaki, at $8.75. Among the seafood choices is salmon Yamato, $7.25. And desserts include chilled mandarin oranges in Cointreau, $1.25 Late suppers, such as a pot of clams steamed with sake, go for $2.95. The restaurant is open for lunch Monday through Friday from 11:30 a.m. till 2:30 p.m. Dinners are served daily from 5 p.m. till midnight. The special supper menu is available after 10:30 p.m.

FOR THE BUDGET: Clifton's Cafeteria, Century City Shopping Center, 10250 Santa Monica Boulevard, Century City, is the newest of a chain of economy cafeterias that has kept the less prosperous of Los Angeles nourished for decades. (The original owner, Clifford Clinton—not Clifton—was famous for years for offering a 5¢ "maintenance" meal in preinflation days.) Now Clifton's has astonished diners by locating at the threshold of swank Beverly Hills. Those attending film and stage performances at Century Center can enjoy an economical meal that might consist of old-fashioned navy bean soup at 55¢; a beef enchilada at $1.08; or tender roast pork with dressing at $1.55. Free parking for three hours. Open every day of the week from 11 a.m. to 8 p.m.

Bel-Air—Moderate

Cafe Four Oaks, 2181 North Beverly Glen, Bel-Air (tel. 474-9317), is the canyon dining retreat creation of former actor/writer Jack Allen, who took over this once greasy-spoon restaurant and made it an outstanding indoor and outdoor dining choice. The four oaks which stood at the house when it was a private home have long since died, but diners are still shaded by a spreading sycamore. The atmosphere is informal, the decor rustic, and the food superb. The menu, which changes seasonally, is recited by attractive and youthful waiters. Entrees might include stuffed filet of sole in hollandaise sauce ($9.75), red snapper baked in fish stock and covered with Creole sauce ($9.25), or veal Normandy ($9.50). The menu is extremely limited (and wisely so), depending on the shopping for that day. However, you're usually given a choice of three or four main dishes, either meat, fish, or fowl. You might start with a hot tomato and cucumber soup (or even peanut butter soup), and there is always the chef's own salad with a special house dressing. Top off the meal with a special dessert, the "Lemon Thing," at $1.75. Closed Sunday and Monday nights, but otherwise open for dinners only from 6 to 9:30. Extremely popular are Saturday and Sunday brunches from 11 to 2. Beverly Glen is above Westwood and U.C.L.A., off Sunset Boulevard, and adjoining Bel-Air.

Westwood Village

Westwood Village is officially Los Angeles, but it has a special relaxed quality and identity of its own. It has slowly grown out of a sleepy college town, embracing the spacious campus of U.C.L.A. Now high-rise office buildings, specialty shops, restaurants, and movie theaters dominate.

Its shopping, movie theater, and restaurant core is dubbed "Westwood Village," one edge of it facing Wilshire Boulevard. Perhaps because of the larger number of students, there are more movie theaters (usually first-run) than anywhere in Los Angeles. Intermixed are innumerable restaurants where you can get anything from a gourmet East Indian curry dinner to a Mexican meal—even a dill-pickle ice cream cone!

Westwood, incidentally, is sandwiched between Beverly Hills, Bel-Air, and Sawtelle.

All the following recommendations are in the budget to moderate classification, depending in most cases on what you order.

Carl Andersen's, 10930 Weyborn Avenue, Westwood Village (tel. 479-1776), has an old-world ambience, most informal and homelike. The facade of stone and shingles is inviting. Inside, many nooks and crannies make for intimate dining. There are even books in high cases ready for your perusal. The owner-chef, Carl Andersen, who established this restaurant in 1939, once cooked for the king of Denmark. He still offers many Danish dishes, though his menu is liberated. At luncheon, you can get some of those famous Danish open-faced sandwiches, including steak tartare ($3.95) and roast duck ($3.75). The dinner price includes soup, salad, dessert, and coffee. Try the fricadeller ("pingpong" meatballs) with red cabbage at $4.50, or the Danish goulash at $6.25. Lunch, Monday through Saturday, is from 11 a.m. to 2:30 p.m. Dinner, Monday through Wednesday, is from 5 p.m. to 9:30 p.m. (till 10 p.m. on Thursday through Saturday).

Paul Bhalla's, 10853 Lindbrook Drive, Westwood Village (tel. 478-8535), is a true adventure in East Indian dining. Owners Joyce and Paul Bhalla offer delicious curries and tandoori preparations. This restaurant is said to be the only place in Los Angeles offering authentic tandoori cooking. This method is similar to an American barbecue, except that it is done in a clay oven. Chicken tandoori ($7.50) is our favorite. Other excellent entree choices are lobster bhuna served with almonds and pure silver leaf ($6.75), and beef or lamb biryani ($6.95). All of the above are served with soup, salad, dal (curried lentils), raita, rice pilaf, Indian bread, chutneys, and condiments. The wine list includes good French and Californian selections. Dinner only is served, Tuesday through Sunday, from 5:30 on. The setting is exotic, accented with memorabilia from India. Paul Bhalla's is one block north of Wilshire.

Bratskellar, 1154 Westwood Boulevard, Westwood Village (tel. 477-9535), is decorated like a medieval castle, with treasures imported from old churches and buildings in Europe—stained-glass windows, throne chairs, a huge clock, and unusual lighting fixtures. One of the interesting features is a floor-to-ceiling (25 feet) wine rack. The clientele is part student, part movie-goer, part businessman, and part shopper. Sandwiches start at $1.85 and go up to $2.95. Dinners begin at $2.95 (for spaghetti) and range up to $6.75 (for a 12-ounce top sirloin steak). The fastest-moving item is the Brat-Kebab, two skewers of beef or shrimp on a bed of rice with fresh vegetables, cole slaw, and garlic roll at $4.50. The Bratskellar is open Monday to Saturday from 11:30 a.m. to 2 p.m. (Sundays, 4 p.m. till midnight).

Old World, 1019 Westwood Boulevard (tel. 477-2033), epitomizes the new kind of California restaurant, forming its own special gourmet qualities. It takes some of the best of Americana and infuses it with health-food standards. This means salads made, whenever possible, with organically grown vegetables, hamburger beef ranked the second best in the city by *Los Angeles* magazine, soups made from earthy, tasty ingredients, "old-world" Belgian waffles using soya and wheat flour, and ice cream with pure ingredients, avoiding chemicals and additives. Room after room is like a Belgian country inn, furnished with antiques, coved black fireplaces, and stained-glass windows. For lunch, try a vegetable casserole topped with melted cheese at $2.75, or a "hi-pro" turkey sandwich at $2.75. For dinner, why not the "swinger steak" at $4.95 (it's 12 ounces of ground sirloin mixed with onions, peppers, olives, and natural cheddar, served with a salad and a baked potato)? Worth noting is the Belgian brunch with champagne at $4.50 (for that late weekend morning). Other Old Worlds are at 8782 Sunset Boulevard in Hollywood (tel. 652-2520) or at 216 North Beverly Drive in Beverly Hills (tel. 274-7695).

The Country's Only Gourmet French Cafeteria

Le Foyer de France, 10858 Lindbrook Drive, Westwood (tel. 474-0948), is unique, even in California. It has been called the country's only gourmet French health-food restaurant. Its cuisine is prepared by Leon Iragui, formerly chef at the fabled Romanoff's and once a private cook to Prince Rainier of Monaco. You present yourself at a buffet counter, where Chef Leon, in his stiffly starched high white hat, along with Basque-born Madame Iragui, help you make selections. They have three requirements: that you do not smoke, that no alcohol be consumed on the premises, and that no tea or coffee be served. In return for these restrictions, you're offered fine traditional cooking, made with fresh ingredients. The buffet table is heaped with such dishes as veal soufflé, quenelles Foyer de France, and bouchée à la reine (a kind of meat patty). A complete dinner costs from $3.95 to $5.50, including two fresh vegetables, a soup (the onion is delicious) or salad, plus homemade French bread. Luncheons are less expensive, ranging from $2.25 to $2.75. Hours are from 10:30 a.m. to 9 p.m. (Friday and Saturday until 9:30 p.m.).

Swensen's Ice Cream Factory, 1051 Broxton Avenue, Westwood Village (tel. 478-6785), is extravagant in its use of rich cream and fresh flavorings. In 1948 Earle Swensen started it all on Russian Hill in San Francisco. Now he's invaded Westwood Village, attracting at least half the student body of U.C.L.A. He offers more than 45 flavors of ice cream, including such oddities as "bubble gum" or "sticky-chewy chocolate." But can you imagine "dill pickle"? Two scoops go for 80¢. Homemade sandwiches are named after famous artists. A Michelangelo at $1.55 is filled with white-meat turkey and avocado, while a Picasso ($1.20) contains tuna fish. We don't think there's any symbolism involved. Open Monday to Thursday from 11:30 a.m. to 11:30 p.m.; Friday and Saturday from 11:30 a.m. to 1 a.m.; Sunday from 12:30 p.m. to 11:30 p.m.

Macho's, 939 Broxton Avenue, Westwood Village (tel. 478-1241), could almost be recommended in the entertainment section, as there's live Mexican and Spanish entertainment Friday, Saturday, and Sunday evenings. Macho's may be the most beautiful Mexican restaurant in Los Angeles, with tables set in a simulated courtyard and on a balcony. The decor is sophisticated and colorful. You get appetizing versions of Mexican food. At lunch you can order a choice of combination plates for $2.95. At night an à la carte specialty, priced at $5.05, is carne en serappi (fresh chopped steak with onions and hot sauce, topped with guacamole and sour cream, wrapped in a tortilla). You might also try the arroz con pollo (chicken with rice) at $4.15. The restaurant is open Monday through Thursday from 11 a.m. to midnight (Friday and Saturday until 1 a.m.); Sunday from 4 p.m. till 11 p.m.

The Best Hot Dog in Town

Pink's Hot Dogs, on the northwest corner of La Brea and Melrose near the heart of old Hollywood, is the kind of place you wouldn't expect to find in a guidebook. Yet its chili dogs at 60¢ are justly famous, served with infinite skill by the "Great Johnny" for the past 22 years. Some 4,000 of these delicious dogs are sold daily between the hours of 8 a.m. and 3 a.m. Outdoor tables are placed at the corner, although most people stand while they eat their treats. Pray the bulldozers stay away from this little nugget of a place!

The Best Ice Cream in Town

Clancy Muldoon, 11834 Wilshire Boulevard, West Los Angeles, makes the best ice cream in Southern California. No qualifications. It's not a fancy ice cream parlor—far from it. Just a long counter where you line up for some of the most original ice cream dishes imaginable. The raspberry cheesecake is famous, and other unusual flavors include root beer marble, cappuccino, and apple strudel. Our recommendation: mocha chip. Mr. and Mrs. Muldoon, with the assistance of their son Terry, produce and sell more than 150 gallons of smooth-riding ice cream per day. A sizable (five-ounce) single scoop —cup or cone—costs 45¢; a double, 80¢. The Muldoons use only 100% natural honey or else raw unprocessed sugar as a sweetener, plus rich cream and fresh eggs. No artificial flavorings are permitted. A banana split costs $1.50; 23-ounce shakes and malts, $1.10. Clancy's place is a long way out Wilshire, past Westwood, but worth the trip if you're a true devotee of ice cream. Open from 11 a.m. till 11 p.m. Sunday through Thursday (from 11 a.m. to midnight on Friday and Saturday and all summer). You can also find the same quality ice cream at Clancy's two new locations: 1524 Wilshire Boulevard in Santa Monica, and at the corner of Sunset Boulevard and La Brea in Hollywood.

The Best Hamburger in the World

Cassell's Patio Hamburgers, 3300 West Sixth Street at Berendo, Los Angeles, in the Wilshire district. On one thing, Angelenos agree: Alvin Cassell serves the best burger in a town where the competition is rough! He has spent the last 30 years creating what is undeniably a gastronomic triumph. The setting is totally unpretentious, the owner preferring to put his profit into the hamburger—not the decor, making the Cassell hamburger a legend in its own time. For $2.35 you are served a sumptuous, all prime USDA-graded steer beef (imported almost daily from Colorado) burger, the cost including all the fixings you desire—two kinds of lettuce, homemade mayonnaise, Roquefort dressing, freshly sliced tomatoes, onions, pickles—all on a help-yourself basis. You can also have all the peaches, cottage cheese, and homemade potato salad you want. You can order your burger medium, rare, well done, or "blue," which is merely whisked over the fire. The beef is ground fresh every day, Monday through Friday. Have some freshly made lemonade (with only top-grade lemons, of course), at 60¢, to accompany your meal. After you've received your order at the pick-up counter, you can dine inside, or at one of the small tables on the umbrella-shaded terrace. It's reassuring to know that, in spite of his fame, Mr. Cassell has refused all franchise offers. Unfortunately, Cassell's is open only for lunch, Monday through Friday, from 11 a.m. to 3 p.m.

San Fernando Valley

San Fernando Valley, called simply "the Valley," has many small communities, including several motion picture and television studios. Most of our restaurant selections here—all in the moderately priced to budget category—lie mainly along Ventura Boulevard, running from Cahuenga Pass (Universal City) along the Hollywood mountains north toward Santa Barbara.

UNIVERSAL CITY—AMERICAN: The **Four Stages,** 30 Universal City Plaza, Universal City (tel. 980-1212), is the ultimate theatrical restaurant in Los Angeles. On the Sheraton-Universal Studio lot, the quartet of dining rooms with one large "sound stage" form facsimiles of movie sets. Adding a touch of movie set realism, catwalks with spotlights are placed overhead.

The Captain's Deck, on Stage One is a replica of a clipper ship, with dining tables set on deck, surrounded by the main mast, ropes, and the "ocean." Stage Two, the Gold Rush room, evokes a frontier scene, complete with swinging doors. You dine in Western saloon chairs. In the Marco Polo room on Stage Three, a scene from a sultan's palace is recreated. At any minute, you expect the arrival of Yvonne de Carlo. On Stage Four, the Grenadier Room, you dine within a royal castle.

Waiters and waitresses appear in delightfully designed aprons and vests, depicting old-time movie stars. They then present you with what appears to be a movie-lot clapboard, putting it on a small easel on your table for your inspection and selections. Items range from New York steak for $8.50 to a well-prepared stuffed deviled crab at $6. Other delicious dishes are the twin filets at $8.50, and the twin lobster tails at $12. If you enjoy fresh fish, the Four Stages presents a fresh catch of the day. Fresh vegetables are also served with each main course. Luncheons, called the "matinee performance," are offered at reduced tariffs, and are served from 11:30 a.m. to 2:30 p.m., Monday through Friday. Dinners are served from 6 p.m. to 11 p.m. nightly. You'll also want to try the special Sunday brunch from 11 a.m. to 3 p.m.

STUDIO CITY: **Moskva Cliff,** 12616 Ventura Boulevard, Studio City (tel. 984-1220), justifies its many awards and citations for its Russian cuisine. A mammoth mustard palace on Ventura Boulevard, it offers two spacious dining rooms, sprinkled with samovars to set the right tone. Whatever your main dish selection, you're given an appetizer, soup, salad, pirojok, dessert, coffee or tea. We'd recommend the eggplant caviar, with shallots, tomatoes, and herbs, served ice cold. For soups, of course, the cold beet borsch is touched with lemon and sour cream. The chef has won his fame for his maréchale at $6.75. It's a boneless breast of capon, stuffed with a delicately seasoned filling of fresh black mushrooms, butter, and rich cream, dipped in egg and croutons, then sauteed crisply and finally baked to allow the flavors to blend. For dessert, the special cake is delicious. Naturally, you'll want Russian tea served in a glass. Open daily at 5 p.m., Sundays at 4. Closed Mondays.

Sportsmen's Lodge, 12833 Ventura Boulevard, Studio City (tel. 877-9846). Originally the attraction here was that you could catch your own trout in the ponds and streams around the restaurant. The artificial ponds and streams are still there, providing an enchanting view in the evening when they're lit. But the lodge no longer needs gimmicks to attract attention. The world—and not just trout fanciers—has come to its door, knowing that the staff serves one of the best meals in town. A sign in the kitchen tells the story: "If you're not proud of it, don't serve it!"

Sitting on plush banquettes you're served the trout stuffed with crab meat at $8.75. Continental, even Polynesian and Asian dishes, are offered as well. The curry of chicken and lobster, for example, is $9.95. Another superb selection is the roast Long Island duckling, with orange sauce and wild rice, at $8.50. Even if you don't like Caesar salad—$1.75 à la carte or 50¢ extra on the dinner—you may want to order it, just to enjoy the theatrical flourish with which it is served.

If you take your meal before 6:30 p.m., prices are lower (they're also lower from 4:30 p.m. to 5:30 p.m. on Sunday). Sunday brunch between 11 a.m. and 2:30 p.m. is a tradition at the lodge, featuring such dishes as cheese blintzes at $4.25 and omelette aux foie de volaille at $4.75. From 10 p.m. on, you can partake of the "after-hours" menu. Open for both brunch and dinner.

ENCINO—STEAKS AND HAMBURGERS: The Refectory, 17237 Ventura Boulevard, Encino (tel. 986-2598), is an integral part of the Spanish-style shopping complex, Plaza de Oro (Square of Gold). The square is village-like, with many courtyards, filled with shrubbery, fountains, pools, and flowers. The restaurant itself is a huge tavern, with overscaled oak beams, creating the feeling of a monastery. Lights are low, and tables are spaced far enough apart for comfort. It's more or less a glorified steak house, featuring Midwestern corn-fed aged beef, along with a help-yourself salad bar. A nun's cut of prime rib goes for $6.95, though you'd pay $7.75 for the monk's cut. Rack of lamb at $6.25 is basted in wine sauce, served with rice pilaf; lobster tail is $7.25. Desserts include a liqueur parfait at $1.50. Dinner only is served. Hours Monday through Thursday are 6 to 10:30; Friday and Saturday, 6 to 11:30; Sunday, 5 to 10:30. Take the Balboa exit from the Ventura Freeway.

Pasadena

While sightseeing in the area, you may want to consider one of the following choices.

Miyako, 139 South Los Robles, Pasadena (tel. 795-7005), offers fine Japanese cuisine in an attractive setting. It gives you a choice of both tatami and armchair service, and fresh flower arrangements are placed about discreetly. From the tatami room, you can enjoy a view of a small Japanese garden, while attended by waitresses traditionally attired in kimonos. Subtle understatement is the order of the day. Lunch is served Monday through Friday from 11:30 to 2; dinner, every day from 5:30 to 10. The gourmet dinner, from hors d'oeuvres to cookies, is $7.95, though you may prefer one of the sukiyaki dinners, $5.75 to $6.75. Lunches are priced around $2.50 and $4. The Miyako is on the same street as the Hilton.

Konditori Patio Restaurant, 230 South Lake, Pasadena (tel. 792-8044), specializes in those delicious open-faced sandwiches. They range in price from $1.45 to $4.45, though many of the local people who work nearby drop in for the "West Coast Special Salad" at $2.85. Baked fresh on the premises, the pastries and cakes are rich and good, and you can take them out into the garden, with its umbrella-shaded tables. Imported beer such as Copenhagen's Carlsberg is sold here. From 7:30 a.m. till 11:30 a.m., you can order breakfasts ranging in price from $1.10 to $3.50 and featuring Swedish pancakes and smoked salmon and eggs. The restaurant is open daily, except Sundays and holidays, till 5:30 p.m.

Marina del Rey—Moderate

When Angelenos want to celebrate, they head for the newly emerging Restaurant Row in this resort. All our recommendations are moderately priced.

The Warehouse, 4499 Admiralty Way, Marina del Rey (tel. 823-5451), is a wharfside restaurant that some have compared to Disneyland. It's not only colorful and dramatic, but serves good food as well. On Friday and Saturday nights, the line is long. This unique international restaurant is the creation of Burt Hixson, a photographer who conceived The Warehouse after visiting 42 countries and traveling 23,000 miles around the world. For him, it is a dream come true. Remembering exotic-looking wharfs on his trips, he erected a two-level dockside "warehouse," where one dines on casks and barrels, or inside wooden packing crates. Most of the tables have a view of the wharf and of the boats in the marina.

Chicken Tahitian, cooked over hickory wood, seems to be the most popular dish at $5.50. Other good entrees are the shrimp Malaysia at $8.95 and the international steak at $7.75. The

Warehouse has gained a deserved reputation for its exotic drinks, especially the house concoction, the Warf Wrat, a combination of coconut, pineapple, and Puerto Rican rums, $1.75. Open from 11 a.m. to 2 a.m. weekdays; 2 p.m. to 2 a.m. Saturdays and Sundays. The special treat is the talented harpist who entertains evenings. You get an excellent dinner, a concert, and a fascinating atmosphere.

Charley Brown's Restaurant, 4445 Admiralty Way, Marina del Rey (tel. 823-4534). Good food, a rustic decor, and the view of the marina's principal channel make this eatery an enduring favorite. No reservations are taken, so you may have to wait, a custom made pleasurable by the dry martinis served at the bar. Steak is the specialty, served with the house salad dipped in a green goddess dressing. A loaf of hot sourdough bread is placed on every table. To conclude your meal, try the crêpes Alaska filled with Häagen-Dazs vanilla ice cream and topped with brandied apples or Bing cherries ($1.25). Dinners range in price from $4.95 to $10.25, this latter price for steak and lobster; lunches from $2.75 to $4.45. Lunch is served Monday through Friday from 11:30 to 2:30; dinner, Monday through Thursday, from 5:30 to 10:30. On Friday and Saturday, dinner is from 5:30 to 11. A special Sunday brunch is offered from 10 to 3. At the latter, you can enjoy peaches in champagne, followed by eggs Benedict with hash brown potatoes and homemade blueberry muffins, for $3.65.

Donkin's Inn, 14130 Marquesas Way, Marina del Rey (tel. 823-4551). Yacht owners dock their vessels here and stroll in for a full-course meal. Naturally, the dockside tables go first. In the evening, stop first at the bar to enjoy the free hors d'oeuvres dispensed between 5 and 7. Those increasingly rare California sand dabs are featured here, and veal is also a specialty. Including soup or salad, dinners range in price from $7.75 for sauteed scallops or breast of chicken in béarnaise sauce (among other entrees) to $11.25 for steak au poivre. Lunch is priced anywhere from about $3 to $4.50. Background music is featured, but the view's the thing. Sunday brunch with champagne goes for $4.75. Open daily from 11:30 a.m. to 11:15 p.m. Thursday through Sunday nights there's disco—in a soundproofed area away from diners—9 p.m. to 2 a.m.

John Oldrate's Cyrano, 13535 Mindanao Way, Marina del Rey (tel. 823-5305). Lively and informal, this restaurant attracts with its continental cuisine and yachting atmosphere. Late at night it's a popular rendezvous for TV and film personalities.

The house specialty is a delicious London broil at $5.95, which comes accompanied by rice, mushrooms, vegetables, hot rolls, and butter. A chocolate mousse ($1.50) is an added treat. Complete dinners are in the $5.50 to $10.95 range, with lunches costing from $3 to $4.95. There's nightly entertainment at the piano bar. Open daily from 11:30 a.m. to 1 a.m. A Sunday brunch is served from 10:30 a.m. till 3 p.m., and a special Saturday brunch is offered from 11 a.m. to 4 p.m.

The Hungry Tiger, 300 Washington, Marina del Rey (tel. 821-0579), is the newest and best of the restaurants created by Bob Prescott, the founder of the Flying Tiger Line and former flying ace in China with Chennault's famed "Tigers." It's right at the marina dock and shopping complex. The architectural design allows tables to have a close-up view of the moored yachts. The ceiling has undulating redwood slats and miniature twinkling lights—a woodsy, glamorous place at which to dine. From the sea come such selections as Alaskan king crab legs at $9.50 and bouillabaisse Parisienne at $8.85. Steaks are also offered. For a New York sirloin, you'll pay $9.50. All entrees are served with clam chowder, French onion soup or a mixed green salad, and an individual loaf of bread, plus two vegetables and rice or baked potato. Open daily for dinner from 5 p.m.

Genji, 310 Washington Street, Washington Square (tel. 822-5152), is something a little different on the Marina del Rey restaurant scene. It's a modernistic Japanese restaurant, the creation of owner George Matsuda, who spent much time doing research to create the proper ambience here. The decor is somewhat involved in symbolism: Genji, a prince of ancient Japan, was married to a girl called Murasaki, which means purple—hence there are a lot of purple and plum shades in the decor. The furnishings are teak and butcher block, and Japanese prints adorn the walls; enhancing the atmosphere is Japanese background music. There's seating up front at the sushi bar, and in good weather you can dine outdoors on the patio.

A combination dinner of sashimi/beef teriyaki/tempura ($9.75) is served with salad, soup, rice, tea (genmai cha, our favorite kind), and green-tea ice cream (another little-known goody). The same meal with tempura/chicken yakitori is $6.75, or featuring a variety of sushi, $5.75. A container of sake with your meal is $1.50; a bottle of Kirin or Asahi beer, 95¢. Luncheon entrees at Genji begin at $2.50.

The restaurant is open daily serving lunch from 11 to 3, Monday through Saturday, with dinner nightly from 5 to 11.

Chapter V

SIGHTS IN AND AROUND LOS ANGELES

NO MATTER WHAT the product—film or sightseeing attraction—Los Angeles has an inbred flair for the dramatic. Beginning in the 1920s, when Hollywood burst into its glory, the larger-than-life approach has been adopted by virtually every exhibitor or entrepreneur.

Ice cream parlors were hidden under the hoop skirts of a two-story-high cement version of Little Eva; Simon Rodia's Towers in Watts were made of scrap metal, tile, mosaics, and glass bottles, foreshadowing the arrival of Pop Art; fake ruins of castles and missions were created by moonlighting studio carpenters to enhance real-estate values.

Faith healings required full-scale scenery and cast, as exemplified by the style of Aimee Semple McPherson. She would stage her life story nightly for an audience sometimes approaching 5,000. Of course, she'd have to omit mention of two or three of her husbands, as that autobiographical bit would not be appropriate for her later lecture on the "sins" of divorce. To illustrate that she was born on a farm in Canada, the curtain would open onto a pastoral setting, with Sister Aimee in a backyard swing—milk bucket dangling from her arm—and a cow in the background. She would then proceed to milk the cow and pass the full dippers to the audience who filed up to the stage. While ladling out the milk, she crooned love songs which she had written herself.

It's just in the Hollywood blood to put on a good show.

Hollywood premieres often attracted worldwide attention. Of one in particular, Ezra Goodman wrote: "For the opening of Howard Hughes' aviation epic *Hell's Angels,* in 1930, he (Sid Grauman) had Hollywood Boulevard roped off for ten blocks, streetcars detoured and 250 searchlights picking out thirty airplanes in the sky, while the Hollywood hills in the background were lit up with Hughes' name."

The Grauman technique has now permeated down to the grocer. What Los Angeles supermarket owner would think of opening for business without revolving searchlights, perhaps guest appearances of film or TV personalities?

The same blockbuster tradition carries over into the sightseeing attractions in and around Los Angeles. Forest Lawn Cemetery achieves "the ultimate"—staging christenings, marriages, and deaths! Too many craftsmen had too much at stake to let the La Brea Tar Pits (an Ice Age fossil site) in Hancock Park remain empty after the bones were removed. The pits are now filled with life-size replicas of the ancient beasts.

So, if you like the dry, classic approach to museums and sights, you've come to the wrong city!

Los Angeles

Although Los Angeles began in and around the Old Plaza and Olvera Street, later development and growth pushed the heart of the city to another area, approximately seven blocks west, on **Pershing Square.** Opening onto the square (now tunneled with parking garages), the deluxe Biltmore Hotel was built, an auditorium for concerts and the Philharmonic Orchestra erected later. Elegant residences lined **Bunker Hill** in the late 19th century, the mansions reached via Angels' Flight, a unique cable car.

Then came the earthquake scare, and city planning authorities prohibited buildings more than 150 feet high. Foreseeing that such a limitation would seriously hamper certain businesses, companies began to head out Wilshire Boulevard and into outlying areas. For a while, many parts of Los Angeles proper became relatively forgotten, falling into disrepair. Beautiful town houses gave way to slums. The 1884 Firehouse deteriorated into a fleabag hotel.

Through skilled building techniques, the earthquake disaster potential ostensibly lessened, and the ban on tall structures was removed in 1957. Large-scale leveling of Bunker Hill began, despite strong protestations that landmark mansions were being destroyed. Starting in the mid-1920s, the **Civic Center** steadily grew, culminated by the 28-story City Hall. You can take an elevator to visit the observation deck Mondays to Thursdays

THE MAJOR SIGHTS

from 10 to 4 (Fridays, 10 to 10; weekends, 10 to 5). Today, the United Bank Building on the corner of Hope Street and Wilshire Boulevard is, at 54 stories, the tallest building west of Chicago.

The shimmering addition of the new $35-million **Music Center** in the '60s marked the beginning of a long-overdue renaissance for downtown Los Angeles. New office buildings have continued this massive restoration.

The **Los Angeles Convention and Exhibition Center** occupies a 38-acre site at 1201 South Figueroa Street.

A WALKING TOUR OF OLD LOS ANGELES: People don't walk in Los Angeles. They drive automobiles. However, make one exception to that rule and visit the **Pueblo de Los Angeles.** Though bogged down by a lack of funds, the old pueblo—the birthplace of the city in 1781—is slowly being restored as a state historical landmark. A walking tour of this most interesting district is made easy if you go first to the **Visitors' Center,** 100 Paseo de la Plaza (tel. 628-1274). Organized walking tours—at no charge—leave here Tuesdays through Saturdays at 10 a.m., 11 a.m., noon, and 1 p.m.

The tour begins on the **Old Plaza,** with its circular lacy wrought-iron bandstand. It was here, so it is believed, that Felipe de Neve, the Spanish governor, founded the pueblo. Opening directly on the square is the **Old Mission Church,** the city's oldest, dating from 1818. It's filled with paintings and ecclesiastical relics, and is open daily to visitors.

But perhaps more so than the above, the block-long, traffic-free **Olvera Street,** said to be the oldest in Los Angeles, forms a tangible link to the origins of the city, particularly its rich Spanish and Mexican heritage. Now transformed into a Mexican market, it is complete with colorful shops, cafes, and "puestos" with craftsmen such as silversmiths, glass-blowers, leather artisans, and candlemakers.

The stalls and shops display merchandise imported from across the border (see our shopping section). The air is filled with the perfume and spices used. And the tiny open-fronted cafes offer simple Mexican food, as señoras quickly put together plates of tacos and frijoles at low prices. There are two full-scale Mexican restaurants as well, the most popular of which is Casa La Golondrina (see our nightlife section). Make sure you drop in on the **Trade Mart** (no admission fee) to enjoy the various exhibits of crafts from south-of-the-border.

The star attraction on the street is **Avila Adobe,** a long, low adobe building dating from 1818, making it the city's oldest. Open every day of the year, it charges no admission. Restored after earthquake damage, it was built by Don Francisco Avila, and is graced with a front veranda and rear garden, brightened by bougainvillea, roses, avocados, and gardenias.

Pico House (named after the last Mexican governor of California), built around 1870 on Main Street, was the first three-story building, a prestigious hotel of the mid-Victorian era sheltering exhausted travelers from the East at the "end of the line." Here guests relaxed in comparative luxury, enjoying the enclosed courtyard with its sweet-smelling vines and flowers. The restoration of the facade has been completed, but craftsmen are still working on the interior.

The **Merced Theatre** is also undergoing restoration. Presently, it cannot be viewed on the inside, but if projected plans materialize, it will once more stage plays.

Other famous buildings in the district include **Sepulveda House** and the **Pelanconi House,** the latter built in the mid-19th century, time of the first two-story brick-built structures in Los Angeles.

At the end of the walking tour, you can stroll over to **Union**

Passenger Terminal, 800 North Alameda Street, just east of the Plaza and Olvera Street. It has been declared a cultural monument—"one of the most beautiful buildings in Southern California." At the old terminal, movie stars would arrive grandly on the Santa Fe *Chief*, with their latest spouses. But this terminal was torn down in 1939 and replaced by the present one—the last "great" passenger terminal built in America. Covering 50 acres, it contains tile roofing, landscaped patios with benches and fountains, and arched passageways. Its architectural style has been described as "early California mission."

THE MUSIC CENTER: With three theaters in one, the county-owned **Music Center** offers Angelenos a proper forum for the performing arts. In many ways, the $35-million complex of buildings marks the coming of cultural age for the sprawling metropolis.

In large part, the Center owes its birth to the fund-raising efforts of Mrs. Norman Chandler, wife of the late publisher of the *Los Angeles Times.* The reigning social queen of Los Angeles, Mrs. Chandler is known for her civic and charity work, as well as for her beautification programs.

In the same complex as the Civic Center, the Music Center is between Temple and First Streets, one block south of Figueroa. The trio of theaters are named after Mrs. Chandler, the Ahmanson Foundation, and Mark Taper.

The **Mark Taper Forum** and the **Ahmanson Theatre** are usually taken up with rehearsals in daytime, but the public is invited to tour the 3,197-seat **Dorothy Chandler Pavilion**. (Six months of the season at the Pavilion is devoted to presentations of the Los Angeles Civic Light Opera Association, with the balance of the year as the winter home of the Los Angeles Philharmonic interspersed with grand opera and other events.)

The acoustically flexible theater, gleaming in glass with splashing fountains out front, is on six levels, including the fifth-floor Pavilion Restaurant. In another part of the building is the aptly named Curtain Call Restaurant. Free tours are conducted on Monday, Tuesday, Thursday, and Friday, May through October. From November through April, the tours are Monday through Thursday. Although the tour tickets are complimentary, the parking in the garages below isn't: 35¢ for a half hour, with a maximum of $1.50.

Of course, the best way to visit the Music Center is via a performance—either a recital, concert, drama, musical, ballet, dance program, opera, whatever. For details, you can refer to the daily newspapers, or call 972-7211.

NATURAL HISTORY MUSEUM: In Exposition Park, the county-administered **Natural History Museum,** the largest of its kind in the West, shelters seemingly countless exhibits.

There are more than 35 halls and galleries which chronicle people and their environment from 400 million years before they first appeared to the present day. Exhibits include brilliant examples of work by ancient Maya, Aztec, Inca, and pre-Inca potters, sculptors, and goldsmiths; arts and crafts of the peoples of the islands of the South Pacific; a complete depiction of insect families and their relationships to other life forms, etc.

At this writing, the museum is undergoing considerable transformation. A new Exposition Boulevard entrance and esplanade is under construction, as are indoor and patio dining facilities, new quarters for the Bookshop and Ethnic Arts Shop, and new galleries. These latter will house exhibits such as fossils of gigantic, extinct creatures from the state of Kansas which was once part of a vast, inland ocean; and the works of photographer Edward S. Curtis, who devoted his life to saving the customs and traditions of the North American Indian from oblivion.

In addition, the fossils from the La Brea Tar Pits, once housed here, are being moved to the new (to give its full official name) **Los Angeles County Museum of Natural History George C. Page, La Brea Discoveries.**

At 900 Exposition Boulevard, the Natural History Museum is open from 10 a.m. to 5 p.m. daily, except Monday. Admission and parking are free. Exposition Park, which adjoins the campus of the University of Southern California, is reached via the Harbor Freeway (get off at the ramp leading to Exposition Boulevard).

WATTS TOWERS: If you had met Simon Rodia, you might have taken him for a simple immigrant. Only he wasn't so simple. A tilesetter who originally came from one of the poorest districts of Rome, and grew up in Watts, he set out late in life to leave something behind in his adopted country ("because I was raised here, you understand?") Perhaps unknowingly, he left his own memorial.

As a result, the **Watts Towers** stand as a unique personal statement of an eccentric man who pieced together pieces of junk, creating his own fantasyland more "real" than anything at Disneyland. In many ways, his folk art foreshadowed the Pop movement—at least, that aspect of the school that transformed this society's everyday items, and even junk, into an artistic statement.

A rugged individualist who ignored the jeers and scorn of his neighbors ("some of the people think I was crazy"), Mr. Rodia scavenged the city for flotsam and jetsam, bits and pieces of iron and tin, old bottles (especially green ones), tin and stone, seashells, colored tiles.

The towers took him 33 years to build ("I no have anybody help me out"). With the instinctive skill of the artist—and without elaborate blueprints—he made his towers soar, holding them together by rods of steel, mixing lime with water, then applying his own mortar, his network of mesh screens and sieves. Two towers soar ten stories high, nearly 100 feet. The others average 40 feet.

The task completed in 1954, Mr. Rodia suddenly and mysteriously left his neighbors in Watts. He was no longer there to guard his life's achievement. In the years following, the towers fell into disrepair, the helpless victims of vandals, who cracked many of the seashells and some of the bottles—just for sport. Tracked down in 1959 in Martinez, California, Mr. Rodia seemed not to care—his spiritual link with the towers apparently was severed after their creation.

As it turned out, the greatest danger to the towers was not from the vandals, but from the municipal building department, which ordered that the towers be leveled as "hazardous to the general public." The owners did not comply. A hearing was called.

The issue became a cause célèbre. The towers that nobody had seemed interested in sparked massive support, the controversy spewing into a public hearing. Directors of museums and news-hungry magazine reporters "discovered" the spires, fanning them into nationwide attention. A decision was made to subject the steepest tower to the "pull test" to determine if it could withstand the pressure. In front of television cameras and newspaper reporters, the crucial experiment was carried out. The tower didn't budge, except for a stray shell.

Simon Rodia's dream was to live.

As recently as 1975, the City of Los Angeles accepted the

towers as a gift from the Committee for Simon Rodia's Towers in Watts, and agreed to restore and maintain them as a cultural treasure.

The towers are at 1765 East 107th Street, and are open daily from 9 a.m. to 5 p.m.; no admission is charged. To reach them, take the Harbor Freeway toward San Pedro, getting off and turning left onto Century Boulevard. Go right on Central, left on 108th Street, then left onto Willowbrook to 107th Street. The drive along Century Boulevard goes through the area of the 1965 Watts riot. For further information, call 569-8181.

Wilshire Boulevard

To Los Angeles, Wilshire Boulevard is what Park Avenue is to New York, the Champs Elysées to Paris. Commencing its run in downtown Los Angeles, near Grand Street, it stretches to Santa Monica. It is an impressive string of hotels, contemporary apartment houses, department stores, office buildings, and plush restaurants.

The realtors of the '30s named one strip—between Highland and Fairfax—**Miracle Mile.** Their ambitious label is increasingly being backed up by reality as new decorator stores and glass-and-steel office buildings locate here. Some of the most prestigious hotels in Southern California stand on Wilshire, starting with the downtown **Los Angeles Hilton** and later embracing the **Ambassador,** with its own parklike grounds. Across the street from the deluxe hotel, you'll find the **Original Brown Derby Restaurant** (see our dining recommendations in the preceding chapter).

The boulevard passes through MacArthur Park, with its own lake and the Otis Art Institute, as well as **Lafayette Park.** Near the eastern edge of Miracle Mile is the Los Angeles County Museum in **Hancock Park,** site of the La Brea Tar Pits. The boulevard also runs through the Beverly Hills shopping section, with its Beverly Wilshire and Beverly Hilton hotels.

LOS ANGELES COUNTY MUSEUM OF ART: A complex of three modern buildings, the **County Museum of Art,** at 5905 Wilshire Boulevard (tel. 937-4250), in Hancock Park (next to the La Brea Tar Pits), is considered the finest and most catholic art museum west of the Mississippi.

The four-story **Ahmanson Gallery**—built around a central atrium—shelters the permanent collection of art, ranging from prehistory to Andy Warhol. Here you'll see a monumental Cambodian sculpture of the Hindu god Vishnu dating from the 10th century A.D., Japanese paintings from the Edo period, African, medieval, pre-Hispanic, and Middle Eastern art.

Enhanced by considerable bequests, the collection is particularly rich in the Impressionists (e.g., Renoir's *Two Girls Reading*). The galleries seem to contain one—or maybe two—contributions by each of a host of major artists, such as Munch, Matisse, Rouault, Chagall, Bonnard, Picasso, Rothko, Léger, Dubuffet, Gauguin, Cézanne, Monet, Miró, Toulouse-Lautrec, Kandinsky, Pollock, and Mary Cassat. Sculpture from the 19th and 20th centuries is also well represented, as in Rodin's *The Kiss*.

On the ground level, you'll find galleries devoted to collections from the Near East, China, Japan, Egypt, Greece, Roman, and medieval days—and some rare Assyrian alabaster bas reliefs. On the Plaza level are paintings from Spain, England, and France, set off effectively by the Early and High Renaissance masterpieces from Italy. On the third level is grouped a collection of 19th-century paintings and 20th-century sculpture. The fourth level galleries attract with their exhibits of textiles, costumes, prints, and drawings, rich in European and American decorative arts, as well as a gallery of Indian and Islamic art.

The museum is closed Mondays, Thanksgiving, Christmas, and New Years. Its daily hours vary: from 10 a.m. to 5 p.m. Tuesdays through Fridays; from 10 a.m. to 6 p.m. on Saturdays and Sundays. No admission is charged except for special exhibits in the Hammer Wing for which adults pay $1; students and

Los Angeles County Museum of Art

senior citizens, 50¢. Tours, covering the highlights of the permanent collection, are offered daily at 1 p.m. (Saturday and Sunday at 1 p.m. and again at 2:30 p.m.).

In the Frances and Armand Hammer Wing major changing exhibitions are presented. The permanent contemporary art collection is also housed here in **Lytton Halls** on the third level. Finally, in the **Leo S. Bing Center,** are facilities for films, lectures, concerts, and an art rental gallery. Incidentally, on the plaza level of the Leo S. Bing Center is a cafeteria, the Plaza Cafe, with outdoor tables which overlook the Rancho La Brea (Tar Pits), coming up next.

RANCHO LA BREA (TAR PITS): In **Hancock Park** is the largest fossil site inherited from the Ice Age (Pleistocene). A "natural history landmark," it is at 5801 Wilshire Boulevard, to the west of La Brea Avenue, on the same grounds as the Los Angeles County Museum of Art. Like a Lorelei, the pits began at least 40,000 years ago luring all sorts of prehistoric amphibians, birds, and mammals to drink—and they stayed forever! Ironically, other predatory monsters, seeing them trapped, jumped into the oily mire to devour them, only to find that it was their "last supper." Although the existence of the pits was known as early as the 18th century, it wasn't until 1906 that scientists began a systematic removal and classification of the fossils. In subsequent years, more than half a million specimens were brought up, most of them of the giant variety: ground sloths, huge vultures, mastodons (early relatives of the elephant), camels (in California?), and prehistoric relatives of many of today's rodents, bears, lizards, and birds. In one pit, the skeleton of an Indian—dating, as best as can be ascertained, from 9,000 years ago—was unearthed.

The current excavation, which began in 1969, has already uncovered more than one million fossils, including many small plants and insects. Even sea shells have been found. All these discoveries have made the La Brea Tar Pits the world's richest known source of Ice Age fossils.

A number of Angelenos have contributed to the construction of replicas of some of the birds and animals in their original setting, and they stand today—fully life-size—to enthrall.

But the tar pits represent more than a museum of perfectly preserved plant and animal life. The discoveries made here have given scientists insight into ecological functions and requirements of many creatures still alive today. They have also spurred further research into archaeological techniques that have made it possible more accurately to date and clean fossils without damaging them. By these new processes, some bones have been dated at 15,500 years, and a human skeleton has been placed at about 9,000 years old.

Tours of the tar pits are also available Thursday through Sunday from 10 a.m. to 5 p.m. Conducted by docents of the Natural History Museum, the tours cover the historical and ecological significance of the excavations as well as some of the techniques involved in uncovering the remains of prehistoric creatures.

In the spring of 1975, as a result of the contribution of philanthropist George C. Page, construction was begun on the new George C. Page (La Brea Discoveries) Museum, adjacent to the pits. When completed in the spring of 1977, the new museum will, for the first time, permit the public to view the restored Rancho La Brea fossils at the site where they were found. From 1913 to 1976, a dozen or so of the La Brea specimens were mounted and on display at the L.A. County Natural History Museum in Exposition Park. These specimens, as well as all others in the 500,000-specimen La Brea collections, are presently being transferred to the new facility.

Some of the features of the Page Museum will include the following: twin theaters for viewing a 15-minute multi-media documentary, *The Rancho La Brea Story;* the La Brea Woman exhibit, consisting of a complete replica of the skeleton of the only human remains found at La Brea, as well as a lifelike reconstruction of the person as she might have appeared when living some 9,000 years ago; 400 skulls of the dire wolf; the Pleistocene Extinction Mural, portraying the animals that once lived in the Los Angeles Basin, but became extinct in the Late Pleistocene. In addition, visitors will be able to view the museum's paleontological laboratory, and also to look directly into the excavation or "dig" that has been ongoing at the Hancock Park site since 1969 Admission to both the Page Museum and the Viewing Station are free. Upon completion, the museum will be open to the public Tuesday through Sunday, from 10 a.m. to 5 p.m. The Viewing Station is open Wednesday through Sunday, the same hours. For further information, call 933-7451.

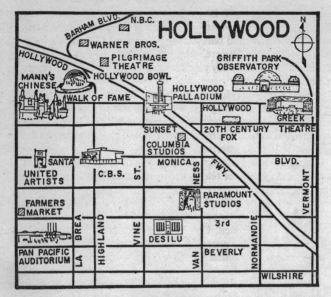

Hollywood

For a city that's not a city (but actually a part of Los Angeles), Hollywood has been chronicled to death.

The legend of Hollywood as the movie capital of the world still persists, though many of its former studios have moved into the nearby San Fernando Valley. It's been a long time since the country waited with baited breath for the urgent bulletins of "Louella Parsons from Hollywood," announcing who's splitting up, who's expecting, etc.

But Hollywood seems unaware of its own demise. Consequently, on its streets—especially Hollywood Boulevard—walk what may be (per square block) the prettiest girls and handsomest guys in America, great numbers of whom want to "break into the movies." And not one of them admits to being more than 30 years old! The film colony bears many traces of its years as the world's "dream factory"—within its confines, you'll still locate such studios as Paramount Pictures.

With its ordinary, everyday architecture, **Hollywood Boulevard** may remind one of Main Street, U.S.A. But look again. The stores may be pedestrian in design, but not the merchandise offered. Hollywood has been called "the porno capital of the country." Hollywood Boulevard has also been labeled "the Times Square of the West." In the era of the silent screen, stars arrived in ermine and tails at the premières at Grauman's (now Mann's) Chinese Theatre, after which they danced at garden court apartments. Today you'll find more pimps and prostitutes than stars.

However, look below your feet on Hollywood Boulevard. You'll be strolling along the **Walk of Fame.** Along the boulevard, bronze medallions with the names of stars and leading character actors dating from the days of the nickelodeon to the present have been inserted.

Under the name of the personality is the symbol of his medium —be it films, radio, or television. In star-struck Hollywood, the walk is amazingly democratic and fair. That is, it honors not only the legends—Chaplin, Pickford, Crawford, Davis—but such beloved character actresses as ZaZu Pitts; leading ladies of yesterday (Kay Francis, Una Merkel); even personalities totally unknown to today's generation, such at Betty Blythe. The latter's *The Queen of Sheba* was as big, for a while, as Valentino's *The Sheik.*

The corner of **Hollywood and Vine** is legendary—its fame larger than it deserves. Architecturally dull, it was known for the stars who crossed the intersection—all the big names in Hollywood. When Greta Garbo walked down the street in trousers, and was widely photographed, the pictures shocked women all over America. After recovering from their horror and the headlines—"Garbo Wears Pants"—women rushed to their astonished dressmakers (or, in some cases, their husbands' tailors) to have the slacks duplicated.

On Vine Street and Hollywood Boulevard stands the **Hollywood Palace Theater,** original home of "The Hollywood Palace" show. Now it is the scene of "The Lawrence Welk Show." For tickets, write to "The Lawrence Welk Show," 1735 North Vine Street, Hollywood, CA 90028. It's also possible to obtain tickets at the box office.

Near the corner of Hollywood and Vine is the disc-shaped **Capitol Records Building,** the first circular office building in the world. On Vine is the **Brown Derby Restaurant** (not to be confused with the Original Brown Derby on Wilshire Boulevard). In its dining rooms, the walls are covered with caricatures of film and recording personalities. Also on Vine is the **Huntington Hartford Theatre.**

THE HOLLYWOOD WAX MUSEUM: One block east of the world-famous Grauman's Chinese Theatre, the Hollywood Wax Museum, 6767 Hollywood Boulevard (tel. 462-8860), perpetuates the movie-world legend. Inside, the most publicized figures are the tableaux of John F. Kennedy at the lectern, and Marilyn Monroe in her famous dress-blowing scene from *The Seven-Year Itch.* A tableau of Leonardo da Vinci's *Last Supper,* as well as scenes depicting the Beatles, Queen Victoria, and Martin Luther King are on display.

However, most of the wax figures are movie stars or celebrities from the entertainment world. Contemporary figures include Raquel Welch, Glen Campbell, Barbra Streisand, and Sonny and Cher. Charlie Chaplin, W.C. Fields, and Mae West represent the stars of yesteryear.

In the Chamber of Horrors—evocative of Madame Toussaud's in London—you'll see the coffin used in *The Raven,* as well as a scene from Vincent Price's old hit, *The House of Wax.*

An added attraction is the **Oscar Movie Theatre,** presenting a film that spans more than four decades of Academy Award winners and presentations. The sound track is composed of a medley of songs which won as the best of their respective years. Flashing before you is everybody from Mary Pickford as *Coquette* to John Wayne in *True Grit,* from Glenda Jackson in *Women in Love* to George C. Scott in *Patton.*

The museum is open daily from 10 a.m. to midnight (Friday and Saturday till 2 a.m.) The adult admission is $3; junior (ages 13 to 17), military, and senior citizens, $2; children six to 12, $1 (under six, free).

Mann's Chinese Theatre, the Bowl, and Mulholland Drive

On Hollywood Boulevard (at 6925), **Mann's** (formerly Grauman's) **Chinese Theatre** was showman Sid Grauman's masterpiece. For the facade, he actually imported pillars of an Oriental temple, placing them in the forecourt. A proper enclosure was created for the signatures and hand and footprints of the stars.

Some personalities went beyond a simple imprint. John Barrymore made an impression of his profile, Betty Grable of her shapely leg, Bill Hart of his gun, and Gene Autry of the hoofprints of Champ, his horse.

Countless thousands of visitors match their feet and hands with those imbedded in the cement. You may find the hands or hands and feet of your favorites: Elizabeth Taylor, Charles Boyer, Barbara Stanwyck, Robert Taylor, Gary Cooper, Bing Crosby, Pola Negri, Loretta Young, Paul Newman, Tyrone Power, Ginger Rogers, Lana Turner, Bette Davis, Marie Dressler, Wallace Beery, Constance and Norma Talmadge, Humphrey Bogart, and many, many others.

Across the street is **Grauman's Egyptian Theatre,** a mock palace of ancient Thebes with a long forecourt, planted with semitropical trees and flowers, the setting for many a spectacular movie premiere, complete with klieg lights and appropriate ballyhoo. In Hollywood's great days, robed Egyptian guards (extras from the studios) paced the upper ramparts. Every usherette—in flowing robes and imitation jewelry—was a potential Cleopatra.

If you're a truly dedicated film buff, you can continue your experience with legendary Hollywood by paying a call at the **Hollywood Memorial Park Cemetery,** at 6000 Santa Monica Boulevard, between Van Ness and Gower Streets. This is where the mysterious lady in black annually pays homage at the crypt of Valentino on the anniversary of his death.

Peter Lorre is buried here, as is Douglas Fairbanks, who captured "America's sweetheart," but didn't hold her. Clifton Webb, Norma Talmadge, Tyrone Power, and Marion Davies are also buried here. Hours are from 7:30 a.m. to 5 p.m.

Nestled in the foothills is the **Hollywood Bowl,** summer home of the Los Angeles Philharmonic Orchestra since 1922. The most popular concerts each season are the Fourth of July Fireworks Family Picnic Concert and the two-day Tchaikovsky Spectacular with cannon and fireworks. Other presentations in-

Hollywood Bowl

clude numerous rock, gospel, and folk music concerts; the traditional Easter Sunrise Service; and the admission-free "Open House at the Bowl" children's festival. The Los Angeles Philharmonic season runs from July through September, with ticket prices starting at $1 on Tuesdays and Thursdays, $1.50 on Fridays and Saturdays. Information on programs, artists, ticket availability, and RTD bus service to the Bowl is available by calling (213) 87-MUSIC.

Reached via Cahuenga Pass, **Mulholland Drive** commences in the Hollywood Hills, a winding scenic mountaintop highway that wends its way through Topanga Canyon, emerging near Malibu Beach. Mulholland Drive—in the stretch across the Santa Monica mountains—provides the most breathtaking view of the entire Los Angeles area, as well as the San Fernando Valley. From these heights, you can see for yourself the validity of the California wish fulfillment of a swimming pool for every home— well, almost. A few seclusion-seeking stars, such as Marlon Brando, have purchased "view" homes on the drive.

In the northern hilly portion of Hollywood is **Hollywoodland,** with a dam and lake surrounded by hillside homes (reached by Beachwood Drive, off Franklin Avenue).

Griffith Park, the Zoo, and Planetarium

Griffith Park, in Hollywood terminology, is a "spec." You've sat through many a Western or war movie that purported to be somewhere else in the world, but was in reality the rugged terrain of what is the second-largest city-owned park in the world (4,253 acres). It has something for everybody!

The park straddles the foothills of the Santa Monica mountain chain, peaking at Mount Hollywood. Although the hills are covered with shrubbery, the lower parts—especially the ravines —are verdant and oak-studded parklands. Its position is north of Hollywood and the Los Feliz residential section. On the San Fernando Valley and Glendale peripheries, the Los Angeles River forms the border.

There are at least four major entrances to the park. The nearest to Hollywood is at the northern tip of Western Boulevard (along Ferndell). A second is at the northern extremity of Vermont Avenue, leading into that part of the park containing the Greek Theatre, the Observatory, bird sanctuary, and Mount Hollywood. Along the Los Angeles River, at the junction of Los Feliz Boulevard and Riverside Drive (also the Golden State

Freeway), is an entrance leading to the Los Angeles municipal golf course and the Zoo. The junctions of the Ventura and Golden State Freeways provide yet another entrance, adjacent to the Zoo and "Travel Town."

From Hollywood Boulevard, you can take bus 91 north on Hill Street to Vermont and Hollywood Boulevard, transferring to bus 23, which will deliver you to the Zoo. If you're going to the observatory, you can transfer to the "Observatory" bus at Hollywood Boulevard and Vermont Avenue. If you go by car, you'll be glad to know there's free parking—and a picnic area—near the junction of the Golden State and Ventura Freeways.

The **Los Angeles Zoo,** in keeping with the character of the film colony, bills its offerings as "a cast of thousands." In wildlife, the 80-acre zoo is virtually unbeatable, including some species, such as the Philippine monkey-eating eagle, that have almost gone the way of the dodo bird. In fact, the sign "Endangered Species" is in front of more than 50 species in danger of extinction because of expanding human population, needless slaughter, and destruction of natural habitats. The protection of endangered animals has firmly established the Los Angeles Zoo as a major station in a network of wildlife conservation.

Animals are exhibited by origin in five continental areas: Africa, Eurasia, Australia, and North and South America. In addition, there is an Aviary with large walk-through flight cage, an Aquatic section, a Reptile House, and the ever-popular Children's Zoo with its baby animal nursery. Admission to the zoo is $1.50; 75¢ for juniors from 12 to 15; 75¢ for senior citizens; children 11 and under are free when accompanied by an adult. Facilities include picnic areas, snack stands, souvenir shops, trams, stroller, and wheelchair rentals. Free parking. The zoo is open every day but Christmas, 10 a.m. to 5 p.m. (till 6 p.m. in summer).

Crowning the hill in the park is the **Planetarium,** on Vermont Avenue, where the "great Zeiss projector" flashes seven shows a year across the 75-foot dome. You can see all the stars visible to the naked eye, take "a trip to the moon," or else go to Jupiter and Saturn. Still other projectors simulate the effects of the Northern Lights, as well as sunrise and sunset. One-hour shows are given daily, except Monday (for show times, telephone 664-1191). The price of admission is $1.50 for adults, $1 for juniors (12 to 17); 50¢ for children five to 12. Those under five are not admitted except to the first show on Saturdays. The Griffith Observatory and Laser Images, Inc., present **Laserium,** a light-show concert under the stars. Powerful lasers produce dramatic effects covering the entire sky. In summer shows are at 9:15 and 10:30 p.m. (closed Sundays). Same times in fall (closed Sundays and Mondays). Tickets are $2.50.

The loveliest section of the park is **Ferndell,** where New Zealand horticulturists planted ferns from around the world—creating a lush setting often used as a background for high-fashion photography. In an atmosphere of sycamore and oak, you can bring your picnic lunch, and dine at tables placed there by the Recreation and Parks Department.

The **Greek Theatre** is especially popular (see our nightlife chapter).

Travel Town is a big attraction for children, who are allowed to climb all over retired rail cars, including an old Los Angeles tram and the Stockton Terminal and Eastern Railroad Engine No. 1, which saw more than 85 years of active duty (believed to be a record for a railroad engine). Also on the grounds are three airplanes. Admission-free Travel Town is open from 9:30 a.m. to 5:30 p.m. daily.

A short drive away, near Los Feliz and Riverside Drive, the young at heart book rides on miniature trains—adults paying 50¢, children under 12, 35¢. For slower locomotion, you can hire a pony on the same grounds.

Beverly Hills

Beverly Hills, as everybody knows, is the adopted hometown of many a motion-picture star, such as Groucho Marx, George Burns, Danny Thomas, Kirk Douglas, Fred Astaire, Joey Bishop, James Stewart, Walter Pidgeon, Buddy Hackett, Dinah Shore, Doris Day, Lucille Ball, Warren Beatty, and Steve McQueen.

Although it contains many commercial establishments, the term "residential city" is apt. The municipality is completely encircled by Los Angeles. Three major boulevards—Wilshire, Olympic, and Santa Monica—traverse its southern border. Approximately two-thirds of the city is in the flatlands, the other third in the foothills of the Santa Monica mountain range.

When the city incorporated at the outbreak of World War I, it contained only 675 registered voters. However, during the '20s, it earned the appellation of "boom town," so fantastically did its population soar. Today it proudly boasts its own city hall, police force, and mayor.

The business section of Beverly Hills lies between Wilshire and Santa Monica Boulevards, with its prestigious hotels, restaurants, and upper-bracket department stores, used to catering to the whims of decades of film personalities.

A drive through the glens, canyons, and hillsides of Beverly Hills may astonish you. Nowhere else in the world are you likely to find such an assemblage of superior domestic architecture— each one a virtual candidate for inclusion in *House Beautiful.* You'll feel that each inhabitant within should be a film star, regardless of whether he is or not. It's a cotton wool world, cut off from the sordid parts of Los Angeles.

The most celebrated of all Beverly Hills residences is **Pickfair,** crowning the ridge at 1143 Summit Drive. The home is still owned and lived in by silent-screen star Mary Pickford, and her second husband, Buddy Rogers.

GREYSTONE MANSION: In a community where dream houses are almost commonplace, the **Greystone Mansion,** Loma Vista Drive and Doheny Road, Beverly Hills, stands out like a medieval castle surveying the city from its perch on a hill surrounded by about 19 acres of formal gardens, orchards, pools, woodlands, and lawns. Built in the late 1920s by Edward Doheny, who had amassed his fortune in oil, the $4-million mansion (authorities estimate it would cost $60 million to build it today) is completely elegant inside and out. From its roof of slate imported from Wales to the handcarved balustrades and rafters, no expense was spared in making Greystone Mansion Doheny's "dreamhouse." Further refinements such as marble floors, crystal chandeliers, winding staircases, and fine oak and walnut paneling create a dignified atmosphere of permanence and stability. The mansion is now occupied by the American Film Institute (thus, it no longer has the original furnishings), but it is open to the public on a group-tour basis at a price of $2 per person (children under 12 pay only $1). Tours are conducted on Saturday and Sunday at 1 p.m. and 3 p.m. Reservations are required, and can be made by calling 271-8174.

Toluca Lake

Ever wonder where studios go when they leave Hollywood? Where motion-picture stars live when they don't own homes in Beverly Hills? In large part, they move to **Toluca Lake,** at the northern base of the Hollywood Hills. From Hollywood, it is easily reached via the Cahuenga Pass, Barham Boulevard, or Lankershim Boulevard—or from other points by way of the Golden State, Hollywood, or Ventura Freeways, which feed into the San Fernando Valley.

In the words of one resident, its boundaries are "phantom-like." Taking its name from two natural, artesian-fed lakes, Toluca Lake as early as the 1920s started picking up the overflow from Hollywood. Today, it encompasses a small, compact, and well-developed area, about a third of which lies within the city limits of **Burbank**, the remainder in Los Angeles proper.

Within its boundaries of hills and streets (Verdugo Road to the north, Buena Vista to the east, Forest Lawn and the Hollywood Hills to the south, Lankershim Boulevard to the west), the secluded community houses such film studios as Universal, Warner Brothers, Walt Disney, Columbia, Cathedral Films, and NBC.

Bob Hope, Andy Griffith, Jonathan Winters, and Ann Blyth own homes in the area, as do Keeley Smith, Frankie Avalon, Dorothy Lamour, and Tex Ritter. The list of former residents (many of whom have now retired, died, or moved on) is impressive: Bing Crosby, Oliver Hardy, Tennessee Ernie Ford, Doris Day, Richard Arlen, W. C. Fields, Helen Morgan, Frank Sinatra, Ruby Keeler, Dick Powell, Bette Davis, Mary Astor, even Amelia Earhart.

From "Beautiful Downtown Burbank" to the backstage movie lot tours at **Universal City,** there is much to see and explore.

The Toluca Chamber of Commerce provides an area map of the Toluca Lake Village aiding do-it-yourself visitors who shun the chartered bus tours. The Chamber office is at 10101 Riverside Drive, Toluca Lake.

Touring the Studios

Universal as well as NBC Television invites the public to tour their "cities within cities." Of the two, Universal City has invested the larger hunk of capital for entertaining guests—and you should see it first if your time is limited.

Regrettably, **Metro-Goldwyn-Mayer,** the most famous motion-picture studio in the world, has had to discontinue its public tours. At 10202 Washington Boulevard in Culver City, it requires that you "know somebody" or else have a part in a film before you can gain admittance.

Similarly, **20th Century-Fox** at Century City, bordering Bev-

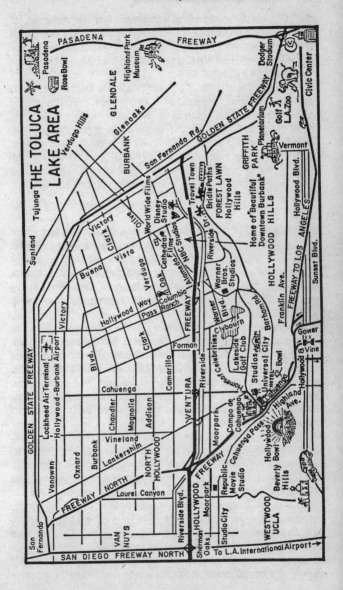

THE TOLUCA LAKE AREA

erly Hills on Santa Monica Boulevard, has discontinued its public tours. New, high-rise shopping, business, and residential complexes rest on what were once lots devoted exclusively to filmmaking—on land formerly owned by Tom Mix, when it was known as "Mixville."

However, if you've got "connections," you might manage to get inside. After all, the interest is compelling, even though the studio has developed much of its surplus land. Fox, of course, is the oldest and certainly one of the most prestigious studios, having turned out some of the greatest motion pictures ever made in America, including the 1950 *All About Eve,* starring Bette Davis. It had special success with blondes—Alice Faye, Betty Grable, and the young woman who replaced her, Marilyn Monroe.

UNIVERSAL CITY STUDIOS: Welcoming nearly two and a half million visitors yearly, **Universal City** has come a long way since its World War I beginnings as a chicken ranch. The largest studio in the world, it sprawls over 420 acres of rugged mountain terrain and valley (entrance at 100 Universal City Plaza, at the junction of the Hollywood Freeway and Lankershim Boulevard, tel. 877-2121).

Many great names in the history of the cinema are linked to Universal. The founder, Carl Laemmle, hired Erich von Stroheim as a director, and he proceeded to make a number of movies that shocked post-World War I audiences with their candor. However, he was dismissed as a "spendthrift." In another era, the studio's sagging coffers were greatly enhanced by Deanna Durbin, only 15 in 1937 when she appeared in *One Hundred Men and a Girl.*

After World War II, and into the '50s, Universal lured audiences back to movie theaters with such pedestrian vehicles as the *Ma and Pa Kettle* series (with Marjorie Main and Percy Kilbride) and the *Francis* flicks (the talking mule teamed with his sidekick, Donald O'Connor), plus a rising set of young leading men such as Tony Curtis and Rock Hudson.

The guided portion of the tour—aboard one of the brightly colored GlamorTrams—lasts about two hours. Usually your tour guide is an aspiring actor or actress. The tour takes you through the entire studio, and you descend at various points along the route, perhaps for a visit to Lucille Ball's dressing room, or a call at the office of Edith Head, grande dame of the wardrobe department.

You'll learn much behind-the-scenes information: what Technicolor "blood" is made of, how moviemakers make rain fall on cue, and how sound effects are added after a film is shot. Perhaps the most interesting aspect of the tour is a guided trip through "movie worlds"—a European Street rebuilt and aged at a cost of $2 million; Six Points Texas, a western town with six intersecting streets; Colonial Street (Smalltown, U.S.A.) The special effects include a flash flood, a torpedo attack on one of the man-made lakes, a storm at sea, a flaming building, a collapsing bridge, a runaway train, and a doomed glacier expedition. The newest thrill is an attack on the tram—as it passes through an eastern seaboard town—by the shark from *Jaws.* Actually, Universal City is giving Disneyland competition.

Those 17 years of age or older pay $5.95, the price dropping to $4.95 for those 12 to 16, and to $3.95 for the five-to-11 age group. In summer, there are continuous tours daily from 8 a.m. to 5 p.m. From Labor Day till mid-June, tours are operated from 10 a.m. to 3:30 p.m. daily. Never on Thanksgiving and Christmas, however.

At the cost of $5 million, Universal City erected a **Visitors' Entertainment Center,** where the GlamorTram will deposit you. Once there, you can spend as much time as you like, perhaps taking in the motion picture museum in the Cinema Pavilion, or going to Screen Test Theatre where members of the audience are cast as "guest stars" in a TV drama. In addition, stunt men—often with bullwhips and pistols—demonstrate their skill, espe-

Hollywood movie-making

cially in taking a fall. Makeup artists do their thing by turning two members of the audience into Frankenstein and his bride.

As the day stretches out, you may want to patronize one of the many outdoor dining areas. And if you want to stay on the lot after hours and perhaps see a few stars at play, head on over to the $13-million **Sheraton-Universal** deluxe hotel, built on the grounds of Universal City. For "making appearances," try the Four Stages Restaurant.

NBC TELEVISION: Good-naturedly spoofed for its grand size by Johnny Carson, who calls it home for his "Tonight" show, NBC-TV's Burbank facilities are the largest color studios in the United States. For a behind-the-camera preview of this complex, you can get to the studios, 3000 West Alameda in Burbank, in about five minutes from either the Ventura, Golden State, or Hollywood Freeway.

As you trip over one of the sets of "Sanford and Son," you are conducted through the studio by a bright, attractive young person. It's not guaranteed that you'll actually meet a star, though it sometimes happens (few actors can resist an admiring audience). Many big-name TV personalities tape their shows here, notably Bob Hope, Johnny Carson, Dick Van Dyke, McLean Stevenson, Jack Albertson, etc.

Aside from the glamor aspects, the tour is most informative, including looks at the scenery shop, the wardrobe department, the news department, and the rehearsal halls.

Continuous tours are conducted daily, except Sunday, from 10 a.m. to 5 p.m. The charge is $1.90 for adults, $1.25 for children ages six to 12, and free for children under six.

Tickets can be obtained for shows by writing to the address above. Tickets for such shows as "Tonight" and "Sanford and Son" are available on a limited basis at the studio, starting at 8:30 a.m. on the day of taping. Shows such as "Hollywood Squares" and many others offer tickets about two days before the taping. The ticket office is open weekdays from 8:30 a.m. till 5:30 p.m. Lines form early in the morning.

Glendale and Forest Lawn

A smallish residential and industrial community, lying roughly between Griffith Park and Pasadena, **Glendale** is the home of a number of ultra-conservative citizens, often satirized on television or made the butt of many a tired joke. Ironically, within the boundaries of the former "ranch" is one of the world's most unconventional and controversial cemeteries, **Forest Lawn.**

The "sacred gardens" are in the hills, about half a block off San Fernando Road, just three short blocks south of Glendale Boulevard. To reach Glendale and Forest Lawn from Hollywood, drive east on Los Feliz Boulevard, crossing over Riverside Drive and Los Angeles Drive. This portion of Los Feliz Boulevard is visited chiefly for its famed "Antique Row." Turn right on San Fernando Road, and the entrance to Forest Lawn will be three blocks on your left.

From downtown Los Angeles, a distance of eight miles, take the Pasadena Freeway, switching onto the northbound Golden State Freeway (along Riverside Drive). Turn right on the Glendale Freeway, then left onto San Fernando Road. Forest Lawn will be on your right, before you reach Glendale Boulevard.

By bus from downtown Los Angeles, take "Sunland" (No. 56), going north on Spring Street, between 11th Street and Sunset Boulevard.

FOREST LAWN: This is a cemetery extraordinaire! Actually, there is a quartet of Forest Lawns (others at Cypress, Hollywood Hills, and Covina Hills), but the best known one is at 1712 South Glendale Avenue, Glendale. The admission-free gardens may be visited from 9 a.m. to 5 p.m.

In the introduction of Adela Rogers St. John's *First Step up Toward Heaven* (the biography of the founder, Hubert Eaton), appeared this description of Forest Lawn: "Imagine the greenest, most enchanting park you ever saw in your life. Imagine hearing the singing birds in the tops of the towering trees, or letting your gaze sweep over vistas of sparkling lawns, with shaded arborways, and garden retreats, and beautiful noble statuary. It sounds unreal—perhaps—an unearthly park-paradise."

Evelyn Waugh in his satirical *The Loved One* saw Forest Lawn differently. In his mythical "Whispering Glades," he depicted an ominous graveyard with "mortuary hostesses," "Before Need" reservations, coffins like "The Egypt of the Pharaohs," and "slumber rooms" where corpses lie in repose.

Of particular interest is the "Last Supper" window—based on Leonardo da Vinci's painting and displayed in the "Memorial Court of Honor" in the Great Mausoleum. The panels open daily at 10 a.m., 11 a.m., and every half-hour from noon to 4 p.m., revealing the work of Signorina Rosa Moretti, the last member of a Perugia, Italy, family known for its secret process of making stained glass.

Thousands of Southern Californians are entombed in the Great Mausoleum, including such celebrities as W. C. Fields, Ed Wynn, Jean Harlow, and Clark Gable. On the art terraces and in the corridors are displayed reproductions of statuary, such as Michelangelo's *Twilight* and *Dawn*, as well as Donatello's *St. George*.

The big draw on the hill—next to the Forest Lawn Museum—is a special theater with the world's largest single curtain (210 feet long, 65 feet high), for the presentation of two paintings. One is *The Crucifixion,* the largest permanently mounted painting in the United States, perhaps the world. Paderewski dreamed it, and Jan Styka painted it. The other is *The Resurrection,* completed by Robert Clark in 1965. The paintings are shown every half-hour from 11 a.m. to 5 p.m. After viewing them, you can explore the museum, with its reproduction of Ghiberti's *Paradise Doors.*

Other attractions include the Court of David, with its reproduction of Michelangelo's famous sculpted masterpiece. Interesting churches include the Church of the Recessional, modeled after a 10th-century building in Sussex, England, and dedicated to the poetry of Rudyard Kipling (see his family album and literary mementos in an adjoining wing), and the Wee Kirk o' the Heather, based on a church built early in the 14th century in Glencairn, Scotland. A stained-glass window depicts the story of Annie Laurie, a 17th-century heroine who "reluctantly married someone else," though "her heart remained faithful to Douglas, love of her youth."

Forest Lawn isn't just for the dear departed. It is estimated that wedding chimes have rung for over 55,000 persons. The memorial churches are also the setting for numerous christenings, church services, ordinations of ministers, and other ecclesiastical functions.

In other words, Forest Lawn gets the business from birth to death.

Van Nuys

At the Anheuser-Busch Brewery, you can stroll leisurely through the **Busch Gardens,** a setting of splendor filled with more than 2,000 rare birds. You can also take a 20-minute tropical boat ride through the lagoons, and bask in the glow of exotic flowers. The tour begins with a 3,500-foot monorail ride through the brewery that turns out the popular Budweiser, Michelob, and Busch beers. You'll literally sail over the fermentation cellars.

Later, you can explore the gardens—best done by taking one of the boat rides leaving frequently. Through the waterways, the guide will point out a 45-foot waterfall, simulating the effect of the Sierras. You'll see such birds as the Chinese mandarin duck (considered by many the most beautiful of his species in the world), the South American king vulture, the scarlet ibis (the sacred bird of ancient Egypt), black and white European storks, the flamboyant giant Macaw, the white-belly sea eagle, and the African crown crane.

Seven times a day, beginning with a 1:30 performance, bird shows are staged, with such performers as the sulphur-crested cockatoos doing their tricks in the 450-seat Amphitheater. Also you can go to the Otter and Penguin House, or else relax at one of the beer pavilions, such as the Busch terrace overlooking the Gorge.

A five-acre, $6-million addition to the gardens contains the nation's largest collection of tanagers, cocks of the rock, umbrella birds, turacous, and hummingbirds. The hummingbirds, incidentally, flit about in virtual free-flight conditions. Two other water-borne rides are the Ya-Hoo Barrel Ride, including a dramatic descent via a 30-foot chute, and the Speed Boat Ride on a gasoline-powered craft operated by individual riders. Other attractions include a huge walk-through "flight cage"—one of the largest aviaries in the nation—and a magic show.

The newest attraction is "Old St. Louis," where it's 1900 again and the atmosphere is country fair. There's an old-fashioned fun house, bumper cars, a sky trolley, and the Crystal Arcade.

The gardens, at 16000 Roscoe Boulevard, Van Nuys (tel. 786-0410), are open daily, 10 a.m. to midnight, from June 15 to September 2. The rest of the year, open weekends and holidays only (except Christmas and New Years) from 10 a.m. to 6 p.m. The general admission prices include all rides, shows, and attractions. Adults pay $5.25, children four to 11, $4.75 (under four, free). At the Roscoe Boulevard entrance is parking, 50¢ for automobiles. To reach the brewery and gardens, take the Hollywood Freeway to Ventura Freeway, then head north on the San Diego Freeway, getting off at Roscoe Boulevard.

Highland Park

For an introduction to the spirit of the great Southwest, head for **Highland Park,** where the following little-known attraction awaits you. You can take the Pasadena Freeway, exiting at Avenue 43.

THE SOUTHWEST MUSEUM: Crowning the crest of a steep hill, overlooking Arroyo Seco, the Southwest Museum was founded in 1907 by Charles F. Lummis, utilizing private funds. It contains one of the finest collections of antiquities of Indians of the Americas. At 234 Museum Drive, it can be approached either via a winding drive or else through a tunnel at the foot of the hill, which opens onto an elevator which will carry you to the top.

Inside the two-story structure, the whole Indian world of the Americas opens onto a panoramic exhibition, complete with a tepee, rare paintings, weapons, moccasins, and other artifacts. You'll find Sitting Bull's pictorial autobiography and a painting by the chief "in earth colors" on the canvas liner of a U.S. Cavalry blanket (a work he did shortly before he was assassinated).

Lummis, who was the director of the Los Angeles Library, collected a great many rare and valuable books on the Southwest, which he turned over to the museum, along with his extensive archaeological collection.

The museum also contains a portrait of General John Charles Frémont, the famous 19th-century explorer and politician, and his well-known wife, Jessie Benton, daughter of a Missouri senator. Frémont is remembered chiefly for his career as an explorer ("From the ashes of his campfires have sprung cities"). He explored the country west of the Mississippi all the way to the Pacific, and is credited with trail-blazing efforts by the Forty-Niners.

The museum is open daily, except Mondays, from 1 p.m. till 4:45 p.m., although it shuts down completely from mid-August till mid-September. Admission is free.

You can also visit **El Alisal,** the rugged home of Charles F. Lummis, founder of the museum, at nearby 200 East Avenue 43. Lummis built this two-story "castle" himself, using rocks from a nearby arroyo and telephone poles from the Santa Fe Railroad. His home became a cultural center for many famous personages in the literary, theatrical, political, and art world. Himself an author, editor (he coined the slogan "See America First"), archaeologist, and librarian, Mr. Lummis was equally at home with Will Rogers, "Teddy" Roosevelt, singer Mary Garden, and Madame Schumann-Heinck, and writers such as Blasco Ibáñez. The house is open free to the public daily, except Saturday, from 1 p.m. to 4 p.m.

Magic Mountain

On a 200-acre site of green rolling hills at Valencia, 35 miles northwest of downtown Los Angeles, is one of the best family fun parks in the West. Opened in the spring of 1971, with its ponds, lakes, and waterfalls, as well as trees and flowering plants, the "mountain" is an attractive garden. But the emphasis is on the rides, some costing as much as $3 million to construct. Of course, everyone wants to ride the Log Jammer, hollowed-out fiberglass logs that careen through the mountain in a log flume water course, ending with a 47-foot plunge into a lake! Rivaling this attraction is the Jet Stream ride. The Sky Tower, on the other hand, takes you to the top of a 384-foot structure, about equal to the height of a 32-story building. From the observation decks, a panoramic view unfolds. And the newest attraction is the Great American Revolution, a roller coaster with a 360-degree loop—the ultimate thrill ride.

Other rides include The Métro, a monorail; The Galaxy, the tallest double-arm ferris wheel in the world; El Bumpo, skimmer boats propelled by air jets over a man-made lagoon; the Grand Carousel, which was originally built in 1912 but restored at great cost; the Sand Blasters, dune buggies propelled by exhaust-free electric motors; the Gold Rusher, a "white knuckler" featuring a runaway mine train; Standard Oil's Grand Prix, sports cars racing around a fully landscaped track; the Funicular, a cable railroad imported from Europe; The Jolly Monster; and the Steam Train, a narrow-gauge steam replica of a turn-of-the-century passenger train. In the interest of ecology, the train burns propane, not coal.

Children's World features 11 rides, everything from a roller coaster to Lunar Lander rides. In the one-acre Children's Farm and Petting Zoo, children are invited to pet and feed the animals in their natural environment. And the new Wizard's Village expands Magic Mountain's offerings to the little kids.

Although there are many snackbars and cafeterias, the best food is at the **Four Winds,** an Oriental restaurant at the summit of Magic Mountain. You can help yourself at lunch to all the salads you want—for just $2.35. The brochette of beef dinner, including the buffet, is only $3.95.

The major entertainment center is the 3,400-seat Showcase Theater, which on special occasions draws name performers. Variety shows, marching bands, magic acts, puppet shows, and local rock groups round out the bill.

You get everything—rides, amusements, special attractions, the showcase entertainment—for just one admission price: $7.50 for adults, $6.50 for children ages three to 11. The park is open in summer from 9 a.m. to midnight daily. Off-season hours vary, so it's best to call ahead (tel. 805/259-7272) for information.

The amusement park is reached from Highway 101 in Ventura by taking State Highway 126 through Fillmore to Castaic Junction, then turning south for about one mile at the junction of 126 and Interstate 5. From either direction, the park is two minutes west of the Golden State Freeway (Interstate 5) at the Magic Mountain Parkway exit.

William S. Hart Park

He was the prototype of the cowboy hero, the Western good guy who loved his horse more than his girl. Before he died on June 23, 1946, at the age of 74, Bill Hart expressed a hope that has since been fulfilled: "While I was making pictures, the people gave me their nickels, dimes, and quarters. When I am gone, I want them to have my home."

Purchased in 1920, his Horseshoe Ranch is now the William S. Hart County Park, whose entrance is at the junction of Newhall Avenue and San Fernando Road, at 24151 Newhall Avenue, Newhall. To reach the ranch, drive north on Golden State Freeway to Highway 14, then north on Highway 14 to San Fernando Road, continuing north to Newhall Avenue.

The park is stocked with farm animals, including a rare buffalo herd. Walt Disney provided the nucleus of the herd when he donated eight of the buffalos in 1962. Visitors are allowed to take along a picnic lunch, enjoying it at designated spots on the 253-acre site.

At the entrance to the park, a shuttle will take you to the museum, housed in the old Hart home, which he called "La Loma de Los Vientos." It's open daily from 10 a.m. to 5 p.m., except on Christmas, New Year's Day, and Thanksgiving. Built in the Spanish-Mexican style, the house contains 14 rooms, stuffed not only with mementos of Hart's career, but with genuine relics of the Old West. The furnishings are pretty much as Hart left them. The museum also owns 18 paintings and five bronze statues by Charles M. Russell, a close friend of the cowboy hero.

As Hart stipulated in his will, no one is charged admission. The park is open daily, expect holidays, from 10 a.m. to 6 p.m. (till 7:30 p.m. during Daylight Savings).

The Spanish Missions

On July 16, 1769, a Franciscan padre, Junípero Serra, established the first in a string of missions that were to stretch along **El Camino Real** (the Royal Road). Eventually, the missions were to total 21, reaching from San Diego to Sonoma.

Tolerated by the Spanish king, the mission chain formed a colonization bulwark against possible Russian aggrandizements in the north. The missions each functioned much like a commune, with the padres and Indians creating their own centers of agriculture and industry. They raised cattle, sheep, and goats, planted citrus groves and olive trees, made soap, blankets, wine, even ironware. The Indians were taught methods of irrigation and many of the communities prospered. Four of the most-visited missions include the following:

SAN JUAN CAPISTRANO: Fifty-six miles south of Los Angeles, the little inland town of San Juan Capistrano is internationally celebrated because of the swallows which return there faithfully on St. Joseph's Day, March 19. The so-called miracle of the swallows draws many visitors to the town. On October 23, the Day of San Juan, the swallows punctually leave for their "mysterious home" in the south, probably somewhere in South America. The chirping swallows have been greatly romanticized, bird watchers loving to cite the streaks of iridescent emerald in their plumage.

The town takes its name from "the jewel of the missions," the Old Mission San Juan Capistrano. After a disappointing start in 1775, it was "refounded" the following year. Construction on a stone church was begun in 1797, but it was destroyed in an earthquake in 1812. The ruins today provide a good nesting place for some of the swallows.

The semitropical grounds are serene and peaceful, haunted by a melancholy loveliness. Once inside, you're likely to be submerged under a whir of pigeons from a fountain named in their honor. Hopefully, you will have purchased a bag of bird food (wheat).

The grounds contain the remains of what is considered the oldest building in California. The altar, dating from the 17th century, is from Catalonia. The mission may be visited from 7 a.m. till 5 p.m., and it charges 50¢ per person (children under 12 free if accompanied by parents).

MISSION SAN FERNANDO: In 1797, Padre Fermin Lasuen founded a mission, 17th in the eventual chain of 21, in what was to be called the San Fernando Valley. At 15151 Mission Boulevard, at the junction of the Golden State and San Diego Freeways, in San Fernando, the mission reached its apex in the same year—1812—that an earthquake struck.

On the grounds you can explore a convent, with rooms like narrow quadrangles. Dedicated in 1822, with an arcade of 21 classic arches and adobe walls four feet thick, it was here that many of the wayfarers along El Camino Real were sheltered for the night—or as long as they wanted to stay. It also served as sleeping quarters for the padres, and contained a dining room and kitchen, as well as a vat and wine cellar.

The mission chapel, its walls seemingly jutting outward, was built in 1806 and is graced with primitive Indian wall paintings in cobalt blue. The adjoining cemetery, with its tiny brook and semitropical vegetation, is the most serene spot (half a dozen padres were buried there, along with hundreds of Shoshone Indi-

Capistrano

ans). In the museum is an exceptional altar, dating from the early 17th century; intricate handcarved wooden vines, and all gold-leafed. You can walk through the peaceful grounds from 9 a.m. to 4 p.m. for a 75¢ admission for adults, 25¢ for children seven to 15.

MISSION SAN GABRIEL ARCANGEL: One of the best preserved of the missions built under the leadership of Padre Junípero Serra, San Gabriel traces its origins back to 1771, when it was founded fourth in the 21-link chain. It's a completely self-contained compound, with a famous set of bells, soap vats, an old kitchen, an aqueduct, a cemetery, a winery, a tannery, and a mission church. Because of its strategic location, it was visited by numerous wayfarers en route to and coming from Mexico.

Construction on the church—distinguished by its buttresses— was begun in 1792. Erected to withstand the ravages of time, the walls are about five feet thick. In the sanctuary is a revered 17th-century painting, an oval-faced, and sad-eyed *Our Lady of Sorrows*—said to have subdued hostile Indians with its serenity. The glittering polychrome statues surrounding the altar were handcarved, and in the copper font the first Indian was baptized in 1771.

In the museum are some "aboriginal" Indian paintings depicting the *14 Stations of the Cross*—painted on sail cloth, with colors made from crushing the petals of desert flowers. The childlike primitives tell their story crudely but vividly.

The mission, nine miles northeast of downtown Los Angeles, is open daily, except Christmas, Thanksgiving, and Easter, from 9:30 a.m. to 4 p.m. You can leave a donation or buy a gift at the curio shop. The mission is at 537 West Mission Drive, San Gabriel, about one mile south of the Huntington Museum at San Marino. The admission charges are 50¢ for adults, 25¢ for children five to 12 (children under five are admitted free).

MISSION SANTA BARBARA: On the edge of Mission Canyon, this old mission lent its name to the seaside resort and residential city 98 miles northwest of Los Angeles. Founded shortly before Christmas in 1786, the "Queen of the Missions" was built in the neoclassical style. Today, it is the headquarters of the Pacific coast district of the Franciscans. It contains a trio of quadrangles in the original style, plus a facade of splayed Moorish windows.

Perhaps its most idyllic spot is the cloister garden, with a circular lily pond, the twin towers along the front reflected in the background.

A church that stood on this spot was gutted in an earthquake that hit in 1812. The reconstruction began in 1815, lasting for five years. The mission was again damaged by an earthquake in 1925. Some $375,000 needed for its restoration poured in, mainly through public contributions. However, because of a defect in the building materials, a quarter of a century later the facade and towers were torn down and rebuilt, and reblessed once again in 1953.

At its heyday, at the dawn of the 19th century, the number of Indians living at the mission totaled around 2,000. Under the direction of the padres, the Indians raised livestock and cultivated the fields. It was the stated goal of each mission to be self-sustaining, making and providing the clothing of its members as well as their foodstuff. Trades such as saddle-making and blacksmithing were also learned.

The mission at Laguna and Los Olivos Streets is open daily from 9 a.m. to 5 p.m., and charges 50¢ for adults (children under 16 admitted free).

While in Santa Barbara, you might want to lunch at **El Paseo**, 818 State Street (tel. 965-5106). It's like old Seville. The setting is in a maze of interesting shops in the paseo arcade. You enter through a patio with a winding, open staircase and flowering trees. Occasionally entertainment is presented on the raised platform. Many Mexican suggestions, ranging in price from $2.95 to $4.95, are featured. And the eclectic menu also features the likes of corned beef and pastrami sandwiches on rye. Consider driving up for the Sunday buffet (noon to 8 p.m.)—all you can eat for $3.95.

If you fall in love with the special Spanish charm that hangs over Santa Barbara, you might want to spend the night, checking in at the **Santa Barbara Biltmore**, 1260 Channel Drive, Montecito, Santa Barbara (tel. 969-2261), one of America's most outstanding hotels. It's a garden paradise, between the Pacific and Santa Ynez mountains on 21 acres of lawns and floral gardens. Rooms are deluxe, with every convenience, many having romantic Spanish balconies. All are furnished in a traditional Iberian style. In the main building, singles go from $40 to $70; doubles and twins, from $45 to $75. More economical are rooms in the Anacapa wing: singles at $30 to $40, doubles or twins at

$35 to $45. Adjacent to the main building is a sizeable recreation area, with two enormous swimming pools, sun terraces, and a nearby sandy bathing beach.

A hotel choice for the budget traveler is the **Upham,** 1404 De la Vina, Santa Barbara (tel. 962-0058), which was called the Lincoln House when it was built in 1871. Mr. John Hall, the owner, says it is "the oldest cosmopolitan hotel in Southern California." It's a big, square, stark-white Victorian house, with many bungalows in its rear garden. Inside, antique furnishings prevail. Bedrooms are appropriately furnished in the old style. Singles with bath range from $12 to $16 nightly; twins, $20. If you want two rooms with a connecting bath, the charge is $18. Luncheons for hotel guests are $1.75; evening meals, $4.50. The homelike atmosphere is reflected in the canopy-tented little cocktail lounge. You pour your own drinks, as the honor system prevails.

Pasadena Area

The grande dame of the Greater Los Angeles area, **Pasadena** is a residential city 11 miles northwest of the downtown district, hugging the foothills of the Sierra Madre mountain range in the San Gabriel Valley. It has street after street of large estates, surrounded by semitropical gardens—a haven for "old money."

Of course, it is known chiefly for its **Rose Bowl,** with its New Year's football game (where the champions of the East meet those of the West) and its annual **Tournament of Roses** parade. Since its beginnings in 1890—with "flower-bedecked buggies and surreys"—the parade has included such "grand marshals" as Bob Hope and Mary Pickford, even Richard Nixon and Shirley Temple. Since the early 1950s, both the parade and play-off game have enjoyed a nationwide audience.

Just south of Pasadena is another primarily residential community, **San Marino,** visited chiefly because of its world-famed **Huntington Library and Museum,** and the nearby **Descanso Gardens** and **San Gabriel Mission.**

From these hill-hugging communities, you can reach the Los Angeles National Forest mountain resorts, such as **Big Bear, Mount Wilson,** and **Mount Baldy.**

HUNTINGTON LIBRARY, ART GALLERY, AND BOTANICAL GARDENS: At 1151 Oxford Road, in San Marino (tel. 681-6601), stands the fulfillment of a dream of its creator, Henry E. Huntington (1850-1927). About 12 miles from downtown Los Angeles, the 207-acre estate of the pioneer rail tycoon—complete with his gardens and classical mansion—has been converted into a cultural center for students, art devotees, and the general public. Mr. Huntington's thirst for original manuscripts, rare books, great paintings, and skillfully planned gardens led to the formation of what may be considered one of the greatest sightseeing attractions in Southern California.

His home is now the art gallery, housing paintings, tapestries, furniture, and other decorative arts chiefly English and French works of the 18th century. In the art gallery, the most celebrated painting is Gainsborough's *The Blue Boy.* Another famous portrait is that of the youthful aunt of Elizabeth Barrett Browning, *Pinkie,* by Sir Thomas Lawrence. Equally well known are Gilbert Stuart's portrait of George Washington; Sir Joshua Reynolds's *Sarah Siddons as the Tragic Muse,* and Romney's *Lady Hamilton.* You'll also find a collection of Beauvais and Gobelin tapestries.

The library is divided into seven halls, with permanent and changing exhibitions from its remarkable collection of English and American first editions, letters, and manuscripts. They include one of the copies of the Gutenberg Bible printed in the 1450s in Mainz; a 1410 copy of Chaucer's *Canterbury Tales;* a First Folio of Shakespeare's plays; Benjamin Franklin's *Autobiography* in his own writing; Edgar Allan Poe's handwritten copy of "Annabel Lee." There are more than 300,000 rare books and about six million manuscripts ranging from the 11th to the present century.

Of special interest are the Botanical Gardens, with verdant semitropical planting, rare shrubs, and trees, studded with 17th-century statuary from Padua and surrounded by azaleas and camellias. You can also stroll through, among others, a Desert Garden, with extensive cacti in all shapes; a Camellia Garden with 1,500 varieties; and a Japanese Garden, with curving pathways, dwarf maples, an arched moon bridge, reflection pools, a 16th-century samurai's house furnished authentically, a Zen Garden, and a bonsai court.

The admission-free museum and grounds are open Tuesdays through Sundays from 1 p.m. to 4:30 p.m. (closed on major holidays and during the entire month of October).

NORTON SIMON MUSEUM OF ART: One of the most important new museums in California is at Colorado Boulevard at Orange Grove (tel. 449-6840). Formerly the Pasadena Art Museum, it sits atop a mound with broad plazas, sculpture gardens, a reflection pool, and semitropical paintings. In the spring of 1974, it was taken over by the Norton Simon Foundation, and closed for extensive repairs, remodeling, and interior redesigning. It reopened in March, 1975, the revamped galleries featuring not only the 20th-century art exhibited here in the past, but art from the pre-Renaissance through the 19th century as well.

Newly installed Indian and Southeast Asian galleries feature great stone and bronze sculptures from India, Nepal, Kashmir, Thailand, and Cambodia. Especially notable is the *Sivapuram Nataraja,* the 10th-century Chola bronze idol depicting the Hindu god Shiva as Lord of Dance, one of this museum's superb collection of Chola bronzes.

In addition, the museum houses eight important paintings by Peter Paul Reubens; an important collection of the sculptures of Maillol; Rembrandt's portrait of his son, *Titus;* and major works by Rousseau, Courbet, Matisse, Corot, Picasso, Raphael, Breughel, Hals, and Claude Lorrain.

The museum is open Thursday through Sunday from noon to 6 p.m. Adults pay $1.50 for admission, senior citizens and students 50¢; children under 12 are admitted free.

DESCANSO GARDENS: Here you'll see one of the largest collections of camellias in the world, more than 100,000 specimens. The rose varieties are spectacular as well, including some from Damascus dating from the time of Christ. You can also admire lilacs, azaleas, orchids, and daffodils, plus many species of native plants—all planted in or around a mature Southern California oak forest. A stream and many paths run through the oaks, and a chaparral nature trail is provided for those who wish to observe native vegetation. Other features of the gardens are monthly art exhibitions in the Hospitality House; an Oriental Teahouse serving Tuesday through Sunday, 11 to 4; the Minka Gift Shop; and guided tram tours, 1 to 4 weekdays (10:30 to 4:30 on weekends). The gardens are at 1418 Descanso Drive, La Canada, and are open daily from 8 to 5 (till 5:30 during Daylight Savings). For additional information, telephone 681-0331. Admission is free, though persons under 18 must be accompanied by adults. Picnicking ,is allowed only in specified areas. The gardens, incidentally, are run by the Los Angeles County Department of Arboreta and Botanic Gardens.

Organized Tours

The quickest, easiest, and most efficient way to explore the sights of Southern California is by an organized sightseeing tour. A number of companies offer such tours, the most outstanding of which is **Gray Line Tours Company,** 1207 West Third Street, Los Angeles (tel. 481-2121 for information), and 1441 S. West Street in Anaheim (tel. 778-2770). In air-conditioned coaches, with commentaries by guides, the tours include such sights as Disneyland, the movie studios, the homes of the stars in Beverly Hills, Farmers Market, Marineland, Forest Lawn, the Movieland Wax Museum, Palm Springs, Hollywood, Sunset Strip, and Knott's Berry Farm.

Rates depend on the point at which you connect with the tours. In all the following cases, we've quoted the rate from the downtown terminal in Los Angeles. The most popular tours are conducted year-round; others are scheduled only in summer.

One of the most heavily booked tours is the **Hollywood-Beverly Hills** jaunt (movie-star homes, the Farmers Market, Sunset Strip, Mann's Chinese Theatre), costing $7.50 for adults, $3.75 for children. One full-day tour includes not only homes of movie and TV stars, but also Universal Studios, the Farmers Market, Santa Monica, and points along the Pacific—all for $18.85 for adults, $17.85 for juniors, and $10.55 for children.

One four-hour tour explores **Pasadena,** the **Rose Bowl,** and the **Huntington Library** (of *Pinkie,* and *Blue Boy* fame), including Old Los Angeles, and a stop at the San Gabriel Mission, founded in 1771. The fare is $7.50 for adults and juniors, $3.75 for children. The tour is conducted on Thursdays only (except holidays) from mid-June till the first of September. Another tour covers **Forest Lawn,** costing adults and juniors $8.05, and children $3.75. The four-hour tour is conducted on Monday and Wednesday from mid-June till the first of September, and on Mondays only during the rest of the year.

The jaunt of most interest is the eight-hour trip to **Disneyland,** including seven attractions. Costing $19.30 for adults and juniors (just $10.65 for children), the tour is conducted daily from May 6 to mid-September (Wednesday through Sunday the rest of the year.

In the same area, another popular tour visits **Knott's Berry Farm** and the **Movieland Wax Museum**, and lasts eight hours. It is conducted daily from mid-June till September 11 (Tuesdays and Fridays only the rest of the year), and costs adults $21.55; children, $13.15.

The **Marineland of the Pacific** and **Queen Mary Tour** leaves daily year-round, stopping off also at the Ports O'Call. The cost is $16.80 for adults, and $9.40 for children for an eight-hour trek.

The above are only some of the tours available: others go to San Diego, San Juan Capistrano, La Jolla, the Santa Barbara Franciscan Mission, and the Ojai Valley. There's also a Los Angeles-Hollywood evening tour. The most expensive offering—the **Night Life Party**, a six-hour spree—leaves daily in summer (Tuesdays through Saturdays the rest of the year), costing $30 for adults and including a full-course dinner at a restaurant, then two nightclub shows, with one drink at each.

Sports

While sports buffs in less favorable climates are moving indoors after Labor Day, the Los Angeles fans can attend outdoor events all year round in the warm California sunshine. Of course, there are indoor sports such as basketball, but Angelenos can also enjoy an afternoon at the racetrack in January while most of the country is shoveling a path through the snow. Most of the sporting events are held on the outskirts of the city or in nearby communities, where you'll find huge parking lots for that Los Angeles necessity, the automobile.

HORSERACING: A day at the track in one of the famous racing parks near Los Angeles is a memorable event—whether you win or lose. More than just a betting window and an oval-shaped track, the race tracks in Southern California are among the most beautiful anywhere. Some have elaborate infields complete with ponds and decorative wildlife, tropical gardens, or elaborate picnic parks. Many have elegant restaurants, and one even has a fashionable shopping mall. Here are three of the most popular:

Set against a dramatic background of rugged mountains, **Santa Anita Park**, Huntington Drive and Baldwin Avenue, Arcadia (tel. 447-2171), offers a combination of European and American styles of racing. The track, in operation for more than 40 years, has its winter season from late December to early April. Gates open at 11 to 11:30 a.m. Races are held Wednesday through

Sunday only. The Oak Tree Racing Association sponsors racing each autumn. During the season, visitors can watch the morning workouts and even take a tour of the stables. Admission to the park is $2.25 for grandstand and infield, $4 for the clubhouse. Children 17 and under are admitted free with a parent. Parking is 75¢. Santa Anita is just 14 miles east of Los Angeles, directly accessible from the Foothill Freeway.

For a day of thoroughbred racing, you can go to **Hollywood Park**, 1050 S. Prairie Avenue, at Inglewood (tel. 678-1181). Eleven miles southwest of downtown Los Angeles, the park is spread across 350 landscaped acres. The thoroughbred season extends from April to July. Post time is 2 p.m., Wednesday through Sunday. From mid-September through December, harness racing is held nightly, with post time at 7:45 p.m. The admission is as follows: grandstand, $2; clubhouse, $4; reserved seats, $1.75. There is space for 30,000 cars in the parking lot, with rates ranging from $1 to $3. Besides the 48 refreshment stands scattered throughout the park, there are also four restaurants.

"Where the world's fastest horses race" is not just an idle claim made by **Los Alamitos**, 4961 Katella Avenue in Los Alamitos (tel. 431-1361). From May through August, the lightning-fast quarter horses race each evening, Monday through Saturday, at 8 p.m. There's also a winter season from December to early February, and a harness racing season from March to May. The park itself is luxuriously designed, with an infield featuring palm- and flower-lined ponds stocked with swans and other waterfowl. The glassed-in Turf Terrace offers racing fans an unobstructed view of the track while they drink or dine.

Santa Anita Park

Admission is $2.25 for grandstand seats, $3.50 for entry to the clubhouse, and $1.50 for reserved seats. Los Alamitos is just west of Disneyland on Katella Avenue.

THE FORUM: When the circus comes to town, you'll find it at the Forum, billed as "the world's most beautiful showplace for sports and entertainment." At 3900 West Manchester Avenue, Inglewood (tel. 673-1300), this massive sports arena is the home of the Los Angeles Lakers and the Los Angeles Kings. Out-of-towners such as the Harlem Globetrotters, Holiday on Ice, and the Ringling Brothers Circus appear here throughout the year. Its also the site of the annual Forum Championship Rodeo. Prices vary with the event, so call ahead for information.

DODGER STADIUM: Remember when they were called the Brooklyn Bums? The latest home for the Dodgers is not Ebbets Field, but this modern stadium at 1000 Elysian Park Avenue, Los Angeles (tel. 225-1400). It's considered one of the best baseball fields in the world, offering every one of the fans (the stadium seats 56,000) an unobstructed view because of its unique cantilever construction. Although the game season lasts only from April through September, the stadium is used year-round for various events. Admission is $4.50 for box seats, $3 for reserved seats, and $2 for general admission ($1 for children). Parking in the 16,000-car lot costs $1 per vehicle.

Across the Desert

After busy days along the Pacific, you may be ready for the special appeal of the desert. If so, the best resort to wind down in is Palm Springs, previewed briefly later in this chapter. However, if you long for more excitement, you can head east to Las Vegas. If that is your plan, consider stopping off at either Apple Valley or Calico Ghost Town, or both, on your trip along Route 15.

APPLE VALLEY: Doesn't it sound like the happiest place in the world? Rimmed by the snow-capped San Bernardino Mountains, this land is for those who want to bask in the sun and breathe pure desert air. The town rose from the desert right after World War II, and uses its vast underground water supply to create this oasis. Horseback riding over desert trails, an 18-hole championship golf course, a haywagon ride to a Western steak fry, songs around the campfire—these are but some of the activities that occupy the vacationer. Apple Valley is some 90 miles from Los Angeles (take Route 15, turning onto 18 at Victorville).

CALICO GHOST TOWN: One of the most famous ghost towns of the Old West lives again! Halfway between Los Angeles and Las Vegas, ten minutes outside Barstow, and just off Interstate 15, Calico was a boom town from 1881 to 1896, when it was abandoned by the silver miners who had settled it so hastily In its heyday, the town was visited frequently by Wyatt Earp, trailed by a string of admiring children. Grubstaked by the county sheriff, a trio of prospectors discovered a silver lode in 1881 that was to produce $86 million of the precious metal in just 15 years.

Today, as in the 19th century, people walk the streets of Calico, past the general store, the old schoolhouse, Lil's saloon, the pottery works, even boot hill. The most popular attraction is the Maggie Mine, where it's possible to explore tunnels dug into the old silver lode. The **Calico House Restaurant** serves a good lunch, and many of the buildings have now become shops selling interesting merchandise.

En route to Palm Springs, consider a stopover at . . .

RIVERSIDE: Riverside is reached by going out U.S. 60, some 50 miles east of Los Angeles. Motorists traveling on U.S. 66 can reach it by a ten-mile drive south from San Bernardino.

Palm Springs

People go to Palm Springs just for fun. One of the world's most renowned resorts, Palm Springs combines sunny deserts with palm-lined canyons. Shaded by rugged San Jacinto and surrounded by a dry, invigorating climate, the resort offers days that are sunny and clear.

Palm Springs is also "the golf capital of the world." More than 100 tournaments are held in the area, including the $100,000 Bob Hope Desert Classic.

Its honorary mayor, incidentally, is Bob Hope; Eisenhower considered the Eldorado Country Club his favorite vacation retreat, and as many movie stars have homes here as they do in Beverly Hills. In the supermarket, you're likely to run into Lucille Ball, Kirk Douglas, Charles Farrell, Cary Grant, William Holden, Elvis Presley, Frank Sinatra, Kim Novak, Jerry Lewis, Dean Martin, even Liberace.

Palm Springs lies 105 miles southeast of Los Angeles. It's most often reached by private car, though you can also go by bus and Amtrak. A multimillion-dollar airport is served by several airlines.

To gain perspective—that is, see for yourself that every sixth family (at least) has a swimming pool—you can glide along the **Palm Springs Aerial Tramway,** a distance of two and a half miles up the slopes of Mount Jacinto. A cable car will carry you and 79 others to a height of 8,516 feet on the world's largest tramway operating on a single span. You'll leave a world of cactus, Joshua trees, date palms, and grazing bighorn sheep, passing through a climate that its promoters have claimed is like going from Mexico to Alaska. At the end of the line, you emerge into the snow, with a panoramic vista of the Coachella Valley, Nevada, Arizona, even Mexico. The tramway is open daily from 10 a.m till 9 p.m., November through May (closed Tuesdays and Wednesdays from June to October). The last tram up the mountain is at 7:30 p.m. The round-trip price is $4 for adults, $3 for juniors (12 to 17), and $1.50 for children (four to 11). To reach it, go to the Tramway Drive, at Chino Canyon, off Highway 111.

There are two places to eat: a snackbar at the bottom of the tramway and the Alpine Room at the top. You can purchase a special ride-and-dinner combination ticket, costing $6.95 for adults; $5.95 for juniors (13 to 17); and $3.50 for children.

HIGH-BUDGET ACCOMMODATIONS: Canyon Hotel, 2850 South Palm Canyon Drive (tel. 323-5656). This is one of the most glamorous resorts in the area, attracting a clientele that includes Elton John, among many other celebs. The 450 rooms are among the loveliest anywhere, done in pastel blue and yellow color schemes and furnished in painted bamboo. Every luxury is included, even an extra phone in the bath.

Facilities on the premises are many. For drinking and dining there's L'Escoffier, serving French and continental haute-cuisine dinners; Bogie's, open for breakfast, lunch, and dinner—by day a steak and seafood house and after 10:30 p.m. a swinging disco; Forty Love, a coffeeshop; Raffles, an exotic nightclub featuring live music for dancing nightly; and the verdant Greenhouse Lounge for drinks and nightly piano bar. But there's lots more

to do than eat and drink. The Canyon has an 18-hole championship golf course and a nine-hole putting green; ten tennis courts
(three lit for night play, two indoors and air-conditioned); a
stable of 300 riding horses; three swimming pools (two Olympic-
size); beauty salons and barbershops; three Jacuzzis; and a fully
equipped health club/spa for shiatsu and Swedish massage, facials, saunas, and mineral baths.

Rates are seasonal and are the same for single or double
occupancy: December 21 to April 20, $59 to $75 (suites $100 to
$350); April 21 to July 5, and September 15 to December 20, $45
to $65. And in summer—not *the* season—you can stay here for
just $25 a night.

The Ingleside Inn, 200 West Ramon Road (tel. 325-1366),
offers the most romantic accommodations in Palm Springs. Once
you enter the imposing wrought-iron gates, you're in a gracious
world of tranquility and fine service. Each of the 26 rooms (some
are villas) is furnished in priceless antiques, many left over from
the days when this was the Humphrey Birge estate. Perhaps your
room will have a canopied bed or a 15th-century vestment chest.
Many have fireplaces, and all have in-room steam baths, not to
mention all the other luxuries you might desire.

On the premises is one of this town's most acclaimed restaurants, **Melvyn's,** a celebrity haunt which was chosen by Frank
and Barbara Sinatra for their intimate after-wedding dinner
party (only about 70 close friends were invited). The decor is
most attractive, with wicker and tapestry-upholstered furnishings, lace curtains on the windows, lots of plants, and a turn-of-
the-century oak-and-mahogany bar with beveled mirrors. A dinner at Melvyn's might begin with the house pâté ($2.50), or
French onion soup au gratin ($1.95). If you're ordering a mul-
ticourse meal, we would suggest the hot spinach salad next ($6
for two). Otherwise you might proceed directly to the entree,
perhaps frogs legs provençale in garlic butter ($11.95), or, if you
prefer something less exotic, broiled lobster tail in drawn butter
($15.95). All entrees are served with soup or salad and a vegeta-
ble. For dessert, French pastries are $1.95. At lunch, in addition
to hot entrees, you can get sandwiches and salads priced at $2.25
to $5.95, the latter for crab Louis.

In addition to Melvyn's, the Inn's other notable facilities are
a swimming pool and Jacuzzi, paddle tennis, croquet, shuffleboard, and a backgammon room/library; golf, tennis, and
horseback riding can be arranged.

Rates for singles or doubles from October 1 to June 1 are from $50 to $100 a night; $40 to $80 the rest of the year.

The **Palm Springs Riviera Hotel,** 1600 North Indian Avenue (tel. 327-8311), is another excellent choice. Situated on 43 acres that include a nine-hole golf course, five tennis courts (free use to guests), and the largest swimming pool in Palm Springs, the Riviera is truly luxurious.

The guest rooms have a resort look with fern-motif drapes, bedspreads, and wallpaper, white bamboo furnishings, and cheerful orange or garden green accents. All rooms are equipped with color TVs, direct-dial phones, modern tub/shower baths, and outside patios.

In addition to the abovementioned facilities, the Riviera has an immense hydrotherapy pool, lots of shops, and a plush dining room overlooking the pool called the Cafe Riviera. Gourmet continental fare is served here, and there's dancing and entertainment nightly in the adjoining lounge.

Rates from December 16 to April 30 are $38 to $48, single; $45 to $55, double. From May 1 to June 30, and September 15 to December 15, they're $35 to $45, single; $40 to $50, double. In the summer, from July 1 to September 14, all rooms, single or double, are a meager $24. Year-round, an extra person in the room is charged $9, and there's no charge for children under 12 in the same room as their parents.

The **Palm Springs Spa Hotel & Mineral Springs,** 100 North Indian Avenue (tel. 325-1461), offers the most health-oriented facilities of any Palm Springs resort. It's situated on land that was formerly considered a shrine by the Cahuilla Indians because of the magical properties of its spring waters. The Spa has three outdoor pools filled with the revitalizing, mineral-filled waters from its underground natural springs, as well as a conventional swimming pool with a sundeck. In addition, there are 30 indoor sunken Roman swirlpools, also filled from the springs. Rounding out these healthful facilities are a vapor-inhalation room, a rock steam room (where mineral waters are turned to steam), a completely equipped gymnasium, and a staff to pamper guests with massages, facials, manicures, pedicures, and other beauty treatments. What is not on the premises—like tennis and golf—is available at a nearby country club. Of course, after you've done all those healthy things, you'll have to be careful not to pile on pounds at the lavish Agua Room, where a superb French cuisine is served at dinner; executive chef Eugene Le

Gallo previously worked at the Stork Club and El Morocco. Breakfast and lunch are served in the Cafe Eugene, adjoining the Agua Lounge.

The rooms at the Spa are suitably luxurious and elegantly appointed. All are equipped with refrigerators, direct-dial phones, color TVs, and baths with Travertine marble sinks.

Rates for all this basking and luxuriating are as follows: from October 1 to December 30, and May 1 to June 1, double rooms are $38 to $46. From December 20 to April 30, they ascend to $50 to $60. And from June 1 to September 30, they plunge to a low of between $22 and $38. If you don't choose to stay at the Spa, you can use the mineral baths for $5 a day.

ACCOMMODATIONS IN THE MODERATE RANGE: The Tropics, 411 East Palm Canyon Drive (tel. 327-1391), is less glamorous than our previous listings, but it's also less expensive. And it does have considerable facilities for a motel: two Olympic-size pools, two Jacuzzis, and shuffleboard. The Conga Room Steak House on the premises serves dinner, and a Sambo coffeeshop adjoins.

As for the rooms—142 in all—they're furnished quite smartly and are outfitted with color TVs, direct-dial phones, tub/shower baths, and, in many cases, refrigerators.

Single and double rates are $32 to $44 from January 15 to June 1; $26 to $36 from October 1 to January 15; and $20 to $32 from June 2 to October 1.

The **Westward Ho Motel,** 701 East Palm Canyon Drive (tel. 327-1531), offers lower rates yet for standard motel rooms and facilities similar to the abovementioned listing. The highest rates here obtain between February and April: singles, $21 to $23; doubles, $23 to $36.

Chapter VI

SHOPPING IN LOS ANGELES

IN SOUTHERN CALIFORNIA, you can combine a shopping expedition with a visit to a sightseeing attraction, which permits you not only to find widely varying merchandise, but to enjoy the atmosphere as well. From Disneyland to Olvera Street to the Ports O'Call Village to the Farmers Market, you can purchase many hard-to-get items from all over the world, as well as Indian, Mexican, Oriental, and Western handicrafts.

OLVERA STREET: In the Pueblo de Los Angeles, Olvera Street offers a quickie shopping trip to Mexico. Believed to be the city's oldest street, it is flanked with shops featuring merchandise imported from all regions of Mexico. The tile-paved Paseo has rows of stalls down its center, selling wares spread out in the fashion of an authentic Mexican market. A wide range of articles is handsomely displayed, and at times you can see the craftsmen at work. The candle-dipping shops are highly scented by herbs, spices, and perfumes used in the beeswax and tallow. At a glass-blowing shop, you can buy trinkets for your what-not shelf (stemmed goblets, plates, and bowls). In addition, you'll find assorted baskets and straw hats, costume jewelry, pottery bowls, decorative tinware (candlesticks, picture frames), and handwoven sandals known as "huaraches." At a number of "puestos," you can purchase select handwoven scarves in primitive, vibrant colors. Shopping here is like participating in a musical pageant, as strolling guitarists and singers entertain with the music of Old Mexico.

NEW CHINATOWN: In shop after shop around the central plazas and lanes, you'll find goods imported from the Orient.

The district lies between North Broadway and North Hill Street (see our restaurant section under "New Chinatown"). Each year newer buildings appear—all built in the classic manner, even the banks! In particular, try the following pagoda-style shops: **Bonds,** for ivory chess sets, teak furniture, and old bronze horses; **Hong Kong,** possibly the best all-around shop for gifts (scarves, fans, bronze bowls, China dolls, dishes, robes, "happi coats"); **Jade Tree,** for prestigious merchandise from the Far East as well as mainland China (bronze Buddhas, chairs and tables, miniature boxes and chests, cloisonné, plus carved ivory, fine jewelry, and high-quality antiques).

Chong Hing Co., 949 Chungking Road, is an owner-operated custom-jewelry shop. Ronald and Ellen Lee make their own exquisite jewelry, good-luck medallions, bracelets, and rings and also sell a good selection of jade figures. **Sam Ward,** 959 South Hill, is a "general store" with not only groceries and vegetables, but also a collection of dishes and teapots. Finally, at **King's Gift Shop,** 504 Chungking Court, opposite the fountain, you'll find a good collection of gifts.

For authentic Japanese products, you can visit Little Tokyo, near City Hall in downtown Los Angeles, where **Rafu Shoten,** 309 East First Street, presents a miniature Japanese department store selection. You can purchase kimonos for men and women, tasseled lanterns, urns, porcelain, figurines, incense burners, and a large collection of Buddha figures.

FARMERS MARKET: At Fairfax and Third Street, the original Farmers Market has, in addition to its food stalls and patio restaurants, more than 50 shops offering top-notch gift buys, ranging from Indian moccasins to trained parrots. The following represent just a sampling of what is available. Go to the **Farmers Market Gem Shop** for American Indian objects, unpolished and cut stones and "findings"; **Walter Wright** for modern gold and silver jewelry with precious stones; the **Western Frontier Moccasin and Leather Shop** for the largest selection of moccasins and handtooled belts in Southern California; the **Sweden Shop** for gifts imported from Scandinavian countries; **Buttons and Bows** for Japanese and Israeli imports, fine gifts, and buttons from all over the world; the **Little Mexico Mart** for straw baskets, huaraches, handbags; **Roos Linen Shop** for linen gifts from all over the world; the **Indian Trading Post** for moccasins, blankets, pottery, jewelry, and Eskimo carvings; and the **Redwood Shop**

for an unusual assortment of gifts in myrtlewood, monkey pod, walnut, teak, rock maple, cherrywood, golden birch, and even redwood trees planted in miniature boxes and ready to grow.

SHOPPING COMPLEXES: Shopping in Southern California is finding its own free form, as reflected by the widely diverse selection of complexes previewed below. Incidentally, these compounds of boutiques often spring up in the most unlikely places.

The **Arco Plaza,** 505 South Flower Street, Los Angeles, is seven subterranean acres of shops. Perhaps it's a forecast of shopping in the future. Take a handy escalator outside at the corners of Fifth and Sixth Streets on Flower. Beneath the Atlantic Richfield/Bank of America Twin Towers at Fifth and Flower in downtown Los Angeles, corridors lead to shops and restaurants. Stores and boutiques are on the second and third underground levels. You'll even find a Catholic church! You can enjoy a sundae at **Theodora's** or a pint at **O'Shaughnessy's,** an Irish pub. French cuisine is served in an old-world setting at **François.** There are art exhibits, fashion shows, educational seminars, concerts—everything enhanced by a colorful background with flowers and plants. Tours are conducted by appointment (tel. 625-2132).

The **Broadway Plaza** is a two-level underground shopping mall. It's under a duo of steel-and-glass towers, one housing the 700 Flower Street Office Building, the other the Hyatt Regency Hotel recommended earlier. In the complex is the **Broadway Department Store,** one of the largest and most complete in Los Angeles, plus 30 specialty shops selling everything from books to jewelry. For women, an excellent boutique is **Back Street,** devoted entirely to newly reproduced feminine attire from the '20s, including off-the-shoulder slinky dresses, scarves, and cloche hats. No Salvation Army discards or "Second-Hand Roses" here! The Hyatt House and Broadway store are bounded by Seventh, Eighth, Hope, and Flower Streets. The glass-covered plaza itself is reached via many escalators. The plaza has not only an indoor sidewalk cafe, but a gourmet restaurant attached to the hotel and a revolving rooftop restaurant called **Angel's Flight.** Daily pipe organ and banjo concerts entertain the shoppers, and there's parking for 2,000 cars.

New Orleans Square, 8543 Santa Monica Boulevard (tel. 659-3283), West Hollywood, is an attractive, two-story building of shops and boutiques. It's a delightful place for a browse, as most of the store owners are selective collectors. **Nostalgia,** in shop No. 1, has everything that was stored in your grandmother's attic—and all items are clearly marked as to price. **African Arts & Beads,** in shop No. 3, has masks, sculpture, antique beads, tribal headdresses, and other items. **Creole,** in shop No. 14, offers beaded and bedazzled denim sportswear for men and women. Other shops in the compound sell items as varied as rare plants and jewelry. New Orleans Square marks the beginning of the famous La Cienega row of art galleries and antique shops. Free parking.

Fisherman's Village, Fiji Way, Marina del Rey (tel. 823-5411), is a recreation of a New England fishing village, with cobblestoned streets. It houses some excellent little shops and boutiques, selling small gift items, such as candles, spices, hand-made wood merchandise, leather, and copper.

Another shopping complex nearby, this one housed under one roof in a warehouse building at the Venice edge of Marina del Rey, is **Port of Craft,** 303 Washington Street, Marina del Rey. It's a cluster of boutiques at the edge of a canal. At least a dozen shops are here, including the **Brown Bagger Restaurant,** the **Gob Shop,** and the **First Impression.** Unusual gifts, antiques, arts and crafts—you'll find them here.

Lido Village, Port O'Call, 3400 Via Aporto, Newport Beach, is a smart new shopping mall with an old look. Chic shops open onto bricked walks, and rows of boutiques and restaurants front the yacht and sailboat wharf. There are two floors, with nearly 50 shops of quality merchandise. One shop is devoted to **Lilly Pulitzer** who makes dresses with fabrics handscreened in Key West, Florida. Others include **Sea Treasures,** the **German Home Bakery, India House,** and **Pappagallo** shoes for women.

Cannery Village, Newport Beach, runs for about five square blocks along the wharf, which is now a complex of nearly a hundred fascinating shops, boutiques, and restaurants. Old bungalows, houses, and stores have been given a new lease on life. Little marine factories have been divided into stalls where artisans, collectors, vendors, artists, dressmakers, and craftsmen make and sell unusual items. A good starting point is The Cannery Restaurant on the wharf, where you'll find many of the shops along 29th, 30th, and 31st Streets.

At **The Factory,** 425 East 30th Street, are some 20 shops housed under one roof—a covered arcade made especially attractive by the **House of Distinctive Plants.** In the same complex is a talented stained-glass artist, Ray H. Gibson, of **Gibson's**

Imports and Stained Glass. He works with unusual and imported glass. To supplement his income, he sells Polynesian objects such as batik placemats brought back from the South Seas. Another shop in The Factory is **The Bon Ton,** selling gourmet and contemporary accessories imported from Europe. The owner, Bill Somerlade, even gives gourmet cooking classes. Jack and Maydee Galloway run **Galloways,** 410 31st Street, a showcase for the items they collect, including antiques and such "things" as jewelry, glassware, stemware, even wine and cheese.

Whole Earth Market Place, 18021 Ventura Boulevard, Encino, is a remake of an old supermarket divided into approximately 80 small stalls displaying handmade arts and crafts. If it's made of wood, glass, metal, leather, enamel, or fabric, you'll find it here! The taste level is evocative of Greenwich Village. Toiling owners preside over their stalls. Even if you don't buy anything, you'll probably meet somebody interesting to talk to. A good place to meet people, while enjoying a healthy meal and live entertainment, is at the new **Cafe Concert.** Set in the back of a large parking lot, the Market Place is open Mondays to Saturdays from 10 a.m. to 10 p.m. (Sundays, 10 a.m. to 6 p.m.).

PORTS O'CALL: At the Ports O'Call and Whaler's Wharf in San Pedro you'll find one of the widest selections of gifts in Southern California—something to suit every taste, sold in a recreation of the past. To reach it, take the Harbor Freeway to its termination, bearing left for two miles after leaving it.

In shops resembling the personally run stores of the late 19th century, you can select from such merchandise as American bottles (everything from the Kickapoo Indians' tapeworm secret to love power jugs!); okra pickles; excellent reproductions of antique pewter; pepper mills; salad spoons and forks; Mexican wrought-iron fixtures and furniture; Iron Mountain stoneware; homemade candles; Hawaiian casuals; imports from India; Western and American Indian souvenirs; Oriental articles in brass, teak, and lacquered wood; paintings; boutique clothing; gunpowder tea from Japan; even wigs. You name it!

Toys for Men, W 34, Berth 75, Whaler's Wharf, at Ports O'Call (tel. 833-4212), is a men's gift shop housed in a replica of Paul Revere's home. Its wide-ranging merchandise includes sweaters, shirts, brightly colored socks, neckties, handcarved cedar gifts, chess sets and other games, leather accessories, jewelry, and far-out cards.

The McCloud Ringworks, W 2, Berth 76, at the south end of Whaler's Wharf, are the local goldsmiths and all-around jewelers, offering some exceptional handcrafted pieces.

Now, for handcrafted items from local California artists and craftspeople, head for **Cobblestone Craft Co.,** in Ports O'Call Village where you will find a wide selection of handwrought sterling jewelry, some of which is fabricated on the premises. In addition, this shop features ceramic and wood items, wind chimes, baskets, toys, household accessories, etc. Also in the same village is the **Whoopsie Daisy** flower and plant shop wherein is a 12-foot lava rock waterfall.

WIDE WORLD IMPORT BAZAAR: At 6307 Hollywood Boulevard in Hollywood (also in Pasadena), is this colorful marketplace of goods from the world over. The list of high-quality wares, at reasonable prices, is endless, so take a look for yourself.

ANTIQUES: **Melrose Avenue** between La Cienega and Robertson Boulevards has more than 100 exquisite and tasteful little boutiques and antique shops, making it one of the finest antique centers this side of Portobello Road in London. What was once a residential street now has converted bungalows, where proprietors have incorporated their gardens and patios into the general scheme. Sturdy shoes are recommended.

The Antique Guild, Venice Boulevard at Helms Avenue, just north of Culver City (tel. 838-3131), bills itself as "the world's largest antique outlet"—over three acres of antiques under one roof. Housed in the Old Helms Bakery Building, an L.A. landmark, the Guild has more than 100,000 pieces from Europe on sale at all times—at extremely reasonable prices. Because the Guild *is* so large, they can buy in quantity, and pass the benefit of volume buying on to the customer. Their buyers are constantly checking out and purchasing the entire contents of European castles, beer halls, estates, and mansions. With new shipments coming in every week, the merchandise is constantly changing, and it's fun to browse through the old armoires, chandeliers, stained glass, crystal, china, clocks, washstands, tables, mirrors, etc., even if you don't want to buy.

In addition to the huge selection of antiques and old-world originals, the Guild also has an Indoor Garden Center selling everything for the home garden; an Antique Jewelry Boutique; a Fine Art Gallery; an Idea Room, filled with unique decorating ideas; and Room Vignettes—period settings and eclectic mixes of the old and the contemporary. Should you get hungry, there's even an indoor sidewalk cafe called The Kitchen for lunch and snacks.

Open seven days a week, the Guild is easily reached by freeway from any point in Los Angeles.

JEWELRY: Craftsmen at **Lawrence Martin Kling**, 901 Westwood Boulevard, in Westwood Village, design and handcraft exquisite jewelry, and if you have your own design, they will make it to order.

CRAFTS OF INDIA, MEXICO, AND NEPAL: Viva Boutique, 8872 Sunset Boulevard, Hollywood (tel. 657-7331), is a chic choice for apparel and handmade and handcrafted art objects. The collection is from Mexico, India, even Nepal. This most tasteful boutique is owned and run by a husband-and-wife team, Lucy and George Chybinski, who alternately make shopping expeditions to bring back one-of-a-kind merchandise. Robes in natural fibers, cotton shirts with bright and unusual colors, nicely styled caftans, handmade jewelry, handwoven blankets, llama wool sweaters, large colored tin butterflies, jeweled and brass birds and dragons, even a ceremonial wedding gown, are among the hundreds of inexpensive and stylish items displayed.

Los Angeles City Hall

Chapter VII

LOS ANGELES AFTER DARK

WITH THE PASSAGE of Hollywood's heyday, nightlife in Los Angeles seems comparatively tame somehow. Once the antics of stars were splashed on the front pages of tabloids around the world—for example, Humphrey Bogart's drunken brawls on Sunset Strip. Readers were titillated to read that Franchot Tone had been arrested for "expectorating" in the face of Florabel Muir, New York *Daily News* columnist; that the king of the big prank, Jim Moran, had impersonated Saud El Saud of Saudi Arabia, giving out fake jewelry to near-hysterical waiters at a Hollywood nightclub; that Darryl Zanuck had "performed" on the trapeze at Ciro's; that Bogey and Baby and fellow rat-packers Frank Sinatra and Judy Garland were up to their well-publicized and wildly impractical jokes at the citadel of Michel ("The Prince") Romanoff.

Nowadays, it seems that many Angelenos frequent nightclubs rarely if at all. Essentially, Los Angeles is an informal town whose denizens prefer to entertain in their private homes. For many families, the emphasis is on the rear patio garden, with a barbecue pit placed conveniently near the oval-shaped swimming pool. Even motion picture stars like to take off their makeup and relax in the evenings, unlike the past, when studios compelled them to dress up and go out with starlets or actor escorts they often detested.

Nevertheless, for gregarious young people in particular, there is a wide range of discotheques, folk-music enclaves, whatever. In summer, the hottest little spots are those along the Pacific strip between Santa Monica and Laguna Beach. Some of these clubs come and go seasonally with exasperating irregularity, but when functioning often feature first-rate entertainment—struggling young groups who may be the headliners of tomorrow.

Most of the action in any season, though, centers around:

SUNSET STRIP: The Strip is not the name of a bottomless night-club, but rather the nickname of a 20-block stretch of Sunset Boulevard, linking the western boundaries of Hollywood with the eastern periphery of Beverly Hills. It is familiar to TV fans because of the now-defunct series "77 Sunset Strip."

In the 1920s, gambling clubs appeared on the Strip; the Crosby brothers constructed their own office building to house various enterprises there, and night spots, such as Ciro's, soon cropped up. Supper clubs, high-rise apartment dwellings (the Sunset Towers, erected primarily for film industry people), decorator showrooms, and boutiques joined the rush. William Haines, of silent-screen fame, turned decorator and opened a Greek revival shop. Car-rental showrooms rounded out the picture.

Today, kids hawk copies of the Los Angeles *Free Press* (most intriguing reading), whereas in the past fans gathered outside expensive clubs to collect autographs of movie stars, many of whom weren't in any condition to sign anything.

Sunset Strip makes for a good stroll, certainly an interesting one for avid people-watchers. Starting at Schwab's Drugstore at Sunset and Laurel Canyon Boulevards, you can walk west, passing a number of head shops, nudie nightclubs, and glorified hamburger joints, and watch the action.

But whether you watch the passing parade, or decide to join it, Sunset Strip is fun.

LIVE GROUPS: Doug Weston's Troubadour, 9081 Santa Monica Boulevard, near Doheny, West Hollywood (tel. 276-6168). In olden days, the Smothers Brothers used to appear at the Troubadour. In what now seems the dinosaur era, the hard-pumping Blood, Sweat, and Tears were "discovered" here. The management books some of the finest talent in Los Angeles—often when they're just about to become nationally famous. Among those who have performed at the Troubadour are Joni Mitchell, Judy Collins, The Byrds, and Linda Ronstadt.

You can purchase a ticket to the two-level sanctum for $3 to $5, depending on who's performing. Inside, there's a two-item minimum. Drinks cost $1.25 and up. There is a dinner menu ranging from $3 to $6, but the biggest selections are in the drinks and desserts categories—cappucino, juices, ciders, ice cream—

but salads and sandwiches are also available. Monday night is talent night (a new show opens every Tuesday), and there's a $2 cover with no minimum for that evening only. Tuesday through Sunday, there are two shows nightly: at 9 p.m. and 11 p.m. Dress casually.

Filthy McNasty's, 8852 Sunset Boulevard, Los Angeles (tel. 659-2055), rather facetiously bills itself as "famous since 1971." And indeed it has been, because it has booked interesting talent from the start. For example, Monte Rock had an engagement there, announcing to the audience that he was going to "sing the songs that made me famous." Live groups play for dancing. Right in the heart of the Strip, Filthy McNasty's provides entertainment and dancing nightly. It's open from 6 p.m. till 2 a.m., but the best time to go is after 10 p.m. You pay from $2 for a cover charge on Friday and Saturday, $1 the rest of the week. There's always a one-drink ($1.75) minimum. Proof of age—21 —is required.

O'Shaughnessy's, "C" Level, Arco Plaza, 515 South Flower Street, Los Angeles (tel. 629-2565), will make you Irish for the night. It's an uninhibited, rollicking place at which to wind down, enjoying Irish ballads and drinking songs. The setting, with its heavy beams, tapestries on the walls, and stone walls, is reminiscent of an Irish castle. You dine on rather hearty but simple Irish fare, plus a few American dishes and drinks, but it is the entertainment and conviviality that counts. Entrees range in price from $3.75 to $8.95. It's traditional to order corned beef and cabbage, however, at $4.75, followed by Irish whiskey pie at $1.25. Open from 11 a.m. to midnight, Monday through Thursday (till 1 a.m. on Friday and Saturday). No entertainment Monday nights.

FOR COMEDY: The Comedy Store, 8431 Sunset Boulevard, Hollywood (tel. 656-6225), is the most important showcase for rising comedians in Los Angeles. Owner Mitzi Shore always puts out the welcome mat. Sometimes Redd Foxx or Jimmy Walker turns up. Mitzi gets the show started nightly at 9, and it's a five-hour marathon with 12 to 15 comedians performing nightly. Sunday through Thursday there's a $2 cover and a one-drink ($1.75) minimum (Friday and Saturday, it's a $3 cover and a two-drink minimum). There's no cover on Monday nights, when anyone in the audience can get up and do five minutes. The main room has overscaled photos of such elite comedians as Chaplin, Joe E. Brown, and Cantor.

There are two more Comedy Stores: one at 1621 Westwood Boulevard, Westwood, and another in San Diego at 4315 Ocean Boulevard, Pacific Beach.

Ye Little Club, 455 North Canon Drive, Beverly Hills (tel. 275-3077), is as modest a little bar and night spot as you'll ever find. But for some unexplained reason, it's homebase for special entertainers who try out their material here. For example, Joan Rivers works out her act here before she appears in Las Vegas or on the Johnny Carson show. The decor is sort of Hollywood Tudor, with a fake oak-beam ceiling and imitation crests on the walls. But owner Marshall Edison has a special flair, and it's a "hot" little club. When Ms. Rivers is performing, there's a $3 cover on weekends and $2.50 on other nights. Drinks average $1.75, and there's a two-libation minimum. For an entertainer less well known, the cover charge is only $1 to $3. Monday is amateur night.

ALONG THE COAST: Concerts by the Sea, 100 Fisherman's Wharf, Redondo Beach (tel. 379-4998), is fashionable and entertaining. On the lower level of the pier is this modern though rustic concert hall, offering great names in jazz nightly except Mondays. It's the coastal jazz festival showcase for such artists as Ahmad Jamal, Tito Puente, and Stan Kenton. The box office opens at 8:15 p.m., and shows are at 9 and 11 p.m. The entrance fee varies from $4 to $7.50, depending on the attraction; Wednesdays it's half price for everyone. Don't be too freaked out about going down to Redondo Beach: it's only a short trip on the freeway.

The Lighthouse, 30 Pier Avenue, Hermosa Beach (tel. 372-6911), makes a sensible and needed contribution to the nighttime scene in this beachfront town. Some good groups perform in this self-proclaimed "World's Oldest Jazz Club and Waterfront Dive," which presents predominantly jazz groups. "Aware" comedians also appear from time to time. Near the pier, the club opens at 8:30 with shows at 9:15, 11, and 12:30. On Tuesday nights there's a student discount. The cover charge and minimum vary each night according to the evening and the performers. Admission is usually in the $4 to $5 range. The Lighthouse is open every night except Monday

A JAZZ SUPPER CLUB: Donte's, 4269 Lankershim Boulevard, North Hollywood (tel. 769-1566), is a contender for the best jazz supper club in the Greater Los Angeles area. Open every night, if often features big-name acts. In the past, such stars as Count Basie, Benny Carter, Carmen McRae, Sarah Vaughn, and Morgana King have put in an appearance here. Most hard drinks go for $1.50 to $1.85. In the food department, you can order mostly steak and seafood dishes, in the $2.50 to $9 range. "Jazz dinners" are served from 7 p.m. to 1 a.m. Dinners are in addition to the cover and minimum. There are three shows nightly at 9:30, 11:15, and 1.

MEDIEVAL NIGHTS: The Abbey, 400 East Washington Street, Marina del Rey (tel. 822-2741), is a dining and entertainment adventure into the past. It was assembled from the original set of *Camelot*, and is filled with a zany collection of medieval treasures. You dine on a bishop's chair in front of a stone fireplace in a great hall, with ecclesiastical arches, heraldic banners, coats-of-arms, ancient weapons—everything evoking King Arthur's Knights of the Round Table. Soft lights flicker from the overscaled wrought-iron chandeliers, and you dine in style, enjoying not only the food, but the entertainment. The menu features a selection of fresh seafoods, lamb, steak, prime rib, and veal entrees, ranging in price from $5.95 to $9.95. Open nightly at 5 p.m.

FOR SWINGING SINGLES: The Saloon, 9390 Santa Monica Boulevard, Beverly Hills (tel. 273-7155), is the city's "swingingest singles bar." It's a recreation of an old saloon or English pub. The bar is long, the atmosphere lively, the experiment a smashing success. The setting is like an operetta version of an old tavern, with etched glass, pewter service plates, fresh flowers on the tables, and hanging copper pots. The main drinking lounge is two stories high, with a portrait of Henry VIII. The staff serves one of the best shrimp cocktails in Los Angeles (Gulf of Mexico shrimp on a bed of crushed ice in a ceramic sea shell), $5. A burger is $3.75; saloon chili, $4.50. Beer on draught is $1 to $1.25.

DISCOTHEQUES: Gazzarri's on the Strip, 9039 Sunset Boulevard, Hollywood (tel. CR 3-6606), is the oldest rock discotheque in Los Angeles—and it's still going strong. Big-name rock stars perform here, and two or three groups go full-steam. Gazzarri's is also known for its light show (the best in L.A.), the Gazzarri Dancers, and its presentation of old-time movies. The admission charge ranges from $3 to $3.50 per person, depending on the current attraction. Parking is available. Closed Mondays and Tuesdays.

The Basement, 4215 Admiralty Way, Marina del Rey (tel. 823-0927). If you're a rich young man with a girl stashed away in an apartment at San Diego, another in North Hollywood, chances are you'll bring one of them to The Basement on Saturday night. One wears good clothes here, and tries hard to look well-heeled. A one-drink minimum is imposed. In addition, men pay a $1 cover on Wednesdays and Thursdays, and everybody pays a $2 cover on Fridays and Saturdays. Incidentally, you must prove you are 21 (it may take several documents, including one with a photograph). Usually there are at least two shows with live groups nightly, Tuesday through Sunday. Always there is dancing. The interior is designed arena fashion, with the dance floor on the lowest level.

ABC ENTERTAINMENT CENTER: At Century City, the **ABC Entertainment Center** has become one of the most important nighttime spots in Greater Los Angeles. Part of the Century City complex, it boasts the **Shubert Theater,** where you can see bigtime musicals as *Gypsy* and *A Chorus Line.* For musicals in the evening, the range is from $8 to $16 (cheaper for matinees). Call the box office at 553-9000.

The center has two movie theaters (telephone 553-4595 for what's showing). Food, entertainment, and plenty of bunnies are offered at **The Playboy Club** (for reservations, telephone 277-2777). On the other hand, **Harry's Bar and Grill** is a faithful reproduction of its namesake along the Arno in Florence, Italy. For reservations, telephone 277-2333.

The **Garden Room** in the Century Plaza Hotel has a trio that plays for dancing Friday and Saturday nights. There's no cover or minimum, but drinks cost $1.85.

Finally, in the same hotel, there's the **Hong Kong Bar,** Century Plaza Hotel, Avenue of the Stars, Century City (tel. 277-2000), with an ambience suggesting a version of a Chinese dockside cellar bar. Yet top performers swear by its acoustics, and the audiences are called "the friendliest in Los Angeles." There's dancing to light rock and disco music—continuous entertainment, Tuesday through Sunday from 9 p.m. to 1:30 a.m. There is a $1 cover charge and a two-drink minimum Sunday, and Tuesday through Thursday. The cover increases to $3 on Fridays and Saturdays. Closed Mondays.

A HILTON BOUQUET: L'Escoffier, 9876 Wilshire Boulevard, Beverly Hills (tel. 274-7777), is the Beverly Hilton's penthouse restaurant offering dining and dancing with a view. The award-winning continental cuisine, the panorama of the city, and dancing to the music of an orchestra promise a memorable evening. Open Monday through Saturday from 6:30 p.m., L'Escoffier offers an à la carte menu with entrees ranging from $12 to $20, or Le Menu Classique, a complete dinner for $20. The ultimate in dining is Le Diner Escoffier, a seven-course meal, for $25. Drinks start at $2. You can dance nightly until midnight (till 12:30 a.m. on Friday and Saturday).

The Library, Beverly Hills Hilton, 9876 Wilshire Boulevard, Beverly Hills, is an incongruity, hidden behind an Edwardian entrance of stained glass just off the main lobby of this modern deluxe hotel. It's like a recreation of a library in an English manor house. Ceiling-to-floor shelves contain actual books (we hope to read more in Dumas' *The Regent's Daughter* on our next visit). Knights in armor stand guard at the back, surveying a crowd likely to include Sargeant Shriver, Muhammed Ali, or Mickey Spillane. Drinks are $1.50, and liqueurs are $1.75. The manager, George Sperdakos, offers a unique drink: "Tea, by George." The award-winning drink is made with Suntory Green Tea liqueur, giving it a tea-like taste. Another special drink is "The Bookworm," a blend of vodka, passion fruit nectar, and grapefruit juice.

MEXICAN NIGHTS ON OLVERA STREET: Casa La Golondrina, 35 Olvera Street, Los Angeles (tel. 628-4349), is the best place in Los Angeles for Mexican entertainment. On the city's oldest street, it is sheltered in the first brick-built building (circa 1850), the Pelanconi House. The cafe itself dates from 1924, when it was founded by Señora Consuelo Castillo de Bonzo. You get not only flamenco and Mexican singing, but authentic south-of-the-border meals as well. On nippy evenings, you hopefully will be seated by the open fireplace, where you can listen to the strolling troubadours as they create a romantic and mellow mood. (For lunch, you can dine on the outside terrace.)

Every night is "fiesta" night, especially on Latin American holidays. Entertainment is presented five times weekly (the Casa, however, is closed Wednesdays and Thursdays, except in summer, from mid-June until mid-September). There's no cover charge. You can just drop in for drinks and the show or dancing. Mexican beer goes for $1.25, hard drinks for $2.

Dinner specialties of the Casa cost as low as $5, providing a choice of four entrees, as well as a taquito appetizer, and guacamole (avocado salad), Mexican beans with cheese, Spanish rice, tortillas, coffee, and ice cream. A popular main course is the house specialty—chili verde, ropa vieja, arroz con pollo, enchilada California, $5. Eastern choice top sirloin steak dinners go for $6.

After dining, you can enjoy a leisurely stroll along the brick-and-tiled "Walk of the Angels," with its colorful shops, restaurants, taco cafes, and flamboyantly garbed attendants. For a final snack, try some of the roasted nuts along "El Paseo." Instrumental groups outside add further zest.

MORE LATIN ENTERTAINMENT: Matador, 10948 West Pico Boulevard, West Los Angeles (tel. 475-4949), is a Spanish restaurant with a miniature flamenco room, where matadors from Tijuana like to hang out. Usually a pair of flamenco dancers and guitarists entertain Wednesday through Sunday, starting at 9 (at 9:30 on Friday and Saturday), with three shows nightly. For nondiners there's a $2.50 cover charge plus a one-drink minimum. However, dining is recommended. Gazpacho is 95¢, and most main dishes are $5 to $7. Most recommendable is the supreme de pollo Granada—that is, chicken stuffed with a pâté in a sauce of mushrooms and artichokes, $6.95. Open Tuesday through Sunday from 5 p.m.

El Gato, 7324 Sepulveda Boulevard, Van Nuys (tel. 781-1580), has the atmosphere of a Mexican fiesta. At "The Cat," you can be entertained by a ten-piece mariachi group Wednesday through Sunday. Almost every table overlooks the reflection pool. Combination meals range in price from $4.25 to $6.95, with soup or salad. In the Mariachi Room a family show is presented Sundays at 6 p.m., starring 60 puppets.

There's disco dancing Wednesday through Sunday nights in

the cantina, and dancing to the mariachi band on Friday and Saturday nights.

DINNER AND DANCING: Hollywood Palladium, 6215 Sunset Boulevard, Hollywood (tel. 466-4311). It's best to call first and check on who is appearing at this famous entertainment landmark. The attractions range from big bands like Ray Anthony and Les Brown, to rock groups like the Beach boys and the Average White Band. However, there might also be a square dance night, Latin dance night, a karate exhibition, a closed-circuit fight, or an award show. And Lawrence Welk does New Year's Eve here. Prices vary with the attraction—from $5 to $10 for admission.

VAUDEVILLE: Mayfair Music Hall, 214 Santa Monica Boulevard, Santa Monica (tel. 451-0621), recaptures the sentiment and gusto of music halls of the 19th century. It all takes place in a gilded music hall, once the Santa Monica Opera House, glittering with an Edwardian elegance, right down to polished brass, walnut paneling, stained glass, crystal chandeliers, and gold-leaf Rococo boxes. In the tradition of English music halls, a "chairman" (master of ceremonies) is seated in a box above the stage. With a gavel, he introduces the cast and show, making wry comments. Musicals and vaudeville reviews are presented nightly at 8:30 (8 and 10:45 on Saturdays). The hall is closed on Mondays and Tuesdays. Admission is $5.50, increasing to $6.50 on Saturdays. Drinks, snacks, and complete dinners are available.

A MIXED BAG: Improvisation, 8162 Melrose Avenue (tel. 651-2583), is a homey nightclub in an obscure location where something different goes on each night. Comedy segments of TV shows—like "Don Kirshner's Rock Concert"—are filmed here, as are many cable-TV shows. Sometimes professional comedians use Improvisation as a workshop to try out new material before a live audience; many are not well known, but you might also catch Jimmy Walker, Liza Minelli, Rodney Dangerfield, or Richard Pryor. Sunday night new talent is auditioned, and Wednesday night is songwriter's showcase, sponsored by the record industry union, B.M.I., record producers and agents. Dinner is available, and of course there's a full bar.

Open seven nights, shows begin at 9:30 p.m.; entertainment is

The World's Most Famous Beanery

Barney's Beanery, 8447 Santa Monica Boulevard (tel. 650-9240), below Sunset Strip in West Hollywood, is the most celebrated beanery in the West. In the early '60s, a Pop-Art exhibition in California by sculptor Kienholtz featured an interior scene of the cafe, complete with a customer on a stool and the apron-clad Barney himself behind the counter. Barney, who died in the winter of 1968, was somewhat of a legend in his own right, publicized in a national magazine standing under a misspelled sign, "Fagots Stay Out." The sign still remains, but the old discriminatory policy has been abandoned.

In a newspaper column, Mike Jackson wrote: "From the outside you would guess that Barney's Beanery is ready for the bulldozer. Once inside, you are sure of it." He traced its history from its opening in 1927, citing some of its former patrons: Jean Harlow, John Barrymore, Clara Bow.

Frankly, Barney wouldn't recognize the place today. Outside is a glaring neon sign, and inside are pool tables, game machines, and a blaring jukebox. You can still get chili and beans for 95¢ or a chili burger at $1.75. Many late-night people drop in for ham (a half-pound serving) and three eggs ($2.95) shortly before dawn. The bar is open from 9 a.m. till 2 a.m., and food is served from 10 a.m. on.

continuous till 2 a.m. On Friday, Saturday, and Sunday nights, special shows sometimes play prior to the regular show (beginning at 8:30 p.m.)—usually improvisational comedy groups. There's a $3.50 drink minimum Sunday through Thursday; a $5 drink minimum on Friday nights; a $5 drink minimum plus a $2 cover charge on Saturday nights.

THEATRICAL PRESENTATIONS: Hollywood Bowl, 2301 North Highland, Hollywood (tel. 87-MUSIC) draws music devotees in the summer. The Bowl was created in the early 1920s when a musician—hiking in the hills—was startled to discover its perfect natural acoustics. Launching into song, he heard his voice carried virtually to the ridges of the mountains. Music lovers banded together, financing tiers of seats to be dug, Greek fashion, out of the mountainside. A stage and shell were constructed, the future home of the Los Angeles Philharmonic Orchestra. Box seats were installed in the front, and since many were re-

A Moveable Feast of Art

The Monday night 8-to-10 promenade along La Cienega Boulevard, bordering Beverly Hills, is a ritual for the art aficionado. It's as important as the "paseo" in a Spanish village. You start at the 900 block at the junction of Santa Monica Boulevard, walking down one side of La Cienega toward Olympic Boulevard to the 500 block, then returning on the other side of the street. The avenue is flanked with art galleries (overflowing onto satellite lanes), antique shops, and the dining rooms of the adjoining Restaurant Row.

It's definitely not conservative—neither the exhibits nor the patrons. Many galleries are a showcase for today's or tomorrow's art forms—highly personal sculpture placed in small glass boxes with doors that open, figures made of discarded railroad ties from Angel's Flight, or sculpture with moveable areas of color which change as they pass over one another, and mix before your eyes.

There are more than 20 art galleries along La Cienega and about half that on nearby side streets. Most of them open during regular business hours. However, there is a policy to alternate evening and weekend openings among themselves. Some galleries, for example, are open on Sundays; others on Thursday nights; and some on weekends only (a few by appointment only). However, the Monday evening 8-to-10 period is the time to see and enjoy the most.

served for film stars, intermission time at the Bowl became an extra added attraction.

Nowadays, internationally known conductors and soloists perform classical programs on Tuesday, Thursday, and Saturday nights. The season also includes many rock, country, folk, jazz, and pop events. Presentations usually begin in early July, ending around Labor Day. Typical performers are likely to include anyone from Weylon Jennings to Zubin Mehta to Sarah Vaughn.

Tips from habitués: a part of the Bowl ritual is to order a picnic basket from **Pepper Tree Lane** (call 87-MUSIC the day before to order), which you can enjoy in the gardens before the concert. Or, if you prefer, you can reserve a table at the **Patio Restaurant** (tel. 87-MUSIC), which serves a buffet supper.

Music lovers can purchase tickets for seats high on the hill, enjoying the panorama of the Hollywood hills along with the performance.

Seats for the classical concerts begin as low as $1, and go up to $6 for seats on the benches. However, for the box seats, you'll pay anywhere from $7 to $11.50. Regular seats at the pop concerts are $1 to $10. On Friday and Saturday, special attractions are often presented. Box office opens around June 1, and stays open Monday to Saturday from 10 a.m. to 9 p.m.; Sunday, from noon to 6 p.m. Parking space can be reserved for $2.50, though at the lots adjacent to the Bowl entrance the charge is $1. Incidentally you can park your car nearby for $1.50, and then take a free shuttle.

The **Universal Amphitheater,** Universal City (tel. 980-9421), was built in 1969 at a cost of $1 million. This 5,200-seat outdoor arena, overlooking San Fernando Valley, is next to the Visitors' Entertainment Center of Universal Studios Tours. No seat is more than 140 feet from center stage. Only top names perform in this acoustically perfect arena, and tickets are often sold out before the concert date. Artists are usually scheduled for from three to five days, and include such super-stars as John Denver, Jose Feliciano, Neil Sedaka, Judy Collins, and Linda Ronstadt. Tickets (generally priced between $5.25 and $8.75) are available in advance at the box office, open Monday through Saturday from 10 a.m. to 9 p.m. and on Sunday from noon to 9 p.m. Open July to September.

The **Greek Theatre,** 2700 N. Vermont Avenue, en route to the Observatory, Griffith Park (tel. 660-8400), patterned after the classic outdoor theaters of ancient Greece, is one of the most important showcases for stellar personalities appearing in the summer. In Hollywood's past, such entertainers were featured as Maurice Chevalier, Judy Garland, and Jack Benny.

Nowadays, you're more likely to hear *Madama Butterfly* (yes, the Theatre also presents opera), Neil Diamond, or even Sammy Davis, Jr. Dance groups and national theater societies also find it a good place to perform.

The season runs from late June till September. For the best seats at special shows, you pay as much as $12.50, although the average ticket costs around $7 to $10. For a perch on the upper fringes, expect to be charged $3.50. By bus, take No. 95 from Vermont Avenue and Hollywood Boulevard. The box office in season is open from 10 a.m. to 10 p.m.

The Southern California Theatre Association manages the **Huntington Hartford Theatre,** 1615 North Vine (near Hollywood Boulevard; tel. 462-6666), across from the Hollywood Brown Derby. Dramatic plays are presented—some top touring companies, others produced in Hollywood with stars from the screen, TV, and Broadway. The theater offers more than 1,000 seats and is considered one of the most attractive and intimate in the country. There's a bar upstairs. Prices for seats range from $6.50 to $12.50.

Theatrecraft, 7445¼ Sunset Boulevard (tel. 876-3575), a professional repertory company, has been staging between five and seven shows per season here for the last 15 years. They've even premiered three New York productions. Seats are in the $3 to $5 range. Performances are on Friday and Saturday nights at 8:15, and Sunday matinees at 2 p.m.

The Whiskey Theater, 8901 Sunset Boulevard, West Hollywood (tel. 652-4202), used to be a discotheque featuring big-name rock performers. It has since entered a new incarnation as a theater offering offbeat and innovative plays like *The Psycho Sluts,* from London, and *Let My People Come,* and *Coca-Cola Grande,* both from New York. Show times at 8:30 p.m. Sunday through Thursday; at 9 p.m. and midnight Friday and Saturday. All tickets are about $5. Closed Mondays.

For Top-Grade Avant-Garde Theater

The Company Theater, 1653 South La Cienega Boulevard, Los Angeles, is the best avant-garde experimental theater in Los Angeles —actually, one of the best in the country. An attractive and vigorous young group performs here, exploring and refining the audience-participation and gut-level theatrical experience. Its productions range from "a trip through the geography of the senses," to "a psychedelic tapestry." Call 274-5153 for current performing dates and place. Prices are always most reasonable.

A MELLOW RETREAT: Bel-Air Hotel Bar, 701 Stone Canyon Road, Bel-Air (tel. 472-1211), is one of the mellower places in Greater Los Angeles. If you want a quiet, romantic evening, drive out for drinks in the bar where a pianist and singer will often do one of your favorite songs. There's no cover, and drinks cost around $1.75 to $2.

Chapter VIII

ANAHEIM, DISNEYLAND, AND ENVIRONS

IN AND AROUND Anaheim, you'll be immersed in a theater of involvement. Disneyland dramatizes everything from a simulated trip to the moon to pioneer America, and Knott's Berry Farm at Buena Park recreates the Old West, complete with train robberies and panning for real gold! The Movieland Wax Museum recreates the legendary scenes of motion pictures in tableaux with dummies. The sights of Orange County are many, ranging from alligator parks to Lion Country Safaris. It's a lot of fun—and ideal for families.

Anaheim

Anaheim, 27 miles south of the Los Angeles City Hall, reached via the Santa Ana Freeway, provides the space needed for so large an entertainment center as Disneyland. Once the heart of an orange grove belt, it offers excellent motels and restaurants, catering to the thousands of tourists who visit the world-famed attraction.

If you're going by car, just get on the freeway heading south, and you'll be in Anaheim in about an hour. If you go by bus, take the "Freeway Flyer" (No. 800) from the terminal in downtown Los Angeles at Sixth and Los Angeles Streets.

The **Anaheim Convention Center**, 800 West Katella, Anaheim (tel. 533-5511), is a 40-acre menage of facilities right next door to Disneyland. Something is always going on here, whether it's a rock festival in its 9,100-seat arena, a special art or antiques fair in one of the two 100,000-square-foot exhibition halls, or a sales conference in one of the 27 meeting rooms. There are even kitchen facilities, a cocktail lounge, and attractive grounds for wandering between sessions.

The **Anaheim Stadium,** 2000 State College Boulevard, Anaheim (tel. 634-2000), cost $21 million to build, but it's worth
every penny to the fans of its home baseball team, the California
Angels. Designed for comfort, easy visibility, and smoother
traffic-flow within the stadium, it seats 44,000 in chair-type seats
for baseball games, and up to 56,000 (with the addition of bleach-
ers) for football and other sports.

DISNEYLAND: Even the most jaded nose can hardly turn up at
Disneyland. It's that special: a world of charm and magic! An
open sesame to one's lost childhood, it is an extravagant doorway
to yesterday and tomorrow.

Opened in 1955, Disneyland—the creation of the late Walt
Disney—has steadily grown until it ranks today as the single top
attraction in all of California. It sprawls across many acres and
is constantly expanding.

Disneyland is split into seven themed lands: Main Street, Adventureland, New Orleans Square, Bear Country, Frontierland,
Fantasyland, and Tomorrowland. Do-it-yourselfers will find it
less confusing to progress clockwise, starting with the point of
entry on Main Street. However, some of the attractions, such as
the Disneyland trains and the Disneyland Monorail, take guests
around the perimeter of the park.

The general admission to Disneyland is $5 for adults, $4 for
juniors (12 to 17 years of age), and $2 for children (three to 11).
There is no charge for children two and under. Instead of paying
separately for each attraction, it is best to purchase one of the
ticket books. For example, the "Big 11" ticket book entitles you
to 11 adventures, as well as your general admission—all for
$6.50 for adults, $6 for juniors, and $5.50 for children. The
deluxe book admits you to 15 attractions, includes the general
admission, and costs $7.50 for adults (a $14.60 value); $7 for
juniors (a $13.60 value); and $6.50 for children (an $11.10 value).
First-timers may want to take Disneyland's Deluxe Guided
Tour, the fee including seven major attractions. An adult or
junior is charged $8 and a child $5.

During the fall, winter, and spring seasons, Disneyland is open
from 10 a.m. to 6 p.m. Wednesdays through Fridays, and from
9 a.m. to 7 p.m. Saturdays and Sundays. The park is closed
Mondays and Tuesdays. During the Thanksgiving, Christmas,
and Easter holidays, Disneyland is open every day on an extend-
ed operating schedule. During the summer season, from mid-

June to mid-September, the park is open every day from 8 a.m. to 1 a.m., with special entertainment for the entire family. For further information, contact Guest Relations, Disneyland, 1313 Harbor Boulevard, Anaheim, CA 92803. You can also telephone 714/533-4456 or 213/626-8605, ext. 101.

Perhaps before you plunge into the Fantasia of Disneyland, you'll board the **Disneyland Railroad** (a D coupon) at the Main Street Station. The train chugs into the turn-of-the-century station—evocative of many a Western movie—complete with black smokestack and bright-red "cow-ketcher." Circling the "kingdom" for one and a half miles, the train goes by Adventureland, Bear Country, Frontierland, Fantasyland, Tomorrowland, including the Grand Canyon diorama (with a more than 300-foot-long painting of the world-famed canyon), plus the steamy "Primeval World," when dinosaurs walked on the earth.

On Main Street, there are a series of old-fashioned vehicles (an A coupon) which will take you through the remarkable recreation of a late 19th-century American town: a horse-drawn carriage, a fire wagon that answers an alarm, a fringed surrey, a horseless carriage, and a double-decker omnibus.

Many begin their adventure by calling on the corner Market House where Main Street life centers around a potbelly stove (you may want to join in on a checker game, while listening to the harmonizing of a barbershop quartet). An assortment of merchandise is sold, such as old-time penny sweets (licorice whips, candy buttons). While there, pick up the receiver of the wall telephone and listen in on the latest party-line gossip, taking you back to 1890.

Disneyland

Walking down the street of colorful shops, you'll pass a penny arcade, and can enjoy the "Walt Disney Story featuring great moments with Mr. Lincoln," at the Disneyland Opera House. The attraction, an "audio-animatronics" figure of the 16th president, is free to all guests. Light refreshments and dinner are available at the Carnation Ice Cream Parlor, Plaza Gardens, Plaza Pavilion, the Plaza Inn, and the Town Square Cafe. For a B coupon, you can stop off at the local Cinema to enjoy a silent movie of bygone days.

At **Adventureland,** you can—among other thrills—take a river cruise through the jungle, visit the "enchanted" Tiki Room, or even scale the treehouse of the Swiss Family Robinson.

On the **Jungle Cruise** (an E coupon), you'll feel like Katharine Hepburn in *The African Queen* as you glide through tropical vegetation, pass waterfowl, a Cambodian temple in ruins, and a host of other surprises.

The **Enchanted Tiki Room** is a delightful musical fantasy, with "audio-animatronics" personalities in a South Seas world (an E coupon). One of the least heralded, but most skillfully designed attractions of Disneyland is the **Swiss Family Robinson Treehouse** (a B coupon), where you climb to lofty heights around a wide-spreading tree, on whose limbs rest the bedrooms and "parlor" of the legendary family.

For refreshments, there's the **Tiki Juice Bar** (try tonga punch), and for Polynesian viands, the **Tahitian Terrace.**

The **New Orleans Square** evokes a glamorized Hollywood version of the French quarter of the Louisiana city, complete with lacy iron balconies, old town house patios, with semitropical planting behind wrought-iron gates.

One of the most exciting attractions in the park is the **Pirates of the Caribbean** (an E coupon). You go for a hair-raising sail that recaptures the lore of piracy, including the blood-letting takeover of a Caribbean town and a swampy bayou setting with drooping Spanish moss. One of the best restaurants in Disneyland is the **Blue Bayou,** overlooking the Pirates of the Caribbean. At the **French Market,** you can feast on an array of tempting Louisiana specialties or try a special Disneyland mint julep.

The **Haunted Mansion** is a tall, gray-and-white mansard-roofed house, where you enter between great fluted columns. For a "spook adventure supreme," you'll find it an imaginative experience. You start by meeting the members of the family, going from room to room. Finally, you're taken on a long graveyard ride in cars through the spirit world, with ghosts rising, wailing, and calling to you! Admission is an E coupon.

Bear Country is Disneyland's newest land and hosts the **Country Bear Jamboree** (an E coupon), featuring such entertainers as "Liverlips McGrowl." In addition you can paddle yourself along the "Rivers of America" on **Davy Crockett's Explorer Canoes** (a D coupon).

In **Frontierland,** the folklore of America comes alive. The most popular attraction is the **Mark Twain Steamboat** (a D coupon), a 108-foot-long sternwheel, triple-decker paddle-wheeler, accommodating 350 passengers. You cruise the rivers of America past the shores of Tom Sawyer's Island (complete with a waterfall) woodlands, Indian territory, Fort Wilderness, and a floating barrel bridge.

For an adventure on cave-riddled **Tom Sawyer's Island,** you'll be poled across the river on a raft (a D coupon). Once there, you can explore Fort Wilderness. For many, the exceptional trip is the **Mine Train** (a D coupon), which takes you through a wonderland of nature, a rugged mountain terrain, rainbow caverns, a painted desert, and under a waterfall.

Another special cruise is the three-masted **Columbia Sailing Ship** (a D coupon), a reproduction of the 18th-century merchant ship that was the first to carry the U.S. flag across the globe—a voyage that lasted three years and went a distance of nearly 50,000 miles. For food, try the **Oscar Mayer River Belle Terrace.**

A don't-miss attraction is the **Golden Horseshoe Revue,** an old-time music hall, complete with a stage show—a nostalgic glimpse of what amused the Forty-Niner—with cancan girls and a sultry soubrette known as "Slue-Foot Sue." Mae West would be right at home here. Sponsored by the Pepsi-Cola company, the saloon charges no admission.

Fantasyland evokes some of the great Walt Disney films. Cross the moat of the turreted **Sleeping Beauty Castle,** and you're suddenly transported into a world of make-believe. Here the big attraction—certainly terrifying fun—is the **Matterhorn Bobsleds** (an E coupon), a race down and around twisting, ice-coated mountain slopes. It's probably the most popular ride at Disneyland.

In this "Happiest Place on Earth," you can experience the same adventures as **Alice in Wonderland** (a B coupon), meeting some mad, wonderful characters; board the **Casey Jr. Circus Train** (a B coupon); sail over Fantasyland in a wing-eared **Dum-**

bo **Flying Elephant** (a C coupon); take a spin on the **King Arthur's Carrousel** (an A coupon); "whirl and twirl" at the **Mad Tea Party** (a C coupon); steer a **Motor Boat** across dangerous currents and rapids (a B coupon); take **Mr. Toad's Wild Ride** (a C coupon) through the London of another era; fly over the English capital in a **Peter Pan Flight** (a C coupon) into a never-never land; or share in **Snow White's Adventure** (a C coupon). You can also take a trip through the world of fairy tales on the **Storybook Land Canal Boats** (a D coupon).

"**It's a Small World**" (an E coupon) takes guests in a slow-moving boat past small groups of miniature "children" from around the globe—all singing the same theme song—climaxing in a united earth of total harmony.

Or, if you prefer, you can go to the **Fantasyland Theater** and enjoy Walt Disney cartoons (a C coupon).

In **Tomorrowland**, the romantic past gives way to the wonders of the future. For a preview of the way you'll be traveling in the world of tomorrow, take the **Disneyland Monorail** (an E coupon), whizzing through space all around Disneyland for a bird's-eye view of the park. Here most guests want to take the **Submarine Voyage** (an E coupon), a breathtaking adventure through "liquid space" on an underwater cruise to the North Pole.

For a timely experience, you can book a **Mission to Mars** (a D coupon), presented by McDonnell Douglas, which will give you a seat in a tremendous rocket for a visit to Mission Control on this far-away planet. A **Rocket Jet** will take you to outer space (a D coupon), while you can visit the world of the atom in the **Adventure Thru Inner Space** (a C coupon). Among the free shows and exhibits, you can visit the United States, through film, in the 360-degree **America the Beautiful** presentation.

And don't forget to visit **America Sings** (an E coupon) in the Carousel Theater. Guests are treated to a comical look at America's music during the past 200 years in this show.

By all means, don't miss Disneyland!

STAYING IN ANAHEIM: Many a family has settled into a nearby Anaheim motel with a swimming pool for their stay in Southern California. They buy big books of tickets, savoring Disneyland in bits and pieces, alternating their adventure there with day trips in other directions. If you'd like to make Anaheim your homebase, you'll want to consult the following accommodation recommendations. Except where otherwise indicated, the following hotels fall in the moderate category.

Disneyland Hotel, 1150 West Cerritos Avenue, Anaheim (tel. 778-6600). By Disneyland's Monorail—"the highway in the sky"—you arrive at this complete resort. It's a dazzling array of buildings, containing 1,000 deluxe rooms and suites, set in 60 acres of gardens. Two tall luxurious hotels provide air-conditioned rooms, and garden-style lanai rooms open onto lush planting. The views are superb; the comfort, top-notch. Garden rooms, doubles, cost from $34 to $44; tower rooms, from $40 to $50 for two persons.

The real story here is the extent of facilities available. Of course, you'd expect the Olympic-size pool, but there's also a two-level cove beach surrounded by sand and tidal pools evoking the Pacific shoreline. A cluster of 25 shops and boutiques lures visitors to the Merchandising Center. The Disneyland Hotel also offers a driving range and miniature golf. After your tour, you can relax in the Oak Room spa. Epicurean dining is offered in six restaurants, and you can enjoy entertainment and the view from the Top of the Park cocktail lounge. A water show— "Dancing Waters"—is staged nightly.

Howard Johnson's Motor Lodge, 1380 South Harbor Boulevard, Anaheim (tel. 776-6120), is probably the most elegant accommodation in Anaheim. In a parklike, six-acre setting, its contemporary design was the creation of the award-winning architect W. L. Pereira. It's almost like a resort, seemingly in Bombay or Sumatra, though it's opposite Disneyland. Coved-roofed balconies open onto a central garden with one swimming pool for adults, another for children. Garden paths lead under eucalyptus and olive trees to a splashing circular fountain. From the upper slatted balconies, you can watch the nightly fireworks display at Disneyland. Rooms are decorated with warmth, each with a wall of natural grained wood. Extra-long beds covered with Pop-Art spreads are comfortable. A small living area, individually controlled air conditioning, and large-screen color television sets round out the amenities. From May 15 to September 15, the highest tariffs are charged: from $26 to $38 in a double- or twin-bedded room.

Inn at the Park, 1855 South Harbor Boulevard, Anaheim (tel. 638-8300), is one of the newest hotels to be built in Anaheim, and it's a magnificent example of resort-style architecture. Close to Disneyland, it rises 14 floors and is richly endowed with parklike grounds, rock gardens, and swimming pools. Recently acquired

A Bit of Olde England

The **Sheraton-Anaheim Motor Hotel**, 1015 Ball Road, Anaheim (tel. 778-1700), is an overblown Tudor extravaganza. It's a Western version of an English coach inn, right on the freeway. The English inn-castle theme permeates both the interior and the black-and-white timbered exterior.

A somewhat bizarre 370-room luxury motel, it incorporates bits and pieces of Olde England. A Midlands castle, Larden Hall, built in 1460, was torn down and shipped to the United States piece by piece to become part of the Sheraton, previously the Royale Coach Motor Hotel. In addition, the motel includes a collection of more than 50 stained-glass windows—removed from a boys' school in the environs of London. An architect capped the weirdly shaped and gabled melange with a stone tower lined with battlements. There are reflection pools as well and a formal English garden.

The designer of the public rooms imported tapestries, fireplaces, weapons, old paintings, antique furniture, and blunder-busses. The rear of the castle opens onto a courtyard, which has a vast oval-shaped swimming pool.

The cost of accommodations at the inn is $23 to $32 for a single, $29 to $38 for doubles. More expensive suites are available as well. The rooms—all containing color TV—are widely spread out on three floors, and the individualized furnishings are comfortable.

Opening onto the courtyard, the Falstaff Room suggests an old-world ambience, with a bill of fare considered a "feast for kings and queens." The price of a dinner varies according to the entree you select, the specialty being the prime ribs of beef at $7.75, including Yorkshire pudding and a baked potato. The entrees include either a crisp green salad or French onion soup, plus a whole loaf of French bread and the cheese board. Other dinners begin at $5.75. For dessert, try the grasshopper pie, at 95¢.

by Wrather Inns, it has been completely renovated and remodeled. In addition to 500 rooms, facilities include a restaurant, coffeeshop, and entertainment lounge. Daily rates are $29 to $36 for a single; $38 to $48 for a double.

Anaheim Viking TraveLodge, 505 West Katella Avenue (tel. 774-8710). Just one convenient block from Disneyland, this branch of the TraveLodge chain provides reliable and reasonably priced accommodations. There are 51 nicely furnished rooms, all of which are equipped with color TV, direct-dial phone, modern bath, and coffee-makers. An outdoor heated swimming pool is on the premises, complete with a slide and diving board.

Rates are seasonal. In summer, single rooms are $26; doubles, $28; twins (double doubles), $34. Off-season (September 16 to May 14), singles are $18; doubles, $20; and twins, $24. Year-round an extra person in a room pays $4, and children under 17 can stay free in a room with parents. Two-bedroom units which can accommodate up to eight persons are $44 to $48 in summer.

WHERE TO DINE: Mr. Stox, 1105 East Katella Avenue, Anaheim (tel. 634-2994), is the most prestigious restaurant in Anaheim, though prices are moderate. It lavishly lays on the charm of early California when missions dominated the culture. The cuisine is excellent, and there's entertainment while you dine, usually a popular singer performing with a trio. At lunch you can order salads ($2.75 to $4.95, the latter price for Alaskan king crab) and sandwiches ($2.50 to $3.50). As a predinner starter, we'd suggest a nippy cheese fondue with chunks of San Francisco sourdough bread at $1.75 per person. Mr. Stox uses Eastern black angus beef, aged to his specific instructions. A roast prime rib of beef, with the soup of the day and creamed spinach, is his special feature at $10.50. As for dessert, few can resist the chocolate fudge cake Grand Marnier ($1). You can round out your repast with coffee Stox at $1.50 (a blend of liqueurs mixed with coffee and topped with freshly whipped cream). In addition, Mr. Stox has an exceptional wine cellar (10,000 bottles). However, from his own oak barrels you can order chablis or rosé by the carafe at $3.75.

Buena Park

Six major sights—**Knott's Berry Farm, Enchanted Village,** the **Alligator Farm,** the **Movieland Wax Museum,** the **Palace of Living Art,** and **Movieworld's** collection of cars and planes—are clustered in the tiny community of Buena Park, 20 miles southeast of Los Angeles City Hall on the Santa Ana Freeway. In Orange County, the small area in flatlands (once orange groves) is just a few miles south of Nixon's Whittier and Santa Fe Springs (the oil town that produced a coterie of millionaires).

Since Anaheim, with its super-colossal attraction, Disneyland, is only five miles beyond Buena Park, many visitors are tempted to combine all the adventures into one day. But unless it's the longest day of the year, and you have unlimited energy, we suggest you divide the trek into at least two days—a full day at Buena Park, another day at Disneyland.

After you leave the Santa Ana Freeway, the first sight is Enchanted Village (turn right off the freeway at the junction of Knott Avenue). After the stopover, proceed on the freeway, then turn off when you come to Highway 39 (Beach Boulevard). The first sight will be the Movieland Wax Museum and the adjoining Palace of Living Art, both on Beach Boulevard. Knott's Berry Farm is between four streets: La Palma Avenue, Knott Avenue, Beach Avenue, and Lincoln Avenue. Across the street from Knott's Berry Farm is the Alligator Farm on La Palma.

To go to Disneyland, in Anaheim, continue on La Palma till you join the Santa Ana Freeway.

To reach Buena Park and Anaheim by bus, take "Freeway Flyer" to No. 56 from the downtown Los Angeles terminal at Sixth and Los Angeles Streets. It's an hour's trip.

ENCHANTED VILLAGE: About ten minutes north of Disneyland, at 6122 Knott Avenue, this newest of Buena Park's attractions is reached by taking the Beach/Artesia off-ramp going south on the Santa Ana Freeway, or via Knott Avenue on the Riverside Freeway. Located on 32 lushly planted acres, Enchanted Village is a place where man and "affection-trained" beast communicate through mutual love, respect, and understanding. Affection-training is the method of founder and "animal philosopher" Ralph Helfer, who has trained animals for movies and television (e.g., the Mercury cougar) and comes closer to understanding their language than anyone since Dr. Doolittle.

The attractions consist of shows, rides (atop a camel or elephant, or aboard the Tana River Raft through lush tropics), and many happenings (like the sudden appearance of Tahitian dancers).

Enchanted Village is entered via a jungle path that winds past waterfalls and over landscaped hills. Your first stop is the 3,000-seat Wilderness Theatre, where the current show is a Bicentennial tribute to animals who played an important part in America's history—like Paul Revere's horse, Smokey the Bear, and, of course, the American eagle. There's music, comedy, drama, and dancing.

At the Gentle Jungle Theatre, affection training is demonstrated by a huge elephant who performs spectacularly for a beautiful girl, not to mention an act starring ten full-grown Bengal tigers working with one trainer.

The Lost Island Theatre show features land and water animals in an encounter with a mythical, but nevertheless menacing, swampland creature.

In addition, there's The Touching Place, where you can pet soft woolly llamas, the aviary where birds perch on your shoulders, and a lake where you can even pet the fish!

If you should get hungry, you can stop for exotic eats and entertainment at the Royal Bengal Restaurant.

All shows, happenings, and exhibits are included in a single-price admission (rides and shops are extra). Adults pay $3.50; children four to 11, $1.75 (under four free). The park is open daily from 9 a.m. to 9 p.m. in summer; Saturday through Wednesday from 10 a.m. to 6 p.m. the rest of the year. For further information, call 714/523-2381.

THE MOVIELAND WAX MUSEUM: At 7711 Beach Boulevard (Highway 39), Buena Park, you can see previews of past attractions—everything from Bela Lugosi as Dracula to Marilyn Monroe in *Gentlemen Prefer Blondes.*

Self-billed as "the world's largest and finest wax museum," and in keeping with the Silver Screen it honors, the museum creates the illusion of a big Hollywood premiere. A Rolls-Royce is parked out front. Inside, the effect is enhanced by the foyer of red velvet, and crystal chandeliers.

"America's Sweetheart," Mary Pickford, dedicated the museum on May 4, 1962. It has steadily risen in popularity ever since, as new stars are added yearly, taking their place with the time-tested favorites. The museum was created by a film addict, Allen Parkinson, who saw to it that some of the most memorable scenes in motion pictures were recreated in exacting detail in wax, with such authentic touches as the ripped dress of Sophia Loren in *Two Women.*

As you walk along the Stars' Hall of Fame, you'll encounter Charlie Chaplin in *The Gold Rush;* Harold Lloyd in *Mad Wednesday;* Jean Harlow in *Dinner at Eight;* Charles Laughton in *The Private Life of Henry VIII;* Valentino in *Son of the Sheik;* Shirley Temple in *Bright Eyes;* Edward G. Robinson as *Little Caesar;* Tony Perkins in *Psycho;* Gene Kelly in *Singing in the*

Rain; Tyrone Power in *Blood and Sand;* Elizabeth Taylor in *Cleopatra;* and Newman and Redford in *Butch Cassidy and the Sundance Kid.*

In tableaux are some of the most popular teams: Bogart and Katharine Hepburn in *The African Queen;* Myrna Loy and William Powell in *The Thin Man;* Garbo and Gilbert in *Queen Christina;* Clark Gable and Vivien Leigh in *Gone with the Wind;* not to forget Laurel and Hardy in *The Perfect Day.* Later sets include "Star Trek" and *Planet of the Apes.* One of the newest exhibits is Tony Orlando and Dawn.

More intriguing than the chariots used in the Charlton Heston version of *Ben Hur,* is a tableau depicting the incomparable Gloria Swanson attending the world premiere of *Sunset Boulevard* wrapped in a $10,000 Russian chinchilla that the former motion picture star donated to the museum. Her wax counterpart is seen getting out of a sedan with her co-stars in the film, William Holden and Erich von Stroheim. Every day at 2 p.m., a red carnation held in the hand of the wax figure is exchanged for a fresh one—the faded one given to a woman visitor as a good-luck charm.

Midway in the galleries is a restaurant, where light meals, beer, and wine are served.

Final warning: Beware of one of the Keystone Cops. He's for real!

The museum is open in summer from 9 a.m. to 10 p.m., Sunday through Thursday (from 9 a.m. to 11 p.m. on Friday and Saturday). In winter, the Sunday through Thursday hours are from 10 a.m. to 9 p.m. (till 11 p.m. on Friday and Saturday). Adults are charged $4.50 for admission; children (four to 11), $2.75; under four, free. For information, call 714/522-1154.

Note: The Movieland Wax Museum, just described, is not to be confused with the Hollywood Wax Museum on Hollywood Boulevard.

THE PALACE OF LIVING ART: For the same admission price you pay at the Movieland Wax Museum, you can visit this adjoining million-dollar attraction. Among the highlights is the 18-foot, 10-ton marble reproduction of Michelangelo's *David.*

In addition, the Palace contains a reproduction of the *Pietà,* this one made in Italy from the same Carrara marble that Michelangelo used for his original. From the Louvre Museum in Paris, more than 40 sculptures have been reproduced. Paintings as well were duplicated in exacting detail, the most celebrated being those old favorites, the *Mona Lisa, Pinkie,* and *The Blue Boy.* They also feature three-dimensional sets with wax figures.

MOVIEWORLD: At 6920 Orangethorpe Avenue, in Buena Park, this multimillion-dollar attraction uniquely combines the "cars of the stars" with the largest collection of movie props outside the studios. You can see cars and props here before you see the movie in which they are used. The autos change constantly, as they are in and out for different movies all the time. Among the 700 antique celebrities you may see on your visit are Ma Barker's 1930 Cadillac; the 1930 V-16 Cadillac used by the Harold Robbins character, Nevada Smith, in the film version of *The Carpetbaggers;* the custom-made Pierce-Arrow of Fatty Arbuckle; the custom-built Mercedes-Benz of Al Jolson; plus "Big Daddy" Roth's "California Cools" custom show cars, including his "Druid Princess."

Open year-round from 10 a.m. to 10 p.m. Admission costs $2.75 for adults; $1.25 for children five to 12; under five, free.

KNOTT'S BERRY FARM: Spend a wild day in the West. At Knott's, the rip-roarin' Wild West is brought back to life for the whole family to enjoy. You can pan for gold or take a spine-tingling ride down Timber Mountain. Walk through Ghost Town and enjoy the Old West. Suddenly shots ring out! It's a shoot-'em-up showdown between the sheriff and two "gunfighters."

On the street a pretty girl plays a steam calliope. A barker hustles you into the **Birdcage Theater** for an old-time melodrama where you boo the villain and cheer the hero. Admission is 85¢ for adults, 60¢ for children. Clamber aboard the old **Butterfield Stagecoach** for a journey through the Old West for a fare of 85¢. Then climb onto the **Ghost Town and Calico Railroad** train that chugged through the Rockies way back in '81. The cost is 60¢ for adults and children. Then amble over to **Timber Mountain** for a free-floatin' log ride through sawmills and logging camps that winds up with a wild lunge down a 42-foot chute (85¢ for everyone).

Knott's began in 1920 when Walter and Cordelia Knott and their family arrived in Buena Park in their old Model T. Starting with 20 acres of leased land, the Knott's began to eke out a living by farming and selling berries at a roadside stand.

Fourteen years later, in 1934, Mrs. Knott served her first eight chicken dinners which marked the beginning of the now world-famous **Chicken Dinner Restaurant.** Today the restaurant serves up to 7,000 dinners in a single day at a cost of $3.95 per person. And Knott's other major restaurant, the **Steak House,** has earned a reputation all its own. In addition to these fine eating places, Knott's offers the **Garden Room Buffet, Cable Cart Kitchen Buffet,** and **Ghost Town Grill** restaurants, plus a number of fast-food take-out stands.

What began as a small family affair more than half a century ago has become the nation's third largest family-themed entertainment park and employs approximately 3,500 persons during the summer. Knott's is still owned and operated by three generations of the Knott family.

A major attraction at Knott's Berry Farm is the full-scale brick-by-brick replica of Philadelphia's famed **Independence Hall.** Completed in 1966 as the fulfillment of Walter Knott's life-long dream, Indépendence Hall is furnished with an authentic reproduction of the Liberty Bell, complete with crack. Tours conducted by Colonial-costumed guides are offered daily for 60¢.

A truly high point in the development of Knott's has been the construction of **Knott's Good Time Theater,** a 2,150-seat indoor facility opened in 1971. The theater hosts top-name celebrity entertainment daily during the summers and every weekend year-round. Entrance is included in Knott's admission price.

Still another attraction is **Knott's Fiesta Village,** a Mexican-themed area in tribute to our south-of-the-border neighbors. A fiesta atmosphere prevails, and rides include the Happy Sombrero Ride, the Fiesta Wheel, the Mexican Whip, and the Merry-Go-Round. Fiesta Plaza dance area offers Latin entertainment as well as rock music and dancing, and Mexican dining in **La Cocinita.**

The newest addition to Knott's is a five-and-a-half-acre expansion project known as the **Roaring '20s Airfield.** Featuring 11 air-themed rides and attractions, it doubles the size of the '20s area. The highlight of the latest development is a 20-story Sky Tower, where guests climb to the summit in parachutes and then drop more than 200 feet. For the less adventurous, there's an enclosed Sky Cabin which revolves 360 degrees as it travels up and down the tower. **The Airfield Eatery,** a replica of a 1920s hangar, is the major dining facility in the new area.

Visiting Knott's costs $5.75 for a Bonanza Fun Ticket Book which includes admission plus a selection of ten rides and attractions. For children 11 and under, it's $4.75. Parking is always free. Knott's is on Beach Boulevard in Buena Park just south of the Santa Ana (I 5) and Riverside/Artesia (91) Freeways. For further information, telephone 714/827-1776.

CALIFORNIA ALLIGATOR FARM: Across the street from Knott's Berry Farm is the **Alligator Farm,** 7671 La Palma Avenue, Buena Park, which fascinates with its collection of reptiles —including one of the world's largest crocodiles in captivity, weighing more than 1,400 pounds and nearly 15 feet long! Inside the gates, you'll find more than 1.000 reptiles.

Occasionally, you can see "The Night of the Iguana"—not the Tennessee Williams play, but a show, nevertheless. The poisonous reptiles, safely in glass cages, are alive and deadly throughout the year. When a jungle or a tropical epic is being shot in California, TV and movie studios sometimes rent alligators and crocodiles from the park, making stars out of such unlikely prospects as "George," featured in Walt Disney's *The Happiest Millionaire.*

The farm is open year-round from 10:30 a.m. till 5 p.m. In September and June, it stays open till 6 p.m., and in July and August till 9 p.m. Admission is $2.75 for adults, $1.25 for children five to 14.

WHERE TO STAY: Farm de Ville, 7800 & 7878 Crescent Avenue, at Highway 39 (tel. 527-2201). Conveniently located at the south entrance to Knott's Berry Farm, with buses to Disneyland running right out front, the Farm de Ville is popular with visitors to Buena Park and attracts considerable numbers of honeymooners (yes, many people do spend their honeymoon in the Anaheim/Buena Park fantasyland). Its 130 rooms, housed in two separate buildings, are immaculate and attractive—stylishly furnished with print spreads, shag carpeting, and large dressing areas. Every room has a color TV, radio, direct-dial phone, tub/shower bath, and coffee-maker. Facilities on the premises include two swimming pools with slides and diving boards for the kids, two wading pools for very little tots, two sauna baths, a coin-operated laundry, and an adjoining Sambo's coffeeshop.

In summer, single and double rooms are priced at just $18 to $24, with each additional person in a room charged $4. Suites and two-room units that accommodate four to six persons cost

$32 to $36. Off-season rates are about $2 less.

LION COUNTRY SAFARI: This "safari" is taken in the safety of your locked "cage"—that is, your automobile. Right in Southern California, it's an African wildlife happening. With the assistance of a taped "instant guide," you drive around a simulated African veldt. Incidentally, if your vehicle happens to be a convertible, you're not allowed inside the preserve, but you can rent a safari vehicle or a sedan at the "Hertz Hut." Should you develop any trouble, rangers in zebra-striped vehicles patrol the grounds, ready to assist you. The safari is off the San Diego Freeway at 8800 Moulton Parkway, in Irvine Ranch in Orange County.

A trip here makes all further calls at zoos merely child's play. When a strutting ostrich—the world's largest bird—comes up to your window, or a pride of lions surrounds your car, you experience the wonder and thrill of intimate contact with animals in their "natural setting," complete with hundreds upon hundreds of imported plants and trees. Opened in 1970, the vast acreage (fully enclosed) is a land of rolling hills with a bulrush-studded river—it's nature in the raw.

The wild animals are completely free to roam at will. Eight reserves separate the animals and birds, which are quite incompatible. The individual sections are known by such names as **Kilimanjaro Plains, Ruwenzori Plains,** and **Luangwa Valley.**

Other animals on hand include many species of the zebra; chimpanzees from West and Central Africa; giraffes; hippos; the cheetah (outside Africa, the largest grouping of this increasingly rare animal is found here); the extremely rare white rhino from South Africa; the largest land mammal in the world, the elephant. The collection is particularly rich in the African antelope, including the black sable and the gray duiker, the latter one of the smallest of the species.

The $12-million safari venture was largely sparked by its chief officer, Harry Shuster, who has been praised for his efforts to preserve rare and endangered species of African game. If you're attending in the autumn or winter months, you may enjoy your visit all the more. Shuster put it this way: "The lions, cheetahs, and other animals become more active during the cooler months, providing an even livelier show within the preserve."

The first Lion Country Safari was launched in Florida, its success sparking the California development. The question of whether the lions or other animals would reproduce in this simulated setting became academic when 14 lion cubs were born in the first eight weeks following the opening. In addition to the natural births, the collection is being enlarged by new acquisitions, including eight siamang (large black gibbons.)

Next to the preserve is the **Safari Camp,** embracing 30 acres and including a Zambesi River Cruise, a Hippo Pedal-Boat, and an African Auto Trek. On the river ride, you're likely to bump into a hippo! The auto trek is aboard a zebra-striped safari vehicle. In Pet's Corner, boys and girls are allowed to fondle a variety of small animals.

At **Trader Robbie's African Curios,** a bazaar near the main entrance, authentic imports are featured, including such unusual gifts as a three-foot carved wooden Kikuyu witch doctor.

The 500-acre African wildlife preserve charges $4.95 for adults, $2.95 for children three to 11, and no fee for children under three years of age. It is open year-round from 9 a.m. till sundown.

Santa Ana

The county seat of Orange County and its second largest city has one of the mildest climates in the States, created by a blending of the Pacific breezes with dry winds from the desert. Santa Ana lies 35 miles southeast of Los Angeles and ten miles inland from the ocean shore. It's on a freeway that bears its name, connecting Los Angeles and San Diego.

Just 15 minutes from Disneyland is the **Movieland of the Air Museum,** at the Orange County Airport, Santa Ana (tel. 545-5021). Launched by Frank Tallman and the late Paul Mantz, this museum traces the history of aircraft from its pioneer age to the space era. Perhaps most interesting are the planes from famous films. Displayed are the Sopwith Tripe, the Nieuport 28, the Fokker D7 (a replica), and the Fokker Tripe "Jenny."

At the cost of $2 million, the museum was designed to provide a showcase for historical aircraft which skilled mechanics keep in working order. Perhaps the most thrilling part of the adventure is to ride in an open cockpit.

The Movieland of the Air Museum is open daily in summer from 10 a.m. to 5 p.m. (in winter it closes on Mondays). The admission charged is $2.25 for adults; 75¢ for juniors, 12 to 17; 50¢ for children under 12.

Chapter IX

ALONG THE COAST FROM MALIBU TO SAN DIEGO

THE BEACHES of Greater Los Angeles are as varied as the general topography—ranging from wide, golden sands, with gentle waves, to narrow rocky strips where the surf dashes high into the sky. Chances are, you'll find a beach for any whim, aquatic sport, or pleasure. If you drive out curvy Sunset Boulevard, you'll reach the Coast Highway and the Pacific. While in the area, you can visit the Self-Realization Shrine, the Will Rogers State Park, and the J. Paul Getty Museum.

Afterward, if you continue north up the coast, you'll reach **Malibu,** a 27-mile "strip" studded with the homes of numerous movie and TV stars. The southern part, **Castle Rock,** was used as the background for many a Mack Sennett comedy and his attendant bathing beauties.

Below Malibu, **Santa Monica** emerges, with its municipal pier and excellent public beaches, interspersed with an occasional star's home (in days of yore, Marion Davies's "colonial palace" and Cary Grant's villa were there). Continuing south, you'll pass through **Venice, Manhattan, Hermosa,** and **Redondo Beaches,** with lifeguards and bathing facilities.

Beginning at Palos Verdes Estates, you can head southwest toward the Pacific along **Palos Verdes Drive,** a curving coastline road that evokes the Riviera. Sightseeing stopovers include **Marineland** and the **Wayfarers' Chapel.** At the end of the drive, you'll pass through **San Pedro,** the port of Los Angeles (visit the Ports O'Call and the Whaler's Wharf) and then reach **Long Beach.**

Further south, **Huntington Beach,** another popular stopover, is scene of the world surfing championships in September (sleeping bags line the beach during the "grunion hunts"). **Newport Beach** and **Balboa** are jumping-off points for the offshore **Catalina Island.** The public beach at **Corona del Mar** is relatively uncrowded, the area a haven for yachtsmen. The coves near the art colony of **Laguna Beach** provide top-notch swimming and sunbathing.

This coastal tour won't really end at **La Jolla** and **San Diego,** but will continue across the border for bullfights at Tijuana.

Note on California customs: There are privately operated bathhouses at most of the public beaches, where you can rent a locker, shower, and towel. But more often than not, the true Angeleno changes discreetly in his car (if you're arrested while doing this, we don't know you). State beaches provide lifeguards, and we'd advise staying within the areas supervised by them. The surf in many rocky places is only for the very experienced. Swimming in Southern California is quite possible all year round, though many swimmers wear wet suits on winter days.

Pacific Palisades

After leaving Beverly Hills on Sunset Boulevard, you will soon pass sprawling **U.C.L.A.** on your left—one of the campuses of the University of California, the largest in the United States. Before you reach the coast, you can stop off for three widely varied, but fascinating, visits at the following attractions.

WILL ROGERS STATE HISTORIC PARK: At 14253 Sunset Boulevard, the **Will Rogers State Historic Park** perpetuates the memory of the "cracker-barrel philosopher." Will Rogers, of course, became a legend to a whole generation of Americans, going from trick rider to rope-trick artist, eventually becoming a philosopher of sorts, with such down-on-the-farm observations as "Americans are getting too much like Model 'A' Fords. They all have the same upholstery—and they all make the same noise."

He settled in Hollywood, buying his own ranch and making films, which led one cinema critic to write: "Will Rogers upheld the homely virtues against the tide of sophistication and sex." He was killed in an air crash with his friend Wiley Post in Alaska in mid-August, 1935.

Mrs. Rogers lived at the ranch until her death in 1944, at which time the home and grounds of the "Cherokee Kid" were willed to the state, and they are now supervised as an historic site by the Department of Parks and Recreation. Visitors may explore the grounds, seeing the Rogers former stables, even watching polo games, usually on Thursday and Saturday afternoons. The house, open at 10 a.m., is furnished with Rogers memorabilia, and what might be described as William S. Hart decor.

The park is open from April through October from 7 a.m. to 7 p.m., and from 8 a.m. to 5 p.m. during the winter months. There is a $1.50 per vehicle fee for entry. This fee includes an audio tour of the Rogers home for all passengers in the car. Informed guides are available to answer additional questions. Incidentally, Charles Lindbergh and his wife hid out in seclusion here in the '30s during part of the kidnap craze that surrounded the murder of their first son.

SELF-REALIZATION FELLOWSHIP LAKE SHRINE: A half-mile inland from the Pacific at 17190 Sunset Boulevard, Pacific Palisades (tel. 454-4114), stands this ten-acre garden oasis. It was established as a shrine in 1950 by an Indian swami, Paramahansa Yogananda. The small lake is surrounded by shady walks which go past exotic flowering trees and plants, with swans gliding silently by. Protruding out into the lake is a windmill chapel where services are held. Sunken gardens are filled with tropical plants, and a museum contains artifacts from all over the world. Special interest centers on the Golden Lotus outdoor temple, a houseboat, the Mahatma Gandhi World Peace Memorial, an India Gift Shop, and the Court of Religions. Atop a waterfall is a life-size statue of Christ. The grounds are open from 9 a.m. to 5 p.m. daily except Monday.

J. PAUL GETTY MUSEUM: It's been waggishly dubbed "Pompeii-by-the-Pacific," but the spectacular reconstruction of a Roman villa hidden in the hills above the Pacific is a serious—and successful—attempt to create an ideal setting for the magnificent J. Paul Getty collection. Opened in January, 1974, the museum recreates the splendor of the Villa Dei Papyri, a Roman villa which was buried in volcanic mud when Mount Vesuvius erupted in 79 A.D., destroying Pompeii and Herculaneum.

Set on ten acres of the Getty estate near Malibu, the museum is surrounded by a colonnaded garden with a graceful reflecting pool and replicas of bronze statues found at the site of the original villa. A dozen different types of marble went into the halls inside the colonnades, and reproductions of the original frescoes adorn the walls.

In forming his vast collection, the multibillionaire devoted his principal interest to Greek and Roman sculpture, as shown in the Lansdowne Herakles, the Mazarin Venus, fourth-century stelae and Greek and Roman portraiture. The museum's decorative arts collection features 18th-century French furniture, tapestries, and Oriental carpets. The painting galleries contain an extensive Italian Renaissance and Netherland Baroque collection as well as several important French paintings by such artists as Georges de la Tour (including *The Beggar's Brawl,* bought by Getty in 1972 for more than $950,000) and François Boucher. The museum's most valuable painting is *The Holy Family* by Raphael, which Getty bought for $200 thinking it was a good copy!

The Getty museum is just 20 miles from downtown Los Angeles, at 17985 Pacific Coast Highway, a mile north of Sunset Boulevard in Malibu. It's open Monday through Friday from June to September, Tuesday through Saturday the rest of the year. Hours are from 10 a.m. to 5 p.m., and there is currently no admission charge. Because of limited facilities, it is advisable to make a parking reservation at least one week in advance (by mail or telephone 454-6541).

Malibu

During the "Panic of 1857," a shrewd Irishman purchased Malibu—then a sprawling rancho—for 10¢ an acre. Today its streets and coastline are covered with platinum. A canny Yankee from Massachusetts, Frederick Hastings Rindge, first saw (in 1891) the possibility of an "American Riviera" developing at Malibu. But a step in that direction didn't occur until his widow (who fought a long, bitter legal battle with California to prevent a coastal road from going through her spread) leased property to actress Anna Q. Nilsson in 1927. In time, a host of other stars, including John Gilbert and Clara Bow, built homes on the Malibu strip, and parties here intrigued tabloid readers during the Roaring '20s.

The movie colony, though not as celebrated as it once was, is still ensconced at Malibu. The area stretches along the West Pacific Coast Highway 101-A, from the Los Angeles city line to the extreme frontier of Ventura County. Flanking the coastal road are a string of motels and restaurants, which are especially crowded in summer. Malibu lies about 25 miles from the Los Angeles Civic Center.

At its greatest point, the strip is only three miles wide; at its narrowest, just one mile. Malibu's wide, sandy beaches delight thousands of visitors yearly, who engage in every activity from nude sunbathing to grunion hunting.

Besides swimming, you can always go boating in Malibu. The **Paradise Cove Sportfishing**, at 28128 W. Pacific Coast Highway, Malibu (tel. 457-2511), books half-day and full-day trips aboard its 65-foot boats *Gentleman* and *Speed Twin*. The half-day fare is $7; the full-day fare, $10. Also available for rent are 14-foot skiffs with 6-hp motors for $25 a day, including bait and gas. Or you can stay and fish off the pier at Paradise Cove, four miles west of Malibu Road.

WHERE TO STAY: **Tonga Lei**, 22878 Pacific Coast Highway, Malibu (tel. 456-6444), is a motel operated in conjunction with a thatch-roofed Polynesian restaurant of the same name. It's ideal for a beach stopover, offering both an exotic dinner and a chance to be lulled to sleep listening to the waves of the Pacific. Single or double rooms on the ocean side go for $30, but only $24 on the highway. Rooms are pleasantly furnished and well maintained.

Casa Malibu, 22752 Pacific Coast Highway, Malibu (tel. 456-2219), is like staying at your own beach club. Right on the highway, it's built hacienda-style, with bedrooms and terraces leading down to the surf and sand. There's a restful inner courtyard, with palm trees and cuppa d'oro vines growing up to the balcony. A sundeck with chaise lounges adjoins. Singles or doubles cost $35 overlooking the water, but only $30 if fronting the patio or coastal highway.

WHERE TO DINE: **Alice's**, 2300 Pacific Coast Highway, Malibu (tel. 456-6646), with an atmosphere both chic and informal, is one of the loveliest restaurants in the area. Directly on Malibu Pier, it contains glass on two sides. Rear tables are on a raised platform so that everyone can view the ocean—intoxicating at twilight. The inn is a garden room on the sea, where gentle vibrations rule. The ambience is winning: soft recordings, hanging plants, bentwood chairs, bare wood tables, bowls of fresh fruit provided with each meal, and decanters of freshly made sangría. For starters, try the kettle of steamed clams in herb broth, $4.95. Dinners begin at $6.25, going up to $8.95 for a classic bouillabaisse served in a cast-iron kettle. Lunch, featured daily from 11 to 5, might be an avocado sandwich at $3.95. Open seven days a week till 1 a.m. (till 2 a.m. on Fridays and Saturdays).

Nantucket Light, 22706 Pacific Coast Highway, Malibu (tel. 456-3105), is one of the newest restaurants to be built here (1974). Right on the ocean, it stands bleakly like a Nantucket seacoast barn built from wooden slats left to be weathered by the ocean. Inside, the New England theme permeates, not with a lot of nautical gewgaws, but with a played-down elegance—oak furnishings, heavy beamed ceilings, lots of plants, and a big stone fireplace. Architecturally, the restaurant was designed to provide each table with a view of the ocean. Seafood dominates the menu, beginning with New England clam chowder at $1.50. You can also order a bucket of Eastern steamed clams at $7.25, with drawn butter, salad, and rice pilaf. An order of baked or steamed lobster is $13.95. Desserts include a homemade carrot cake, $1.25.

The Country Wine Cellar (and Continental Delicatessen), 22853 Pacific Coast Highway (tel. 456-2953), is one of Malibu's prettiest and least pretentious dining choices. It has three dining areas. Most intimate is the winery, with heavy, beamed ceilings, inlaid ceramic-tile tables, and, not surprisingly, bottles of wine stacked against the walls. However, for other moods, you might prefer the enclosed cafe area with a slatted roof through which the sun streams in; it's hung with fuschia and ferns. And for those who don't suffer at all from agoraphobia, there's a lushly planted outdoor garden area.

It's a lovely place to start the day with a breakfast of eggs and onions, served with toast topped with cheddar cheese ($2.10). At lunch, soups, salads, and sandwiches are reasonably priced. You can get the same at dinner, along with entrees like chicken Cordon Bleu ($4.50), shrimp scampi ($6.50), and beef stroganoff ($6.50). A lighter meal here might consist of quiche Lorraine and salad ($2.95), or crêpes filled with chicken, fresh mushrooms, onions, and grated cheese ($3.50). For dessert, a New York inspiration is "Grimbles," a fruit- and cream-filled pastry puff (85¢). All the desserts are homemade, and all the vegetables served are fresh.

Since there is a winery on the premises, you have a large

selection of wines to choose from (occasionally, you can even get free samples).

The Country Wine Cellar is open daily from 8 a.m. to 9 p.m., except on Mondays when it closes at 6 p.m.

Tonga Lei, 22878 Pacific Coast Highway, Malibu (tel. 456-6444), is an old-timer, a Polynesian restaurant that has provided an exotic background for many a film star wanting to ocean gaze. The atmosphere is Pago-Pago—a wealth of bamboo, hanging coconuts, and thatching—with shades of Dorothy Lamour. Drinks are exotic and powerful. Polynesian dinners for two range in price from $5.95 to $7.95 per person. At lunch you can order sweet-and-sour pork, with barbecued spare ribs, fried shrimp, fried rice, tea, and cookies for $2.50. Open daily for lunch and dinner.

Topanga

Discovery Inn, 156 South Topanga Canyon Boulevard, Topanga (tel. 455-9079), midway between Malibu and Santa Monica, stands in the still rugged and unspoiled Topanga Canyon, a retreat for naturalists. Originally, composer Richard Dehr ("Marianne," "Green Fields"), took over this rustic bungalow, turning it into an exceptionally fine restaurant (it's now under new ownership). He turned his back to the highway, opening the three rooms toward the base of the mountain, with a garden as the important vista. In each room, there's a potbelly stove on a raised brick hearth. About 20 choices are offered for dinner (no lunches), and in every case you'll get a homemade soup, salad, fresh-baked rolls, rice, and fresh vegetables. Only farm-fresh, organic vegetables are used, along with the finest of prime meats. Everything, incidentally, is prepared to order—so patience is urged. Especially recommendable is the cheese walnut loaf, deliciously vegetarian at $6.75. The chicken Florentine at $7.50 is also good. For dessert, try the carob cake at 55¢. Open daily except Tuesday from 5 to 10.

Inn of the Seventh Ray, 128 Old Topanga Canyon Road (tel. 455-1311), offers the "best of freshly energized food . . . to raise your body's vibration." The "seventh ray," in case you're wondering, is the energy that will bring the golden age into being. If you'd like further elucidation, one of the blissful-looking waiters or waitresses will be glad to go into it. Suffice it to say that you're getting more than just an ordinary meal here.

The vibes are certainly peaceful and the creekside setting

beautiful. Inside it looks like a country church with a peaked ceiling, stained-glass windows, candles flickering on every table, and a fireplace blazing. Carefully selected music—classical or Oriental—is played in the background. If you dine outdoors, which most people do, the music is piped through a speaker. The tables overlook the creek and lots of untamed foliage. Trees overhead provide shade, and there are fresh flowers on every table.

As for the food, it is lovingly prepared, using only the finest and purest ingredients. All the bread is homemade with freshly ground organic grains. Preservatives, sugar, food coloring, or bleached flours are verboten. Even the fruit wines are unpasteurized. We suggest you order a glass ($1) as an apéritif. There are eight entrees, all served with soup or salad, hors d'oeuvres, lightly steamed vegetables, brown rice, and homemade bread. They're listed in order of their vibrational value, the lightest and least dense (those are better for you) first. The number one, or purest, item is "Five Secret Rays," lightly steamed vegetables served with herb butter and tamari nut sauce ($4.25). Skipping along a vibration or two we come to number four, "Om-ri-tas," described as coming "direct from the violet planet, a space ship of nature's perfect vessel." It turns out to be half an eggplant filled with olives, nuts, and cheeses in white wine sauce ($6.25). Numbers five and six are fish and seafood entrees, seven is chicken rosemary, and the eighth and densest item is a ten-ounce New York steak, cut from beef fed on natural grasses only, braised in a scallion, mushroom, and wine sauce ($9.25).

Whether you believe in vibes or not, all the food is very good and you're sure to enjoy the tranquil mountain views. The Inn is open daily for lunch and dinner.

Santa Monica

In the northwestern corner of Los Angeles, Santa Monica draws both visitors and permanent residents who romp on its three miles of good sandy beaches, basking in what has been described as "the most ideal year-round climate in the world."

At the municipally owned **Santa Monica Pier,** fun-seekers go for fishing, boating, and swimming. You can look back at the coastal road, scene of the wild chase in *It's a Mad, Mad, Mad, Mad World.*

Santa Monica's history as a resort goes back to the 1870s.

Today it's a popular residential and convention city, activities centering around a $3-million **Civic Auditorium,** previously the setting for the Academy Award presentations.

Many hotels and apartment houses, with such Southern Californian overstatement names as Shangri-La, line the coast. Four major boulevards from Los Angeles (Wilshire, Santa Monica, Olympic, and Pico) lead to the ocean front and the 14-block-long **Palisades Park.**

Also, right on the beach, is a string of palatial homes, many built by movie stars in the '30s. On the north, Santa Monica is bounded by San Vicente Boulevard, on the south by Venice, and it extends 33 blocks inland toward Los Angeles.

To reach Santa Monica by public transportation, take RTD bus No. 83, leaving from Seventh and Flower Streets in downtown Los Angeles.

MEDIUM-PRICED ACCOMMODATIONS: Royal Inn, 1819 Ocean Avenue, Santa Monica (tel. 451-8711), is a 167-room modern hotel at the intersections of Pico Boulevard, Ocean Avenue, and Main Street. Sleek and glittering, it offers one of the best accommodations in the area, with a decidedly luxurious overlay. Rooms are warm and pleasant, in high-key harmonious colors, with color televisions as well. Singles are $24 to $32; doubles are $28 to $38. To whisk you up eight floors are exterior glass elevators. The hotel's facilities include a therapy pool, heated swimming pool, and cocktail lounge. A Sambo's coffeeshop is on the premises.

Surf Rider Inn, 1700 Ocean Avenue, Santa Monica (tel. EX 3-0331), is a U-shaped motel, its open side on two levels of terraces embracing sandy Santa Monica beach. There's a good-sized heated swimming pool enclosed within the "U." Accommodations are available in three buildings. The Lanai has large rooms with two double beds, or one double and two dual-purpose twin beds; a shoji screen room divider creates a private sitting room. These rooms also contain private balconies with ocean views or entrance to the pool deck. One person pays from $22 to $28; two persons, $25 to $30. In the Island Building, comfortably furnished rooms, with either queen-sized or twin beds, rent for $18 for one, $20 for two. The economy rooms are housed in the Kona, where singles go for $14 to $16, and some special family units are available.

Huntley House, 1111 Second Street, at Wilshire Boulevard

(tel. 451-5971), offers 178 rooms and suites right near the beach.
There's no swimming pool on the premises, but the ocean is a
stone's throw away. The rooms are large and attractive (many
have ocean views), and all have color TV, direct-dial phone, and
other modern amenities. Atop the hotel is a Mediterranean-style
rooftop restaurant called Villa Escala, with terra-cotta tile floors,
leather-upholstered chairs, hanging plants overhead, and photos
of old Mexico lining the walls. Of course, the view is a salient
feature. Considering the surroundings—and the menu, which
pictures a sumbreroed Mexican—you'll be surprised to open the
menu and see items like quiche Lorraine ($4.75) and lemon veal
($8.95). All entrees are accompanied by beer cheese soup, salad,
bread and butter, and a choice of rice, potatoes, or noodles.
There's not a taco or enchilada in sight. For dessert, however,
you might try something rather exotic: cheesecake with mango
sauce (95¢). Luncheon items range from $2.45 (for ham and
Swiss on rye served with homemade beer) to $4.25 (for a steak
sandwich on sourdough bread). In addition to Villa Escala, a
coffeeshop is open from 6 a.m. to 3:30 p.m.

Single rooms at Huntley House cost $20 to $30; doubles, $27
to $32; and suites, $55 to $65.

Roman Inn, 530 Pico Boulevard, at 6th Avenue (tel. 399-
9344), was until recently a Ramada Inn. It's now under new
ownership, and "lookin' good!" Each of its 189 rooms is done up
nicely with floral-pattern drapes and matching bedspreads; murals of sailboats on the wall enhance the resort feel, and even the
bathrooms are attractively turned out with gleaming marble sink
and mattress-ticking wall covering. Rooms are large, and offer
all modern amenities—color TV, direct-dial phone, tub/shower
bath, etc. Some have balconies, and others open out on the pool.
The pool, by the way, is Olympic in size. There's also a Jacuzzi,
a game room off the lobby, and a cheerful coffeeshop on the
premises. Other bonuses here: ample free parking and proximity
to the beach. Singles pay $30 a night; doubles and twins, $36.

Holiday Inn, 120 Colorado Street, at Ocean Boulevard (tel.
451-0676), is extremely well located (adjacent to the Santa Monica Pier) and offers handsome standard accommodations and
facilities. Each room has a color TV, etc., and on each floor
you'll find ice and soda machines. There's also a laundry room
(on the fourth floor), a swimming pool (of course), and a restaurant misleadingly named Top of the Pier (it's off the lobby) that
serves breakfast, lunch, and dinner; a cocktail lounge adjoins.
Rates are seasonal: May 28 to September 6, singles are $28 to

$39; doubles, $34 to $40. The rest of the year rates are about $3 less. Kids under 18 can stay free in a room with their parents.

BUDGET LODGINGS: Kensington Motel, 1746 Ocean Avenue, Santa Monica (tel. 393-9831), overlooks the Pacific, and offers direct access to the bathing beach as well as two pools, one for children. Ninety furnished units here, 55 of which have kitchens. High-season rates are in effect from June 1 to September 10. Tariffs are complicated, going from a standard double-bedded room ($12 to $15) to two rooms with one bath ($25 to $28). The apartments range in price from $15 to $35, the latter for an ocean-view bedroom and living room, with the already-mentioned completely equipped kitchen, and a color TV.

DINING AT SANTA MONICA: Madame Wu's Garden, 2201 Wilshire Boulevard, Santa Monica (tel. 828-5656). From the moment you enter the courtyard, you're in another world. You will relax to the sound of a gently splashing fountain; it surrounds a tree that was politely allowed to grow through the roof. Delicate jade flowers and artifacts are displayed in glass cases set in the walls.

Madame Wu is well-known for her Oriental cuisine. Visiting dignitaries often seek out the serenity of this fine restaurant and its elegantly appointed bar, and film and TV personalities are seen here frequently.

The menu features mostly Cantonese dishes, with a few Szechuan and Hunam specialties. Try going exotic with beef lo mein (soft noodles blended with beef and mixed Chinese vegetables) at $4.25. Madame Wu's is particularly noted for its tossed shredded chicken salad ($4.75), most unusual and delicious.

Some fixed-price dinners—ranging from "imperial" to "gourmet"—are also available from $6.95 to $8.95 per person. Open for lunch, Monday through Friday; dinner is nightly until 10 p.m.

Le Cellier, 2628 Wilshire Boulevard, Santa Monica (tel. 828-1585), is lost in a sort of no-man's-land, about 20 blocks from the beach. But those who find this gem of a French restaurant will be beguiled into thinking they are dining in a little restaurant in Vence or Dinan. The setting itself is pedestrian looking, but the food is divine. Everything is under the scrutiny of the chef-owner, Monsieur Bellordre. You can order better onion soup here than you ever had at Les Halles—and that's saying a lot;

it's mellower and subtler, and the cost is $2.25. Three major dinner favorites include sweet-and-sour roast duckling with a lemon-and-orange sauce at $8.25; bouillabaisse Marseillaise at $8.50; and an individual whole baby lamb rack, $8.95. At lunch we'd recommend a cheese soufflé with a mixed green salad, $4. Dinner is served until 10:30 p.m.

The Old Venice Noodle Company, 2654 Main Street, Santa Monica (tel. 399-9211), is a colossal turn-of-the-century extravaganza that Barnum would envy. A bewildering assemblage of nostalgic American artifacts has been installed in this former brick factory building. The eclectic decor features perhaps the largest collection of old stained-glass windows of any restaurant in greater Los Angeles; a converted 4th and Broadway trolley car with tables; chairs from barbershops, graveyards, and ice cream parlors; church benches; coffee grinders; opulent chandeliers; clusters of huge fern-filled copper pots; nooks with brick fireplaces and books; pink-fringed lamp shades—you name it. Spaghetti dinners, with salad, sourdough bread, coffee, and spumoni ice cream, range in price from $1.95 to $6.25 (the latter for an eight-ounce New York steak with your pasta), and include a selection of savory sauces. Luncheons, served Monday through Friday, 11:30 a.m. to 2:30 p.m., feature a meatball sandwich at $1.95.

Zucky's, 431 Wilshire Boulevard (tel. 393-0551) is the place to go if you've got a yen for the likes of kreplach or kugel. It's one of L.A.'s top delicatessens, and we particularly like the fact that it's kosher-style, not strictly kosher. That means that you can order dairy items—like cheese blintzes ($2.60), as well as meat and fish.

Zucky's makes a pretty good pastrami or corned beef sandwich on rye ($2.25 for either). Other traditional favorites that momma used to make are stuffed cabbage ($3.45), potato pancakes with sour cream and apple sauce ($2.20), and cream cheese and lox on a bagel ($2.45). For dessert there's New York-style strawberry cheesecake (75¢), or perhaps a Napoleon (50¢).

The decor is typically modernistic Jewish deli with bright lighting and orange-leather booths; the ambience is one of lively hubbub. Zucky's is open 24 hours a day to satisfy your deli cravings. You can also have breakfast round the clock here with freshly squeezed orange juice.

Gypsy's, 1215 4th Street, off Wilshire (tel. 451-2841), the funky-exotic creation of owner Tina Todd, would be unique anywhere in the U.S., but it is especially so in Los Angeles. Few

---

Where the Known Go to Be Unknown

Chez Jay, 1657 Ocean Avenue, Santa Monica (tel. EX 5-1741). Because of its casual atmosphere, this restaurant is where the known go to be unknown! For a real feeling of Los Angeles beach life, you could not do better than take a meal here in an atmosphere that is both cool and carefree. Perhaps of all the eateries on the top of the Palisades, this one, run by Jay Fiondella, is the most famous and most fun.

Sawdust on the floor, starched, checkered tablecloths, flickering candlelight, and the friendly faces of the large crowd of habitués create the ambience. The food is really good, typically Californian. For dinner, try the sand dabs sautés amandine, $6, or the butter steak, with "fines herbes," $7. The price of the entree includes a soup or salad, plus vegetables and garlic toast.

You won't be the first beachboy to make Chez Jay your second home. It's open for lunch five days a week, Monday through Friday, from noon to 2 p.m. Dinner is served nightly, Sunday through Thursdays, from 6 until 11; Fridays and Saturdays, from 6:30 till midnight.

Indian restaurants have blossomed on the West Coast, and of those we've sampled most have been mediocre. Gypsy's is a pleasant exception.

The decor consists of a clutter of East Indian artifacts and fabrics, interspersed with lots of plants and enough candlelight to make anything look exotic. The interior dining room is the most intimate, and hence, preferred.

As for the food, it's delicious, and there's lots of it; it's fun to go with a group of friends and enjoy a congenial meal, lingering over many courses. There are ten complete dinners offered; all include an appetizer, salad, poories (Indian bread), dal, vegetable bhaji (deep-fried vegetable fritters), and rice. The chef's specialty is tandoori chicken, marinated in seasoned yogurt, coated in saffron, and barbecued ($5.50). For the same price, you might order lamb korma, a North Indian dish of lamb chunks, cooked with braised onions, poppy seeds, yogurt, and cream, delicately spiced with saffron. Vegetarians can get a fresh vegetable curry dinner here for $4.50. A side order of mango chutney is 60¢, and a dessert of gulab jaman (milk balls in sweet syrup) is 75¢.

Gypsy's serves dinner nightly except Monday from 6 to 10 p.m. Reservations are advised.

Venice

Now merely a dingy mockery of its former self, Venice is an oceanside community south of Santa Monica, bordered by the beautiful new Marina del Rey. The character of Venice has undergone a remarkable change since the turn of the century, when it was founded with the intention of resembling its namesake in Italy. It was graced with canals, quaint one-lane bridges, and authentic imported gondolas piloted by gondoliers. An Italian-style rococo hotel, the St. Marks, attracted the celebrated people of its day. Self-enchanted silent-screen star, Mae Murray (*The Merry Widow*) became one of the first to build a Venetian-style palazzo there in pistachio colors.

Suddenly oil was discovered, and block after block of residences gave way to derricks. As a beach resort (not to mention a harbinger of Disneyland) Venice died a miserable death. Its canals today are slimy and filled with refuse. In the '50s Venice attracted the beatniks and in the '60s the hippies. As late as 1974, it was still making headlines because of nude bathing there (subsequently outlawed).

WHERE TO DINE: Mikasa, 12468 Washington Boulevard, near Centinela (tel. 391-8381). The name sounds like a Mexican eatery, but, as it happens, Mikasa is Japanese, and one of L.A.'s best Japanese restaurants at that. The food is first-rate, and the prices are remarkably low for what you get. All of which is adequately attested to by the long lines waiting to get in every evening. The decor is simple and unpretentious; it's a small place with just ten or so leather booths, a few shoji-screen dividers, paper lanterns overhead, and pretty-colored umbrellas on the walls.

An excellent buy here are the combination dinners. All of them include soup, salad, sunomono (marinated cucumber salad), and green tea. For $4.35 you might get a dinner of beef teriyaki/shrimp and vegetable tempura; fried fish/beef teriyaki; or chicken teriyaki/sashimi (the sashimi here is excellent, by the way). A sukiyaki/sashimi dinner is just $4.95—the lowest price we've found for such a meal on either coast! And for $5.50 to $6 you can get a three-item deluxe combination like beef teriyaki/tempura/sashimi—a real feast. Worthy side orders (in addition, of course, to a decanter of hot sake—$1.50) are the spinach in sesame-and-soy dressing (95¢) and cold bean curd ($1).

Mikasa is open for dinner nightly except Tuesday from 4:30 p.m.

Marina del Rey

Almost like a community created overnight has Marina del Rey burst onto the scene. Not only are there 6,000 boats in the world's largest small-craft harbor, but a Restaurant Row that rivals La Cienega Boulevard.

The recreation and convention center lies right on the coastal stretch between Santa Monica and Los Angeles International Airport, minutes via the San Diego Freeway.

Marina del Rey also has a unique shopping and recreation development known as **Fisherman's Village** at 13755 Fiji Way, containing over 30 specialty shops built in the style of an Old English whaling village. Imports from around the world are sold here. These shops line cobblestoned walks along the waterfront and are interspersed with waterside restaurants. In the center is an authentic 60-foot lighthouse.

As mentioned, the village is right on the waterfront, with a magnificent view of the marina and main channel. Visitors can take a water sightseeing trip around the marina, aboard the *Marina Belle* excursion boat, leaving every hour on the hour seven days a week. Adults pay $2; children six to 12, $1; under six free.

It's also possible to go out on fishing trips, the boats leaving the marina at 7:30 a.m., returning at 2:30 p.m. The cost is $10 for adults, $6 for children. There are sailboats for rent as well. A 21-footer goes for $18 for the first two hours; $5 per hour after that. Power boat rentals cost $10 per hour for a 16-footer, seating four passengers.

Kids will enjoy a puppet show featuring characters from "Orange Phillip Monkey."

For hotel and restaurant recommendations in Marina del Rey, refer to our L.A. hotel and restaurant sections.

Redondo Beach

This oceanside resort is south of Santa Monica, Marina del Rey, and the Los Angeles International Airport. It was established by Henry E. Huntington, the railway tycoon. After a big land boom, the town settled into life as a modest beach resort. It has always attracted fishermen, and more recently it has become industrial.

The **Redondo Beach Pier** is a maze of architecturally attractive restaurants, shops, and a concert auditorium. For a description of "concerts by the sea" presented here, refer to our nightlife section (Chapter VII). The restaurants here feature not only seafood, but an international cuisine including Polynesian, Mexican, and Japanese.

WHERE TO STAY: Portofino Inn, 260 Portofino Way, Redondo Beach (tel. 379-8481), rises from a man-made arm of land in the center of the yacht harbor. Every bedroom here has a balcony with a view of the boats, and all beds are extra-long, with orthopedic mattresses. The decor is traditional, though some rooms are done in a nautical theme. A few rooms have handpainted, carved headboards, with nets stretched toward the ceiling, and 66 of the 132 rooms come with equipped kitchenettes. Singles range from $28 to $36; doubles, $34 to $42. Public drinking and dining facilities include the Oar Room Coffee Shop (breakfast served here at all times of the day); the Crow's Nest Bar (mood music), and the Portofino Restaurant, specializing in steak and seafood, where you can order a good meal. An open-air, heated swimming pool overlooks the ocean.

WHERE TO DINE: Beachbum Burt's, 605 North Harbor Drive, Redondo Beach (tel. 376-0466), was inspired by Burt Hixon, the international photographer who roamed the South Seas. It holds forth nightly under one of the largest palm-thatched rooms in America. A section in the bar rolls back at the press of a button, and you dine under the stars. The building itself is tremendous with flaming torchiers, tall palms, and overhanging balconies and railings. Sidney Greenstreet, Gauguin, Tennessee Williams, or the fictional Sadie Thompson would feel right at home.

Inside, it's even more Pago-Pago, with both a Veranda Bar and a Balcony Bar. There's entertainment nightly, beginning at 9 p.m., and central casting must have been called to provide the "beautiful people" who serve you. Start your meal with an exotic drink. The mai-tai is a specialty at $2.25. Hixon and the master chef, Xavier Koch, have come up with some interesting dishes, including ginger chicken Gauguin at $5.50, and spareribs rarotonga, $6.75. Most diners order the "American mud pie" at 95¢ for dessert.

The **Red Onion**, 655 North Harbor Drive (tel. 376-8813), is just down the road a stretch from Burt's, and almost as zany in concept. The decor is elaborate in the extreme, with slowly rotating fans suspended from bamboo ceilings; stucco walls hung with hundreds of photos of Mexico; an eclectic selection of chairs, many of them rattan and bamboo; an open brick-and-tile fireplace; Persian carpets; and lots and lots of plants. Though a bit overdone, it works well, and enhancing the ambience even more is the harbor view afforded from many tables.

The fare, in case you haven't guessed from the above description, is Mexican, and it's both tasty and plentiful. An amazing bargain here is the afternoon buffet served weekdays between 4 and 7 p.m. For the price of a drink you can eat all you want from a bountiful buffet of salads, rice, beans, enchiladas, tacos, chips, etc.

If you come at other times, or wish to have a regular sitdown meal while the buffet is going, there's an extensive menu. Best to order a margarita ($1.25) right away, and peruse at leisure. You might begin with an appetizer of guacamole ($1.50). Then go on to one of the combination plates priced between $2.10 and $4.95—the latter for a deluxe order that includes a taco, tamale, enchilada, chile relleno, Spanish rice, beans, soup or salad, and tortillas.

Another option is a hot entree like scampi with Spanish rice ($5.95) or arroz con pollo—a chicken-and-rice casserole ($4.75). Both are served with soup or salad. Lighter fare is available, too, ranging from a simple cheeseburger ($1.75) to a beef or cheese enchilada (95¢). And that's not the half of it—perhaps it will take two margaritas before you've made up your mind.

The Red Onion has yet another menu for brunch, and it's also popular for dancing nightly; there's a live band Tuesday through Saturday, disco Monday nights. Open daily from 11 a.m. to 2 a.m. (Sundays from 10 a.m.).

Marineland

Billed as "the world's only four-ring sea circus," Marineland is a huge oceanarium, right on the Pacific, between Redondo Beach and San Pedro. If you're heading south down the coast from Redondo Beach, take the Palos Verdes Drive. If you're inland, Marineland is reached via the San Diego Freeway (take Hawthorne Boulevard to the sea) or the Harbor Freeway to San Pedro.

At this famed attraction of Southern California, just 30 minutes south of Los Angeles, you can see several shows inside for the price of a single admission: $5.50 for adults; children four through 11, $3.75; children under four, free. It's open Wednesday through Sunday, from 10 a.m. to 5 p.m., November 1 to April 1; daily from 10 a.m. to 7 p.m., June 1 to September 7; daily 10 a.m. to 6 p.m. the rest of the year.

In the true Hollywood tradition, there are many performers, and even a "star system" has developed. For example: "Orky" and "Corky" the famous killer whales; "Flipper" and his dolphin friends; "Bubbles" the pilot whale; performing sea lions doing their thing in the Sea Arena. You can also watch a diver feeding the hungry creatures in what is called "the world's largest fish bowl."

To round out the bill you can see walruses captured in the Bering Straits, otters, octopuses, lung fish, rainbow-hued creatures of the deep, jewel tanks swarming with eels, alligators, and Humboldt penguins.

For a panoramic view of the area—a vista stretching from Orange to Ventura Counties—take the Sky Tower ride, whirling on a spindle 344 feet above sea level.

Finally, you may want to spend the night at the **Marineland Motel**, Marineland (tel. 377-1571), right across the parking lot. It provides cliff-dwelling accommodations, each boasting a spectacular view of the ocean. The rates: $17 for one person, $19 for two, and $21 for three (plus tax).

The Wayfarers' Chapel

Built on a cliff with a broad, steep face, the Wayfarers' Chapel, along Palos Verdes Drive South in Rancho Palos Verdes, is a special oasis. In a spot above the lashing waves of the Pacific, Lloyd Wright, son of a more celebrated father (Frank Lloyd Wright), erected a chapel, leaning heavily on glass, surrounding redwoods, and vegetation to create a stunning effect.

The chapel is a memorial to Emanuel Swedenborg, the Stockholm-born 18th-century philosopher and theologian ("the Trinity in one person"), who claimed to have cavorted with spirits and heavenly hosts in his visions. About 12 years after the mystic died, his followers founded the Church of the New Jerusalem. The movement never gained overwhelming numbers of converts, but, though few, the Swedenborgians range around the world, as revealed by a map in the museum and reference library behind the chapel.

Surrounding the building, and planted on the hillside, are rare plants, some of which are native to the Holy Land.

The "glass church" is open seven days a week from 11 a.m. to 4 p.m., charging no admission. Services are held regularly on Sundays at 11 a.m.; telephone 213/377-1650 for more information.

San Pedro

Further down the beach is **San Pedro,** the port of Los Angeles. The partial setting for Richard Henry Dana's *Two Years Before the Mast,* it is nowadays a port handling an estimated two million tons of cargo every month.

PORTS O'CALL AND THE WHALER'S WHARF: In this port city the Ports O'Call and the Whaler's Wharf were created, the latter resembling 19th-century New Bedford, Mass. The wharf is riddled with elm-shaded streets, simulating America's past. The shops (see the shopping chapter for a sampling of the merchandise) are skillfully designed, recapturing brilliantly the atmosphere of a New England seacoast village. The stores are shingled, Colonial, with lantern lights, tavern signs, and small-paned windows.

In a part of the village the promoters attempted to evoke Early California and seaports along the Mediterranean. The latter effect is achieved by bougainvillea and banana plants, bazaar stalls, abundant flowers, and luscious semitropical fruits.

Part of the fun is watching the steady stream of international shipping pass in and out of the port, along with yachts, tuna clippers, and fishing boats.

To reach the Ports O'Call, take the Harbor Freeway to its termination, bearing left for two miles after leaving it. The admission-free village and wharf are open 11 a.m. to 9 p.m. daily year-round.

For meals, you can stop off at the **Ports O'Call Restaurant,** at Berth 76 (tel. 833-3553), which has good selections from the carving board or else from fertile vegetable fields. Luncheon specials are in the $2.35 (for a Tahitian burger) to $4.25 (for a prime rib sandwich) range. At dinner, you can order such dishes as a Java seafood curry with scallops, shrimps, crabmeat, lobster, and condiments ($7.25). Another good dish is baby ribs of pork glazed with a South Pacific sauce ($6.25). A fine dessert is the coconut ice cream at 60¢. A flagon of the house wine with your meal is $3.75. A red Chinese junk is moored in a charming pond near the footbridge to the entrance and a red rickshaw is near the door.

An alternative suggestion is the **Yankee Whaler Inn,** at the Ports O'Call Village (tel. 831-0181), a recreation of a 19th-century whaling inn, lodged on the waterside at the extreme end of the Village. Set apart as it is by a little bridge, it misses much of the usual tourist jam. The facade is weathered clapboard and shingle—a northeastern look.

There are five places at which to dine and drink, plus a deck bar with open fireplaces, and a brick terrace on the waterside. Lunch is served seven days a week between 11 and 4; dinner, till 10 Sundays through Thursdays (on weekends, till 11 p.m.).

Suggested entrees are poached salmon hollandaise ($6.50), and California red snapper covered with baby shrimps and brown butter, with parsley potato ($4.95). A cauldron of steamed clams goes for $6.25. Included in the price are clam chowder or salad, and hot sourdough bread.

Long Beach

Combining beach resort attractions with oil derricks, Long Beach (20 miles south of Los Angeles on San Pedro Bay), is the new home of the **Queen Mary,** at the terminus of Pier J. She completed her final voyage on December 9, 1967, after a 14,500-mile journey that took her around South America via Cape Horn.

The City of Long Beach purchased the vessel at a cost of $3 million. The city is calling the *Queen Mary* "81,000 tons of fun." If you're driving, you must pay $1 to park in the lot. A combination ticket costs adults $4, and children, $1.75. For this one admission you are entitled to explore the **Queen Mary Museum, Jacques Cousteau's Living Sea,** and the **Upper Decks.** The *Queen Mary* is open every day of the year from 10 a.m. Pier J is at the southern end of the Long Beach Freeway.

On the Upper Decks, you can view the luxury suites, as well as stroll along the Promenade Deck. Two long malls of shops await you. The Living Sea exhibits were designed by Jacques Cousteau, the famous ocean explorer. A three-level panorama was created across the lower decks, and it's the world's largest marine exhibition. It's virtually an undersea city, including a futuristic marine farm.

You can also dine aboard the ship in one of three restaurants.

A Roaring '20s Luxury Liner

Directly across from the Ports O'Call, on Terminal Island (take the Vincent Thomas toll bridge, 25¢, to Ferry Street, then the first right after the toll plaza, and follow the signs), is the **S. S. Princess Louise Restaurant,** Berth 236 (tel. 831-2351), which recaptures the luxury-liner living of the roaring '20s. With its four wide decks and "tons" of rooms, the liner is enjoying a busy retirement, hosting banquets, fashion shows, and serving diners who come to sample the specialties of the French chef. Launched in 1921, the *S. S. Princess Louise* was called "The Queen of the Northern Seas," and traversed a route from Vancouver, British Columbia, to Skagway, Alaska.

Lunches are in the $2.95 to $4.95 range, including such dishes as a turkey-and-ham casserole, an avocado pear with crabmeat, and, at the latter price, prime ribs of beef. Dinners, in the $6 to $10.50 range, including soup (perhaps a cooling gazpacho), an entree, a salad, and dessert, as well as hot sourdough bread with whipped butter. Specialties include duck à l'orange at $7.25, Princess Louise clam bake at $8.45, and crêpes of English sole at $7.45.

While dining, guests enjoy views of the busy harbor. In addition, there's a bar with a small dance floor on the forward deck where a combo entertains nightly except Mondays. After the meal, you can visit the Crown Jewel Room, where you'll find replicas of the Crown Jewels of Great Britain, and even these are insured for half a million dollars. The hours are 11:30 to 3 and 5:30 to 10:30, Monday through Thursday. Fridays, dinner is served till 11 p.m. Saturdays, it's open from noon to 3 and from 5 till midnight. Sundays, a champagne brunch is served from 11 a.m. to 3 p.m. ($4.75 for adults, $2.95 for children); dinner till 10 p.m.

The **Lady Hamilton** at lunch offers fresh oysters at $3.35, bouillabaisse Marseillaise at $6.25, and a seafood platter at $4.85. An English trifle at 75¢ is the traditional dessert. Midday fare in the **Lord Nelson** runs to English specialties such as beefsteak and mushroom pie at $2.95. In the evening, the traditional dish is roast prime ribs of beef, $8.25; veal Oscar is $6.95. The **Sir Winston** serves dinner only; it's basically a steak and seafood house offering entrees like steak Diane ($9.75), and fresh trout noblesse ($7.95). Flambé desserts include cherries jubilee ($2) and crêpes suzette ($2.75).

From Pierpoint Landing, you can take a 1½-hour **Long Beach Harbor Tour,** costing $2.50 for adults and $1 for children (5 to

11). Departures are at 10 a.m., noon, 2 p.m., and 4 p.m. On the weekends only, visitors can hop aboard a genuine double-decker bus, brought over from London on the *Queen Mary*, for a "Sea-Lane" harbor tour lasting about an hour.

To the south, **Seal Beach,** with its pier, is a favorite spot with surfers. From the pier, you can walk down Main Street, joining the malt and burger crowd at one of the many cafes.

Catalina Island

Cove-fringed Catalina lies about 26 miles off the California shoreline. Noted for its flying fish and porpoises, as well as its undersea gardens, it marked its rise as a resort when it was purchased in 1919 by William Wrigley, of chewing gum fame. It is only 15 minutes by air from Long Beach or San Pedro, and Catalina Air Lines makes regular flights.

From June 15 to September 15, **Davey's Locker** operates a cruise to Catalina aboard the *Island Holiday.* For reservations and information, go to the Balboa Pavilion, 400 Main Street, Newport (tel. Avalon 451). The boat operates daily in summer, leaving Newport at 9 a.m., returning at 7 p.m. The round-trip fare is $11 for adults, $5.50 for children under 12 (no charge under five).

. The boat arrives at **Avalon,** the capital, on Avalon Bay at Catalina Island. The **Catalina Operations Co.,** Sightseeing Ticket Office, Pleasure Pier, in Avalon (tel. Avalon 1111), offers a combination tour ticket at $6.50 for adults ($3.75 for ages five to 11) that includes a glass-bottom boat ride to see the marine life, plus a drive up a mountain terrace road, and a trip to watch the sea colony along the rocky eastern tip of the island. On the glass-bottom boat, you can see a virtual marine forest.

In addition, several important ship lines operate 500- to 700-passenger vessels to Catalina, the voyage lasting approximately two hours. Leaving from Long Beach, the *Long Beach King* and the *Long Beach Prince* charge adults $10 for a round trip; children $5. Another large ship, the *Monarch,* departs from San Pedro, charging adults $8.50 round trip; $4.25 for children. For information about departures, telephone 775-2654 from Los Angeles.

If you'd like to spend the night on the island, consider the **Zane Grey Pueblo Hotel,** Box 216, Avalon (tel. 831-8822). Ken and Karen Holliday lovingly care for this place, fully aware that they are living in the former home of the novelist, Zane Grey.

He spent his last 20 years here, enjoying the isolated life, the view of the ocean and harbor below the house. The Hollidays have converted the home into a comfortable guest house, even installing a swimming pool. But they still respect its former role by not offering television or phones in the rooms. The accommodations—singles costing anywhere from $20 to $34; doubles, $20 to $38—have queen-sized beds and private baths. Some suites are available at prices ranging from $30 to $40.

Newport Beach

Seemingly, the goal of every high school surfer is to make it big at Newport Beach! It's the "in" spot, attracting collegians, the dune-buggy crowd, grunion runners, and beautiful people—all of whom meet at the Pier, drinking Coors beer. Members of the hip crowd form their own colony, renting the plethora of beach bungalows and apartments. On any Sunday afternoon, a fairly clever and personable stranger can attend at least ten cocktail parties without an invitation!

About 35 miles south of Los Angeles, Newport Beach (embracing **Balboa** as well), nests on a sandy beach strip opening onto the Pacific. Sheltered in the bay between the sand bar and the mainland are Balboa Island and Lido Isle.

A major point in your exploration should be the **Balboa Pavilion** with its much-photographed landmark cupola. Established in 1905, it was once a fashionable spot for Mack Sennett-type bathing beauty contests. Redecorated in 1969, it is the setting for the yearly "Flight of the Snowbirds," and attracts fishermen, sightseers, and hungry diners.

At the Pier, you can take a ferry to **Balboa Island,** the ride costing 40¢ for cars, 10¢ for passengers.

The best way to see the bay is to buy a ticket for a harbor cruise. In summer, there are several trips daily leaving from the **Fun Zone Dock,** near the ferry landing. Some of the waterfront homes you pass are owned by motion-picture and TV stars. A 45-minute cruise costs adults $3; children under 12, 50¢. In winter, the cruise is on weekends only.

WHERE TO STAY: Del Webb's Newporter Inn, 1107 Jamboree Road, Newport Beach (tel. 644-1700), is not only the preferred place to stay, but also the heartbeat center of life in this beach town. It's a resort complex, with two heated swimming pools on its grounds. Each of the skillfully designed bedrooms has air conditioning, color TV, radio, in-house movies, and a view. Singles range from $32 to $38; doubles, from $36 to $40.

In the Wine Cellar, gourmet meals are featured Tuesday through Saturday (a different menu every week of the month). Lunch is served daily, and there's entertainment and dancing nightly in the Lido Lounge.

In addition, you can have lunch and dinner in the Bistro, the Café de la Paix, or Marine Restaurant. Incidentally, on Sundays, between 9 a.m. and 2 p.m., you can enjoy an all-you-can-eat champagne hunt breakfast at the Marine for $3.95.

Giving some stiff competition to Del Webb's Newporter Inn are two new luxury hotels that were completed in 1975. The first of these to go up was a new **Sheraton Newport**, 4545 MacArthur Boulevard (tel. 833-0570). In a style that is becoming increasingly popular in new hotel architecture, the Sheraton has its rooms centered around a courtyard lobby, with ivy-draped balconies reaching seven stories upward to a skylight roof. It's quite attractive, as are the rooms and other facilities here. There are 210 rooms in all, decorated with flair in three color schemes—orange and yellow, green and blue, or red and white. Furnishings are oak, with two leather armchairs in each room, and all amenities from color TV to modern bath.

Facilities include two night-lighted tennis courts which guests can use at no charge; an adjoining golf course; a pool; Jacuzzi; and two restaurants—the Festival Cafe, a coffeeshop open from 6:30 a.m. to 11 p.m., and a handsome, oak-paneled steak and seafood restaurant. There's also Alexander's Banana, looking like an old New York bar, and featuring live rock music for dancing Tuesday through Sunday nights and a guitarist Monday nights.

Because the Sheraton has stiff competition in establishing itself, they're offering some appealing extras—like a free cocktail party from 5 to 7 p.m. Monday through Saturday nights, at which guests can drink all they want.

Rates are competitive, too: $28 to $32 for singles; $32 to $36 for doubles. Included in that price are the abovementioned free cocktail parties; complimentary buffet breakfast every day of your stay; airport limousine service; free local calls; free coffee and *Wall Street Journal* delivered to your room each morning; and free parking. Package plans are also available, including a Friday-and-Saturday-night plan that gives you Disneyland admission with 11 attractions, a new compact car with 200 free miles for Saturday and Sunday, and unlimited cocktails Friday or Saturday night, plus all the abovementioned regular-rate complimentary benefits. The price: $50.50 per person, based on double occupancy. If children are along, they can stay free in the same room with parents, but there is a charge of $6.50 for their Disneyland tickets.

Just a month after the Sheraton appeared on the scene, another major hotel opened its doors in the area. The **Marriott,** 900 Newport Center Drive (tel. 640-4000), is a 377-room, $10-million luxury establishment. Like the Sheraton, it features the new architecture—rooms are centered around a nine-story atrium, and balconies are hung with ivy and bougainvillea vines. The focalpoint of the courtyard is an Italian-Renaissance fountain.

All rooms contain oversized beds, color TV, AM-FM radio (both with bedside remote control), and direct-dial phones; most have balconies (the hotel is designed so that 80% of the rooms have an ocean view). The decor is strikingly attractive, using rust-colored carpeting and brightly patterned drapes and bedspreads.

Facilities include an immense swimming pool and hydrotherapy pool set on a palm-lined sundeck; ten tennis courts (no charge for use weekdays—$5 weekends); and an 18-hole golf course nearby at the Irvine Country Club. **Fashion Island,** with a theater, playground, 60 shops, and ten restaurants, is just across the street. However, there are two fine restaurants right on the premises. The King's Wharf features a steak and seafood menu at lunch (a $4.50 buffet) and dinner. Capriccio is stylized Mediterranean in decor with heavy wrought-iron chandeliers suspended from arched ceilings and substantial-looking leather furnishings. It has an outdoor terrace for open-air dining. Meals (continental fare) are served from 6 a.m. to 2 a.m. (till 3 a.m. Friday and Saturday nights).

Adjoining the King's Wharf is the Main Brace, a nautical-theme discotheque that is also used for a seafood buffet nightly from 5 to 7:30 p.m. It's open nightly for dancing from 9:30 p.m. Over 1,000 people come every Sunday, as well, to partake of a sumptuous 70-item buffet served from 10 a.m. to 2:30 p.m. Adults pay $6.95; children, $3.50.

Rates for single rooms at the Marriott are $32 to $40; twins and doubles are $38 to $46. Like the Sheraton, the Marriott also has an "Escape Weekend" plan for $59.50 per person, based on double occupancy—this one includes meals rather than Disneyland or a car.

Lido Shores Hotel and Marina, 617 Lido Park Drive, Newport Beach (tel. 673-8800), is right at the yacht basin. You'll like the openness of the rooms; many have a Hawaiian-modern look, with ceiling-to-floor picture windows opening onto a view of the boats or swimming pool. Rates for single or double rooms range from $31 to $45, with the higher figure for a bayfront lanai suite.

All rooms are bright and cheerful with color TVs, direct-dial phones, and baths with tub and shower.

WHERE TO DINE: The Cannery, 3010 Lafayette Avenue, Newport Beach (tel. 675-5777), is housed in a remodeled 1934 fish cannery which used to turn out 5,000 cases of swordfish and mackerel a day. The two-story restaurant, its center like an open well, still has its large furnace and ovens, even belts holding shiny cans. Overscaled windows were installed to open up the view. Artisans and painters gather here throughout the day, ordering drinks in the reception lounge and sitting on feed-sack cushions. In the upper room, tables surround a corner platform where a Trinidad steel band plays in the evenings. The chef's special catch of the day goes for $6.95. Another good main dish is the seafood cannelloni at $7.95. At lunch, you can ask for the house special, crab Madagascar (crêpes stuffed with fresh crabmeat), $4.75. Sunday brunch is a ritual: $2.95 for adults, $1.95 for children.

Chanteclair, 18912 MacArthur Boulevard (tel. 752-8001), is designed like a provincial French inn. A rambling stucco structure with a mansard roof, built around a central garden court, it houses several dining and drinking areas: a grand and petit salon, a boudoir, a *bibliothèque*, a garden area with a skylight roof, and a hunting lodge-like lounge. Furnished in antiques, it has five fireplaces and Persian carpeting. Further enhancing the elegantly intimate ambience is a harpist who plays in the early evening on weeknights. All of which combines to create a truly lovely setting for dining:

The cuisine is classically French. At lunch, served weekdays only, you might order chicken-filled crêpes with Mornay sauce ($3.75), steak tartare ($7.25), or a plate of assorted cold hors d'oeuvres served with soup or a champagne cocktail ($5.75).

Dinner is an experience in fine dining; we think it's a worthwhile splurge, but you can easily run up a tab of $50 or $60 for two people. You might begin with the house pâté ($4), or perhaps an order of Beluga caviar with blinis and garniture ($12.50).

We're also partial to the salads—a spinach salad flambé ($2.75) or Belgian endives with roquefort, oil-and-vinegar dressing ($2.50).

For an entree we recommend the braised quail in white wine sauce ($11.75); another favorite is the rack of lamb served with a bouquetière of fresh vegetables and potatoes Dauphine ($12). There's a considerable listing of domestic and imported wines to complement your meal; if you don't know what to select, the wine steward will be happy to help you choose. A soufflé Grand Marnier ($2.50) is the perfect dessert.

Chanteclair is open nightly for dinner from 6 to 11 p.m. (5 to 10:30 on Sundays).

Marrakesh, 1100 West Coast Highway (tel. 645-8384), is a variation on the theme of Dar Maghreb, a Moroccan restaurant previously described in Los Angeles restaurants. The decor is exotic, with dining areas divided into intimate tents, furnished with Persian carpets, and authentic Moroccan pieces. Seating is on low cushioned, sofas, and the entire meal is eaten without silverware—you use your hands! It's something of a ritual feast, which begins, appropriately enough, when a server comes around to wash your hands. Everyone in your party shares the same meal—an eight-course feast priced at $11 or $12. It consists of Moroccan soup; a tangy salad that is scooped up with hunks of fresh bread; b'stila (a chicken-filled pastry topped with cinnamon); a choice of four entrees (baked squab with rice and almonds; baked chicken with lemon and olives; baked fish in a piquant sauce, or rabbit with prune sauce); lamb and vegetables with couscous; fresh fruits; tea; and Moroccan pastries.

A simpler $8 four-course meal is available, but this is no place for light eating, and we suggest you fast during the day, eat slowly, and enjoy the whole dinner. It's delightful to lounge on the cushions and linger over course after course (a bottle of wine helps); Moroccan music enhances the exotic ambience. Open for dinner nightly.

Le Saint-Tropez, 3012 Newport Boulevard, Newport Beach (tel. 673-7883), is like a French country inn. The table settings are classic. Freshly cut flowers are placed about, and logs burn in a brick fireplace. You're welcomed by the owner, René Barge, who will introduce you to the cooking skills of his remarkable Parisian chef, Joseph Viellemaringe. We'd recommend his medallion of veal Normande (made with calvados, cream, and mushrooms) at $9.75, or his rabbit stew at $9. Abalone de Monterey ($9) is also superb. The chef uses only the freshest of

Eatin' on a Riverboat

Reuben E. Lee, 151 E. Coast Highway, Newport Beach, is a free-floating, genuine replica of the famous Mississippi riverboat, the *Robert E. Lee.* It offers two restaurants—the Seafood and the Sternwheeler.

Pink and white awnings shelter the gangplanks outside, and the promenade decks have turn-of-the-century ornate cut-out wood trim. The total effect sets the mood for adventure. The Seafood Restaurant (tel. 675-5790) is in the bow of the ship and is decorated in red-tufted Victorian, the waitresses in mini-yellow crinolines with ruffled aprons.

Dinner entrees include a steaming tureen of vegetable chowder, a small tossed salad, a choice of potatoes or steamed rice, with mushrooms and a basket of baked rolls. Most seafood devotees try the New Orleans bouillabaisse at $7.50 (a tasty concoction made with whole shrimps, lobsters, scallops, clams, fresh fish filet, and crab legs, all skillfully blended with tomato sauce and laced with wine). The Seafood Restaurant serves lunch until 4:30 p.m. Monday to Saturday, and dinner nightly till 11 (midnight on weekends).

At the stern, the appropriately named Sternwheeler (tel. 675-5811) effectively uses glass for a good view of the water paddles. Its decor is "mauve era." Offering extremely good crêpes, the lunch menu includes the "Paddle Wheel," combining chicken, cream sauce, and mushrooms, for $3.25. At dinner you might opt for prime rib of beef au jus, priced at $8.25 to $9.25, depending on the cut. Open from 11:30 a.m. till 11 p.m. (from 5 p.m. till midnight on Saturdays and from 4 p.m. till 11 p.m. on Sundays).

produce (which he selects himself in true Gallic fashion). An excellent selection of French wines is offered as well. Dinner is offered nightly, except Mondays, from 6 p.m.

ROOMS AND FOOD AT BALBOA: Balboa Inn, 105 Main Street, Balboa (tel. 675-8740), at the foot of Balboa Pier is a delightful and well-located hostelry. Built in the '30s, it was designed by the same architect who did the landmark Union Station in Los Angeles, Walter Hagedohn. The building reflects his Spanish-colonial design. The inn had a colorful history in the '30s and '40s, attracting such stars as Jean Harlow and Errol Fynnn, the latter always in need of a hideaway. The building has been restored to as close to its original state as possible. The ground floor is occupied by a restaurant, Mi Casa, which provides inexpensive Mexican meals. The inn is attractive, with a tiled roof and rooms opening onto either the potted-palm courtyard or the swimming pool and ocean. Skill and taste are reflected throughout. Though the furnishings are somewhat austere, there is beauty as well as sophistication. In all, 34 units are offered. They have no phones or TVs, but the desk takes messages, and tube addicts can rent a set just down the street. Rates begin at $20 and go up to $40 for a large kitchen apartment that sleeps up to six persons. Lower rates can be obtained on a weekly or monthly basis.

Tale of the Whale, Balboa Pavilion, 400 Main Street, Balboa (tel. 673-4633), has a prime position in the old pavilion, the center of Balboa social life since 1905. Once a homebase for such big names as Count Basie and Benny Goodman, it is now a leading seafood restaurant. Tables are placed so that you have a spectacular view of Newport Harbor, and almost any kind of fish dinner you can conjure up is available. We're fond of seafood brochette—scallops, swordfish, shrimp, lobster, and white sea bass on a skewer ($6.95). Sole from the Oregon coast stuffed with shrimp and crab and baked in a wine sauce at $5.95 is also good. Desserts range in price from 50¢ to 85¢.

Luncheon entrees are priced from $2.50 to $4.50. The restaurant is open daily from 7 a.m. to 11 p.m.

Costa Mesa

Costa Mesa, in Orange County, is a university and residential colony adjoining Newport Beach and Upper Newport Harbor. It's about 40 miles south of Los Angeles on the San Diego Freeway. Take the Bristol Street off-ramp, continuing on via Newport Boulevard.

Your first stop should be **The Briggs Cunningham Automotive Museum,** 250 East Baker Street (corner of Redhill Avenue; tel. 546-7660), Costa Mesa, which houses what some experts consider the choicest collection of automobiles extant in its 30,000-square-foot exhibition hall. The exhibit ranges from 1898 to the present. You'll see such ostentation as the super-deluxe 1927 Bugatti "Royale," sports cars, classics, antiques, whatever—the range is eclectic. The vintage automobiles are kept in good running condition by skilled mechanics.

At a gift shop in the lobby, you can purchase books on the

automobile, prints, and models, as well as car badges and other items. The museum is open Wednesday through Sunday, 9 a.m. to 5 p.m. (closed Mondays and Tuesdays). It charges $2.50 for adults. Students and military personnel are charged $1.50; children, five through 12, pay 50¢; children under five are admitted free.

SOME FINE RESTAURANTS: Though the following are actually in Newport Beach, they're right at the edge of Costa Mesa and convenient to that area's attractions.

Harry's New York Bar & Grill, 4248 Martingale Way, Newport Beach (tel. 979-5000). Its namesake may be in the genre of gentlemen's clubs, but this Harry's is a garden oasis. Its central core is three stories high with a clerestory, allowing light to stream down onto the bar and adjoining dining areas. Potted palms, hanging ferns, a gigantic art-nouveau gas chandelier, original paintings, photos on the walls, stained glass, brass draught beer handles, old sheet music—an organized clutter designed to cash in on nostalgia. Harry's never seems to close, throwing open its doors at 7 a.m. for an array of fabulous breakfast dishes, including eggs "almost benedict" at $2.75. Luncheon specialties include corned beef and cabbage at $3.25 and Harry's own "colcannon potatoes" (a Celtic combination of chopped onions, bacon, and sauerkraut—grilled like potato pancakes). Deli sandwiches are also popular, going for $2.25. Dinner specialties include Harry's tartare steak with a creamy mustard sauce at $5.95. Desserts feature a rhubarb cobbler at $1. Harry's closes at 2 a.m. (dinner, 5 to 11).

Blackbeard's Galley & Grog, 4250 Martingale Way, Newport Beach (tel. 833-0800), would please Charles Laughton with its gangplank entry and nautical theme. In the entry is a settle beside an open fire—cozy, if you have to wait for a table. With pegged wooden floors, many of the dining rooms are like old taverns with brick walls and beamed ceilings. Near the open hearth of the main fireplace are ten mounted antique ship models. One room has an antique lifeboat suspended overhead; another is the "captain's quarters," with gold-velvet draperies, tufted booths, and old English prints. Sandwiches at lunch run between $1.95 and $3.95. For an additional charge of 75¢ you can draw from the kettle of black bean soup. Each day of the week a different specialty is featured. For example, on Friday, you can order sand-dabs Barbados, with saffron rice, avocado, and banana at $4.85. The house specialty, including a selection from the salad bars, is a Caribbean pork chop at $5.65 (a 16-ounce pork chop taken from the heart of the loin, marinated, then baked slowly, grilled in a savory sauce, and garnished with fresh pineapple and banana simmered in buttered rum). Open every day.

Laguna Beach

Laguna has long been the gathering point for painters, potters, sculptors, and etchers who have created a colorful colony where the leisure life reigns supreme. Its boutiques, galleries, little theaters, and coffeehouses were commonplace at the same time that Greenwich Village was attracting worldwide attention as a haven for New York's artists. Tall eucalyptus trees, palms, and bougainvillea grow abundantly.

WHERE TO STAY: Capri Laguna, 1441 South Coast Highway, Laguna Beach (tel. 494-6533), is a cluster of cliff-hanging bedroom units facing a sandy beach. Almost all rooms open onto balconies, some private. Prices are wide ranging, because of the difference in facilities. For example, poolside apartments, with kitchens, and dining and dressing areas, range from $28.50 to $33 for two in summer, though you pay from $20 to $25 for poolside rooms. More expensive beachfront apartments, even ocean-view penthouses, are available as well. The decor is bright and modern, and all rooms have direct-dial phones, color TV, and baths with tub and/or shower. On the inner courtyard side is a small open-air swimming pool. On winter evenings, guests gather in front of a rugged stone fireplace in the lounge. Across the highway is a shopping complex with 50 arcade boutiques, art galleries, and studios.

Laguna Motor Inn, 1575 North Coast Highway, Laguna Beach (tel. 494-3537), is a resort-style motel complex on the beach side of the highway, with a spacious garden and a swimming pool. Here you can dip in the clear water, or else sunbathe beside tall banana trees. Rooms overlook the gardens, which are abundantly planted with flowers and greenery. In summer, double-bedded accommodations for one or four persons cost $20. There are four apartments with fully equipped kitchens that can accommodate up to seven people and cost just $30 per night. Furnishings throughout are eclectic and quaint. All rooms have black-and-white TV, and modern bath, but no phone.

Laguna Beach Motor Inn, 985 North Coast Highway, Laguna Beach (tel. 494-5294), is right on the coast road, with oceanside terraces, plus a 20-by-40-foot swimming pool and a secluded beach cove. The highway rooms are cheaper and less desirable, but otherwise it's a quiet retreat with a patio garden ideal for sunny breakfasts under the banana trees. Now owned by the Hyuns, a Korean family, the Inn has some charming Oriental touches—like framed calligraphy and paintings on rice paper in the halls and rooms. In summer, singles or doubles are $25 to $34; $18 to $28, off-season. Highly recommended.

WHERE TO DINE: Victor Hugo Inn, 361 Cliff Drive, Laguna Beach (tel. 494-9477), is in the best possible position. Its dining rooms open onto terraces which lead down to the Pacific surf. Each terrace is ablaze with geraniums and roses and subtropical greenery. For Laguna "society" and outstanding artists this is a favorite place for that "special luncheon or dinner." You'd think the Hugo memorabilia in the reception lounge, along with an oil portrait and genealogical charts, would indicate the owner was a direct descendant—not so, it's just the whim of a decorator. Dinners include a choice of soup or salad, and a beverage. Chicken sauteed with mushrooms goes for $6.50. Duckling flambé is $9.50. At lunch prices are cheaper. Reservations are recommended.

The Cottage, 308 North Coast Highway, Laguna Beach (tel. 494-3023), is a landmark—a time-worn early-California frame building with Oriental roof lines. A tall monkey-star pine tree shades the old-fashioned garden. The decor is a melange of artifacts. For example, the table lamps were originally made for the Del Coronado Hotel in San Diego at the turn of the century. The theater seats served for 40 years in the Laguna Playhouse. Be sure to see the photographic collection in the waiting room, including a series devoted to Eiler Larsen, known as "The Greeter," a famous character in Laguna. Other walls are decorated with original oils by Laguna artists. Open from 8 a.m. (very popular for breakfast) to midnight, The Cottage serves good food at prices surprisingly low. Dinner entrees include grilled halibut ($5) and filet mignon ($7). At lunch you might choose from a selection of sandwiches ($1.40 to $2.25), though salads and hot entrees—like tempura vegetables ($2.75)—are also on the menu.

La Jolla

"La Hoya" (that's how it's pronounced) is an oceanside residential portion of the coast, at the northern edge of San Diego. It successfully retains its "old-money" image, although adventurous young people are moving in on the coterie of millionaires and retired citizens. For half a century, the wealthy have been building beautiful retirement estates here, having selected the site for its lushness and rugged coastline, its beaches and cultural facilities. Along Prospect Avenue, running parallel with the coast, are about three blocks of fascinating boutiques, shops, restaurants, cafes, and art galleries. A tasteful, restful, interesting place to visit.

The **Scripps Institution of Oceanography** is world renowned for the research it does in the oceans. It invites visitors to view its aquarium of marine life, many of the specimens captured on scientific expeditions (open daily from 9 a.m. to 5 p.m., at 8602 La Jolla Shores). No admission is charged. Nearby are fine beach and picnic areas.

WHERE TO STAY: La Valencia, 1132 Prospect, La Jolla (tel. 454-0771), is a minor miracle. Too often great old hotels are allowed to deteriorate until they are torn down. In this case La Valencia has been renewed with beautifully coordinated styling in its bedrooms, all given that decorator touch, with reproductions of antiques, coordinated fabrics, and wallpaper interspersed with furnishings imported from Italy, Spain, and France. Highest rates are charged from July 1 to Labor Day; from $40 to $49 for one to two persons. The hotel's entrance is in the center of the village, though its rear faces the ocean. You enter via a tiled loggia with a vine-covered trellis. On your left is a small garden with a fountain and flowering subtropical shrubbery. It's old Spain revisited. At the back, garden terraces open toward the ocean. Here, a free-form swimming pool is edged with lawn, flowering trees and shrubs, and a flagstone sunning deck. Other facilities include sauna, whirlpool, a nine-hole putting green, and three delightful restaurants: the rooftop Skyroom, where a superb buffet lunch is served weekdays for $4.50; the Mediterranean Room, with its adjoining patio for al fresco dining; and the Cafe La Rue.

Sea Lodge, 8110 Camino del Oro (tel. 459-8271). Beginning at the arched stucco registration desk adorned with ceramic tiles, this terra-cotta-roofed resort is Spanish through and through.

Overlooking the Pacific on a mile-long beach, the beauty of the property is enhanced by fountains, fine landscaping, open-air walkways, much tile work, graceful archways, and Mexican antiques. There's a large courtyard, the setting for an immense pool, sundeck, and umbrella tables for poolside luncheons. Other facilities here include three tennis courts, a sauna, a small putting green, and Ping-Pong; there's a nine-hole golf course next door at the La Jolla Beach and Tennis Club.

The Sea Lodge's dining room, La Sala del Mar, is exceptionally lovely, with arched windows looking out over the beach and a peaked, beamed, barn ceiling overhead. The decor is Spanish, with plush leather booths and gold cloths on the tables. Breakfast, lunch, and dinner are served here daily, and the bar is open till 2 a.m.

As for the rooms, they're spacious, equipped with carved wooden beds, large dressing rooms, refrigerators, ceramic tile baths, balconies or lanais, and all modern amenities. Each has one barnwood wall, and rooms on the third floor—the most desirable—have high, sloped barnwood ceilings.

Rates at the Sea Lodge vary with the season. January 1 to March 31, and September 16 to December 31, singles pay $34 to $42; doubles, $39 to $47. April 1 to June 15, singles pay $32 to $38; doubles, $37 to $43. June 16 to September 15, singles pay $42 to $51; doubles, $47 to $56.

WHERE TO DINE: Elario's, 7955 La Jolla Shores Drive (tel. 459-0541). On the top floor of the Summer House Inn, Elario's offers posh rooftop dining. The view from the windowed walls alone provides a dramatic and elegant decor, but it's further enhanced by beautifully appointed, gold-clothed tables, crystal chandeliers overhead, and stained-glass panels at the top of the long windows. There's entertainment nightly—Sunday and Monday a guitarist, Tuesday to Saturday a combo for dancing.

A $3.85 buffet lunch is served weekdays, but you can also order à la carte from an extensive menu. A sandwich, such as French-dip roast beef, served with french fries and a pickle, is $2.50; on the other hand, you might opt for eggs Benedict ($3.25), or shrimp, lobster, or crab Louie ($3.65).

At dinner, we suggest you begin with one of the many hors d'oeuvres offered, perhaps the fettucini Alfredo ($3.75)—always hard to pass up—or stuffed mushrooms with crab salad, Swiss cheese, and cream sauce, served under glass, no less ($3.95). For a main course, it's hard to beat the rack of lamb surrounded by a bouquetière of vegetables ($19.75 for two). Also very good are the classic French bouillabaisse ($9.75) and the many veal specialties ($7.25 to $7.50). The wine list proffers about 70 selections priced at $5 to $500 a bottle.

Elario's is open daily from 7 to 11 for breakfast, 11:30 to 2:30 for lunch, and 6 to 10:30 for dinner. A special Sunday buffet brunch ($4.85) is served from 10 to 2:30.

Rheinlander Haus, 2182 Avenida de la Playa (tel. 454-6770), is a gemütlichkeit German eatery with incredible amounts of cluttery decor. It has beamed ceilings; shelves high on the walls lined with pewter and china plates and other knickknacks; elaborate chandeliers on which torch-carrying Rhine maidens are perched; an eclectic selection of velvet tapestry-upholstered wooden chairs, painted in different colors; ruffled white curtains on the windows; and lots of little paintings on the walls. Every table is set with a different set of beautiful old plates and glasses, and no element of Bavarian kitsch has been overlooked—even the waitresses are outfitted in traditional dirndls. There's extra seating outdoors on the brick patio, at checker-clothed umbrella tables. Caged birds provide a constant background of chirping here.

So much for the decor; the food is authentic German cuisine at its best. The house specialty is the "Feinschmecker platte" ($19 for two), that includes Bavarian chicken, Spencer steak, and wiener schnitzel Cordon Bleu served with potato pancakes, applesauce, and a vegetable. Since that will already leave you too full to budge, you might as well complete the damage with a piece of homemade Black Forest cherry cake (85¢).

At lunch the menu includes deli sandwiches ($1.85 to $2.95) served with German potato salad, as well as hot entrees like sauerbraten ($3.95) and cold plates like a herring salad platter ($2.95). The Rheinlander also features a prix-fixe $3.75 Sunday brunch with a choice of four entrees, served with a fruit cup, homemade bread, champagne, and coffee.

The Rheinlander is open daily for lunch, dinner, and Sunday brunch in summer; the rest of the year it's closed on Mondays.

El Chalan, 5621 La Jolla Boulevard (tel. 459-7707), provides an opportunity for most of us to try a new cuisine—Peruvian. And it's a good place to try it, since owners Victor Villar and Carlos Vinazza, both Peruvians, are most scrupulous about the high quality of their food. It's a charming place to eat, the tables handsomely appointed with red cloths, vases of fresh flowers, and white-linen napkins wound in crystal water glasses. A tassled red curtain across the front window enhances the intimate ambience created by wood-paneled walls and the warm glow from wrought-iron chandeliers overhead.

A meal here might begin with ceviche—pickled fish cooked in lime juice and spices ($1.55)·or a delicious appetizer of papas rellenas—deep-fried meat-stuffed potatoes ($1.35). Among the entrees are several preparations of a fish called totuava—very tasty—priced at $6.50 to $7.50. Other unique dishes are shredded chicken in peanut-and-cashew sauce ($4.75), and duck in white wine sauce with rice, peas, and tomatoes ($6.95). Only fresh vegetables are served here, and desserts are homemade. The wine list offers a reasonably priced selection of domestic wines.

El Chalan is open Wednesday through Monday from 5:30 to 11.

San Diego

The oldest city in California and the third largest on the Pacific Coast, San Diego has a Spanish/Mexican heritage. A freeway connects San Diego with Los Angeles, 120 miles to the north. San Diego is about 15 miles north of the U.S.-Mexican border at Tijuana.

The city boasts one of the most famous natural harbors in the world, making it home base for the 11th Naval District. So many ships and personnel have been sent to San Diego, it is now known as an "unofficial capital of the navy," and is one of the largest military complexes in the world.

You can watch the Recruit Brigade review, a full-dress military parade, every Friday of the year. Every weekend, and on legal holidays, the navy schedules open house aboard one or more ships at Broadway Pier. Friday and Monday, incidentally, are the best days for watching ships enter or leave the harbor.

San Diego also enjoys yet another unofficial title, that of "golf capital of the U.S.," owing to its 65 excellent courses. Fishermen are also attracted, because the deep-sea fishing is the best in the West. Furthermore, sandy beaches and bays make San Diego a center for sailing, skin-diving, surfing, sunbathing, and swimming.

The **San Diego Visitor Information Center,** off Interstate 5 at the end of the Clairemont-Mission Bay Drive off-ramp, offers visitors to San Diego a one-stop service center for hotel reservations, entertainment sightseeing information, fishing licenses, boating permits, and even tickets for bullfight and sports events, not to mention Mexican auto insurance. You can view spectacular Mission Bay from the observation tower at the center, or stop for a snack at the outdoor luncheon patio before continuing your travels in Southern California.

THINGS TO SEE AND DO: Cabrillo National Monument, ten miles from downtown San Diego (at the southern end of State Highway 209), commemorates the discovery of the California coast by Juan Rodriguez Cabrillo in 1542. From the restored Old Point Loma Lighthouse, you can view in one sweeping glance the ocean, bays, islands, mountains, valleys, and plains that comprise the area. And mid-December through February you can view the migration of the California gray whale. Open daily from 9 to 5:15. Perhaps you should go here first to get acquainted with the area before seeking a specific destination.

You can watch the glistening skyline of San Diego fade in the distance if you take one of the **Harbor Excursions,** departing year-round from Broadway Pier, at the foot of Broadway and Harbor Drive (tel. 234-4111). The two-hour, 25-mile cruise takes you past Harbor and Shelter Islands, under the longest orthotropic bridge in the world, past naval installations on North Island, and out into the Pacific. A one-hour, 12-mile cruise covers part of the same area. The longer excursion departs every day at 10 a.m. and 2 p.m. Prices are $4.50 for adults and $2.25 for children five to 11. The one-hour cruise leaves the pier every 45 minutes in summer and four times daily in winter, and the rates are $2.75 for adults and $1.40 for children five to 11.

Mission San Diego de Alcala, 10818 San Diego Mission Road, Mission Valley, in nearby Oceanside, is the first in the chain of 21 missions started by Father Junípero Serra in the 18th century. Open daily from 9 to 5, the mission has a museum containing original records dating from 1769, the year of its founding, as well as liturgical robes, books, and other relics.

Mission Bay Park, just north of San Diego on Route 5, is a massive aquatic park made up of 4,600 acres of land and water ideal for recreation for the whole family. Within the park are resort hotels, sightseeing and deep-sea fishing vessels, golf courses, restaurants, nightclubs, and facilities for all water sports. But the biggest attraction in the park is Sea World, an 80-acre entertainment center where the performers are killer whales, dolphins, seals, penguins, and Japanese pearl divers. One price of $5.50 for adults ($3.25 for children four to 12), admits you to all shows and exhibits. Open from 9 to 7:30 daily in summer; 9:30 to 5 in winter.

Balboa Park

Its 1,400 acres of cultural attractions, semitropical gardens, and towering palms and eucalyptus trees make Balboa Park one of the biggest attractions in the city. Just one and a quarter miles north of downtown, it can be easily reached in minutes by car or bus. The landmark of the park—and symbol of the city itself —is the **California Tower,** an elaborately decorated carillon tower atop the California Building. The 100-bell carillon chimes each quarter-hour and plays a short recital every day at noon.

Inside the California Building is the **Museum of Man** (admission 75¢), containing exhibits telling the story of people through the ages, with emphasis on the Indian cultures of the Americas.

The **Aerospace Museum,** off El Prado, the "main street" of the park, is the home of flying machines, from the first airplanes to modern NASA spacecraft. Among the exhibits is a reproduction of Lindbergh's *Spirit of St. Louis* (the original was designed and built in San Diego).

Further along and across the wide Plaza de Balboa is the **Natural History Museum,** containing exhibits of plants and animals of Southern California, along with a few dinosaur bones. The recently opened Sefton Hall of Shore Ecology features a tide pool, a kelp forest, and other seashore exhibits.

Along the north side of El Prado are two art galleries: the **Timken Gallery** contains a permanent collection of paintings by Old Masters plus an impressive array of Russian icons; the adjoining **Fine Arts Gallery** is devoted to a few Old Masters and a variety of "traveling" exhibits. Outside the gallery is an interesting sculpture garden.

Continuing along El Prado, you'll come to a path leading to the **Old Globe Theater,** the only functioning replica of Shakespeare's original Globe Playhouse. Each summer it is the site of the acclaimed National Shakespeare Festival, with outstanding productions of Shakespearean plays in the 400-seat playhouse, and lighter works in the 245-seat Cassius Carter Center Stage. From October through May, the theater is given over to a wide variety of contemporary plays. For information and reservations, telephone 239-2255 any day, from noon to 8:30 p.m.

The hours for the museum and galleries in Balboa Park are all
the same: 10 a.m. to 4:30 p.m. Museums are open daily except
holidays. Galleries are open daily except Mondays and holidays.

San Diego Zoo

With more than 5,000 animals, this world-famous zoo contains the largest collection of wildlife anywhere, yet it's right in
Balboa Park, just minutes from downtown San Diego. You can
wander through the 100 acres, which are also lavishly landscaped as a botanical garden (some of the plants provide food for
the animal residents), and admire the baby orangutan, koala
bears, the finest collection of primates ever assembled, and more
than 3,000 birds with plumage of every imaginable color.

For a quicker, and possibly more fascinating view of the animals, you can take the **Skyfari Aerial Tramway** across the tree-
tops of the zoo (75¢ for adults, 50¢ for children four to 15).
There's also a bus tour in which driver-guides point out some of
the more exotic creatures living along the path of the three-mile
tour ($1.50 for adults, $1 for children). Admission to the zoo is
$2 for adults. Children 15 and under are admitted free. There's
also a **Children's Zoo** with a petting section and a nursery where
baby animals are raised. Admission for adults is 25¢; ages four
to 15, 15¢; under four, free.

From July to Labor Day, the zoo is open from 9 a.m. to 6 p.m.
Between Labor Day and October 31, it shuts down at 5 p.m.
From November to February, it closes at 4 p.m., and from
March to June, 5 p.m.

The Reuben H. Fleet Space Theater and Science Center

Learning by doing and experiencing is the theme of this city-
owned entertainment complex on the Plaza de Balboa in San
Diego's Balboa Park. Named for the pioneer in aeronautics—
now a San Diegan—who inaugurated the world's first aerial mail
service in 1918, this super-planetarium features the Space Transit Simulator theater (another world's first), which allows visitors
to experience a trip to outer space without leaving the confines
of the comfortable 350-seat auditorium. The simulated trip at-
tains a reality never before possible because of the elaborate
system of devices used, including a $235,000 water-cooled Imax
projector; 70-mm film, the largest available; a fisheye lens; a
$270,000 computer-controlled Star Ball projector that can

project 10,000 stars from any point in the universe at any time in history; zoom projectors; and a 76-foot projection dome.

In addition to the space trip, the giant dome also is used as a projection screen for fascinating filmed travelogues, such as *Garden Isle,* a flying expedition to Hawaii, with closeup looks at towering cliffs, waterfalls, and even the inside of an active volcano.

Adjoining the theater is the 8,000-square-foot Science Center, with more than 30 exhibits that beat, blink, float, whisper, and reveal, to make science come alive for visitors of all ages. This is no "hands-off" museum. Here you can match wits with a computerized teaching machine, create designs with sand pendulums, or examine the iris and pupil of your own eye.

Admission to the Space Theater is $2.50 for adults, $1.75 for juniors ages ten to 17; $1.25 for kids four to nine. The building is open from 10 a.m. to 9:30 p.m. daily, year-round. For information on shows and show times, call 238-1168.

The **Maritime Museum,** 1306 North Harbor Drive, San Diego (tel. 234-9153), is a nautical museum on display in its natural habitat—on the water. Moored at the dock near the fish markets, the museum consists of three restored historic vessels, including the *Berkeley,* the first successful propeller-driven ferry on the Pacific coast, launched in 1898, and the steam yacht *Medea,* an innovative vessel built in 1904. The biggest attraction, however, remains the *Star of India,* the oldest merchant vessel still afloat. Since her launching in 1863 off the Isle of Man, the British-built ship has been around the world 21 times. You can purchase a boarding pass admitting you to all three ships for $2 for adults, 50¢ for children under 12 (under five free). Servicemen pay only $1.50. The vessels of the Maritime Museum are open daily from 9 a.m. to 9 p.m.

Old Town

The spirit of the "Birthplace of California" is captured in the six-block area northwest of downtown San Diego. Although the Old Town was abandoned more than a century ago for a more convenient business center near the bay, it has again become a center of interest—this time as a State Historic Park. Some of its buildings have been restored, and the combination of historic sights, art galleries, antique and curio shops, restaurants, and handicraft centers make this a memorable outing.

Enclosed by Congress, Twiggs, Juan, and Wallace Streets, the park is traffic-free, its narrow streets and wide plazas open to pedestrians only.

The Old Town is easily reached from Interstate Routes 8 or 5. Take the Old Town Avenue exit off I-5, or the Taylor Street exit from I-8. Ranger-led tours leave daily at 2 p.m. from the Park Visitor Center, Machado-Silvas Adobe on San Diego Avenue between Mason and Wallace Streets (tel. 294-5182). A special guided walking tour, offered by the Old San Diego Historical Society, leaves from Whaley House, 2482 San Diego Avenue (tel. 298-2482), each Saturday at 1:30 p.m.

Shelter Island

On the lee side of Point Loma, Shelter Island is actually a peninsula a mile long and 300 feet wide, studded with palm trees and fringed with the white triangular sails jutting up from its many marinas. A favorite center for all types of water sports, it offers public mooring and launching ramps as well as three of San Diego's private yacht clubs. Offshore and deep-sea vessels are available to the saltwater enthusiast. There's even a public fishing pier for those who don't want to leave the shore. You can also enjoy a taste of the sea at one of the fine seafood restaurants.

Harbor Island

More sophisticated than its older sister, man-made Harbor Island is a mile-and-a-half-long peninsula, minutes from the airport, and just across the bay from the towers of downtown San Diego. Besides its landscaped park areas and beaches, the island also contains several luxurious hotels, some of the best nightlife in San Diego, and some excellent gourmet restaurants. If you arrive from the sea, you can dock at two of the largest and most fully equipped marinas in San Diego.

Wild Animal Park

An offspring of the world-famous San Diego Zoo, the Wild Animal Park, 30 miles north of downtown San Diego via U.S. 163, is an 1,800-acre wildlife preserve dedicated to the preservation of endangered species. Animals from Africa and Asia roam free here, much as they would in their native habitats. You can watch gorillas at play in the giant Gorilla Grotto, or wander through the giant aviary where more than 100 exotic birds fly freely in a lush African setting.

You can visit the striking **Nairobi Village**, a 17-acre complex of native huts, exhibits, shows, and shops. While you're in the Village, visit **Mombasa Cooker** and **Thorn Tree Terrace** for dining with a spectacular view of the park. But, for the conservation-minded, the most impressive experience must be the five-mile "safari" on the **Wgasa Bush Line** monorail, passing through sweeping savannahs and veldts, past herds of animals and flocks of wild ground birds. The monorail stops several times during the trip so that visitors can view, photograph, and ask questions of the well-informed guides.

The Wild Animal Park is open daily from 9 a.m. to 9 p.m. in summer, till 5 p.m. in spring and fall, and till 4 p.m. in winter. Adults pay $5; kids pay $2.50. Price of admission includes the monorail.

Tijuana

If you'd like a short trip south of the border but would like to be back in San Diego by nightfall, you can take one of the **Tijuana Joyride** tours offered by Greyhound, ranging in price from $6.50 to $12.50. The shopping-and-lunch tour, priced at $9.50, includes round-trip transportation to Tijuana, sightseeing (a visit to the bull ring, Caliente Race Track, and a glass factory), shopping along Revolución Avenue (discounts on merchandise), and lunch at Caesars, home of the salad of the same name. For information on this and other tours, call 239-9171.

A DELUXE HOTEL CHOICE: **Little America Westgate**, 1055 Second Avenue, San Diego (tel. 232-5011), has rightfully been acclaimed by experts as one of the great luxury hotels of the world. In downtown San Diego, the 20-floor structure seems inspired by such outstanding deluxe French hotels as the Ritz of Paris. Its basic decor is a skillful combination of Louis XV, Louis XVI, Georgian, and the most elegant of the English Regency period. The Fontainebleau has been called "the most elegant dining room built in this century." Off the lobby is the Westgate Room, with its adjacent Plaza Bar. More than 200 antiques and art objects have been collected from around the globe to give the hotel its ebullience—a world of glittering crystal, paneled and gilt walls, and tapestries. The tasteful decor overflows into the bedrooms, which are equally distinctive and glamorous. Based on size and the style of furnishings, singles range in price from $34 to $44; doubles or twins, $39 to $49.

THE MODERATE RANGE: The **Sheraton-Harbor Island Hotel,** 1380 Harbor Island Drive, San Diego (tel. 291-2900), is the newest and largest Sheraton to open in San Diego (there are two more). On a 14-acre site on man-made Harbor Island, it stands on the east side of San Diego Bay, only five minutes from downtown. The 12-story tower encloses 378 handsomely furnished guest rooms, ranging in price from $30 to $41 in a single, from $38 to $51 in a double, according to the time of year. In addition, the adjacent "Lanai Village" offers 122 rooms. Tower rooms have balconies to soak up the view, though all accommodations offer color television, individual air conditioning, and either king-size or two double beds. The hotel's gourmet restaurant is the Portola, commanding a view of the marina and featuring two outdoor patios. At the top of the tower, the Butterfield Stage Saloon opens onto a spectacular view of the city and harbor.

The **Bahia Hotel,** 998 West Mission Bay Drive (tel. 488-0551), enjoys a lovely situation on the peninsula of Mission Bay. It's an extremely pleasant place to stay, offering 335 rooms and good facilities. Every one of the 335 rooms here has a picture window, and most offer views of the bay. Half the rooms have kitchens; all have a bath with dressing area, color TV, direct-dial phone, etc. There's an Olympic-size swimming pool on the premises, as well as a health club, game room, and shuffleboard court (tennis courts are in the planning stage). There's also a dock where you can tie up your boat, or rent one. And then there's the *Bahia Belle,* a sternwheeler that cruises the bay (running every hour on the hour in summer; reduced schedule in winter) stopping at two other hotels. At night there's dancing to live music aboard the *Belle.* The fare is $1.50, which includes as many stops as you like.

Off the cozy fireplace lobby is a coffeeshop serving breakfast, lunch, and dinner. But the Bahia's main restaurant is the unique and elegant Mercedes Room, as much a shrine for that automobile as a dining facility. At the entrance, glamorously lit, and on a stage, is a 1902 sports and racing model—one of the first four-cylinder automobiles manufactured (estimated value, $50,-000). There's Mercedes logo carpeting, as well as Mercedes posters and drawings of antique models on the walls. As for the cuisine, it's continental fare such as Mercedes owners are used to; you might order half a roast duckling à l'orange in sauce bigarade, served with rice pilaf and a broiled brandied peach ($7.70). Soup or salad, bread and butter, and a beverage are included.

If you're vacationing with kids, by the way, they'll adore the Bahia—it's the only hotel we know that has a seal (name of Otis) in a pond.

Rates for one or two persons from July 25 to September 12 are $34 for a room with a queen-size bed, $34 to $38 for extra-large twin beds, and $36 to $40 for double doubles. The rest of the year, queen rooms are $26 to $30; extra-large twins, $28 to $32; and double doubles, $30 to $36.

The **Catamaran**, 3999 Mission Boulevard (tel. 488-1081), directly across the bay, is under the same ownership (car aficionado Bill Evans), and offers almost identical facilities. The restaurant here is the Polynesian Room, and an added attraction is a display of Mr. Evans's antique cars. No seal here, however. Rates are the same as at the Bahia.

Sheraton Half Moon Inn, 2303 Shelter Island Drive, San Diego (tel. 224-3411), is San Diego's version of life on a South Seas island. You can, if you wish, dock your yacht and go for a swim in this garden paradise. Surrounded by subtropical plantings, 176 spacious and well-furnished rooms open onto lovely views. Singles range in price from $28 to $38; doubles, $36 to $46. On the grounds are heated pools for both adults and children, even a nine-hole putting green. Dining is at the Port Royale, offering continental and American cuisine with specialties like prime rib ($9.50) and bouillabaisse ($7.95). There's live music for dancing nightly, except Mondays.

U.S. Grant, 326 Broadway, San Diego (tel. 232-3121), is a grand turn-of-the-century downtown hotel, with many historical associations. Its Edwardian charm has been called "uncommonly opulent." It has been elaborately refurbished, capturing the spirit of another era. Its rooms were designed when guests arrived with trunks and hat boxes. The new styling of the accommodations is excellent. Rates for one range from $19 to $25; for two, from $24 to $30, depending on the type of bed you select. The ornate lobby is ablaze with opera-red flocked wallpaper, marble pillars, bronzes, crystal chandeliers, and warm-toned woods. The public rooms range from the serenity of the Garden Room, to the U.S. Grant Grill, to Grant's Tomb, a tavern-like eatery serving terrific and inexpensive sandwiches.

HOTEL CIRCLE (MODERATE TO BUDGET): Mission Valley is the most centrally located resort area in San Diego. Around its Hotel Circle are many restaurants, motels, and hotels. It also contains the newest and largest shopping complex in the country, the 80-store Fashion Valley Center. Hotels recommended below are good for the budget.

Town & Country, 500 Hotel Circle (tel. 291-7131). At 1,000 rooms (housed in two high-rises and several ranch-style buildings), this is the largest hotel in San Diego. It's something of a "superhotel," offering just about any convenience or facility you might desire. Each attractively furnished modern room is equipped with color TV (on which first-run movies are shown free of charge), direct-dial phone, tub/shower bath, and coffeemaker; the daily newspaper is delivered to your room each morning. A free shuttle bus takes guests back and forth between the hotel and airport and nearby shopping centers, and on-the-premises facilities include many shops, barber and beauty salons, sightseeing desks, transportation desks, car rental, etc.—even a gas station.

In addition, there are three swimming pools, a therapy pool and sauna; guests can use the Atlas Health Club for men and women just across the street, too (they pay $3 for use of regular facilities and $3 for use of tennis courts).

When it comes to eating and drinking, Town & Country is as well equipped as in other areas. There are four restaurants: Le Pavillon for gourmet French dinners, entertainment, and dancing; the Gourmet Room for continental lunches and dinners daily—a piano bar in the adjoining lounge at night; the V.I.P. Room, serving deli lunches weekdays, becomes a nightclub Tuesday through Saturday nights featuring rock bands for dancing; and Crystal T's Emporium, a restaurant-cum-discotheque with a funky-elegant decor. In case you're still hungry, there are two coffeeshops.

The rate for singles at Town & Country is $32; doubles and twins pay $37.

Fabulous Inn, 2485 Hotel Circle Place, San Diego (tel. 291-7700), is a four-story modern complex at the extreme western end of Hotel Circle. There are 142 rooms, each with individual balconies, color TV (with in-house movies available), air conditioning, and direct-dial phones. There's even a generous-sized swimming pool, and a nine-hole golf course, and tennis facilities are across the street. Singles pay $17 to $24; doubles, $20 to $35.

Circle 7/11 Motel, 2201 West Hotel Circle, San Diego (tel. 291-2711), is one of the newest and chicest in the area. Its units have a mansard shingled look with dormer windows. The rooms themselves are brightly decorated, with plenty of amenities such as direct-dial phones, individual air conditioning and heating, and free color TV. Rates for one range from $18 to $26; for two, from $21 to $26; and for three, from $23 to $28; the higher tariffs in all cases for suites with kitchens. On the premises is Rickey's Family Restaurant.

Motel 6, 2424 Hotel Circle—North, San Diego (tel. 297-4871), is a low coral and blue, rancho-style motel, with an exterior balcony partially enclosing a swimming pool terrace. Rooms are simply but pleasantly furnished in a contemporary style, with television and air conditioning. The rate for one is only $8.95. However, two persons pay from $10.95 (a double bed) to $11.95 (two double beds). This latter room is rented for three to four persons for only $13.95, one of the best buys in San Diego.

SOME LEADING RESTAURANTS: Lubach's, 2101 North Harbor Drive, San Diego (tel. 232-5129). Some people consider this the finest dining establishment in the city. Go here not for the decor, but for the food—which is terrific. Bob Lubach has won many honors for his continental cuisine. The service is unpretentious, but the dishes make up for the lack of flair. One specialty most recommendable is totuava sea bass sauté in lemon butter at $8.25. We also heartily endorse the calf's sweetbreads financière at $8.95 and the roast duck with black cherries Montmorency, $7.95. The luncheon menu features open-faced sandwiches, ranging in price from $2.75 to $5.95. Closed Sundays. There's background music, and jackets are required.

Anthony's Star of the Sea Room, 1360 Harbor Drive, San Diego (tel. 232-7408). If we gave stars, we'd award this one four, assuming five to be the top. The Ghio family welcomes you to a dramatic setting overlooking a panorama of the San Diego harbor. What you get here are delicacies from the sea. These tasty seafaring morsels aren't exactly cheap, but they are worth every penny. Next to the three-masted schooner, the *Star of India,* the restaurant on the Embarcadero is renowned for its abalone gourmet at $10.95. Also good is the fresh local seabass or (in season only) totuava at $7. For a beginning, we'd recommend the "pick o' the sea" hors d'oeuvres—a tasty selection personally selected by Mrs. Catherine Ghio, costing $3.25 per person. For dessert, try the fresh stemmed strawberries (in season) at $2.50 per serving. Open daily except holidays from 5:30 p.m. until 10:30 p.m. (for reservations call after 2 p.m.).

Anthony's Fish Grotto, 1360 Harbor Drive (tel. 232-5103), is less expensive and more informal. It was established in 1946 by the Ghio family. Featured here are fish delicacies from the family's own direct source, the Ghio Seafood Market. Reservations are not accepted—you just arrive. Fish and chips, done in a light batter, is praiseworthy here—only $2.80. The house specialty is shellfish casserole à la Catherine (made with lobster meat, crab legs, and scallops), $5.75. A fine dessert is Anthony's cake zabione, 50¢. Open daily, except Tuesdays, from 11:30 a.m. to 8:30 p.m.

Tom Ham's Lighthouse, 2150 Harbor Island Drive, Harbor Island, San Diego (tel. 291-9110), is built at the tip of Harbor Island beneath a lighthouse. You get not only excellent meals here, but can enjoy a museum as well. A collection of marine artifacts was gathered from around the world, forming a nostalgic reminder of San Diego in the early 1800s. Featured on the menu are many New England and early California specialties. The clam chowder, included in the price of your dinner entree, is based on a recipe from Barnstable, Massachusetts. The house specialty is carne asada (cuts of marinated beef tenderloin pan broiled and served with a special Mexican sauce), $7.95. Desserts feature Yankee apple pie at 95¢. Open daily, serving both lunch and dinner.

Casa de Pico, Bazaar del Mundo, Old Town, San Diego, occupies a portion of the former home of General Pio Pico, the first governor of California during Mexican rule. It overlooks a grassy patio, recapturing the beauty of colonial architecture. Specialties of the house, featuring mixed combinations, include the cheese crisp at $2.35 and carne asada at $4.95. Open Sunday through Thursday from 11 a.m. to 10 p.m. (Friday and Saturday until 11 p.m.).

HOW TO SAVE MONEY
ON ALL YOUR TRAVELS

Saving money while traveling is never a simple matter—which is why, almost 14 years ago, the **$10-a-Day Travel Club** was formed. Actually, the idea came from readers of the Arthur Frommer Publications, who felt that such an organization could bring financial benefits, continuing travel information, and a sense of community to economy-minded travelers in all parts of the world. They were right. By combining the purchasing power of thousands of our readers, we've been able to obtain a wide range of exciting travel benefits—including, on occasion, substantial discounts to members from auto rental agencies, restaurants, sightseeing operators, hotels, and other purveyors of tourist services throughout the world.

In keeping with the money-saving concept, the membership fee is low, and it is immediately exceeded by the value of your benefits. Upon receipt of $8 to cover one year's membership, we will send all new members by return mail (book rate) the following items:

(1) The latest edition of any *two* of the books listed on the following page.

(2) A copy of ARTHUR FROMMER'S GUIDE TO NEW YORK.

(3) A copy of SURPRISING AMSTERDAM AND HAPPY HOLLAND—a 224-page pocket-size guide by Ian M. Keown.

(4) A one-year subscription to the quarterly Club newsletter—THE WONDERFUL WORLD OF BUDGET TRAVEL (about which more below).

(5) A voucher entitling you to a $5 discount on any Arthur Frommer International, Inc. tour booked by you through any travel agent in the United States and Canada.

(6) Your personal membership card, which, once received, entitles you to purchase through the Club *all* Arthur Frommer Publications for a third to a half off their regular retail prices during the term of your membership.

These are the immediate and definite benefits which we can assure to members of the Club at this time. Even more exciting, however, are the further and more substantial benefits which it has been our continuing aim to achieve for members. These are announced in the Club's newsletter, THE WONDERFUL WORLD OF BUDGET TRAVEL, a full-size, eight-page newspaper that keeps members up-to-date on fast-breaking developments in low-cost travel in all parts of the world. The newsletter also carries such continuing features as "Travelers' Directory"—a list of members all over the world who are willing to provide hospitality to other members as they pass through their home cities; "Share-a-Trip" —requests from members for travel companions who can share costs; "Readers Ask...Readers Reply"—travel-related queries from members, to which other members reply with firsthand information. It also offers advance news of individual, group, and charter programs operated by Arthur Frommer International, Inc., plus in-depth articles on special destinations (most recently, Newfoundland, the Caribbean, and Wales).

If you would like to join this hardy bunch of International travelers and participate in its exchange of information and hospitality, simply send $8 along with your name and address to: $10-a-Day Travel Club, Inc., 380 Madison Ave., New York, N.Y. 10017. Remember to specify which *two* of the books in section one above you wish to receive in your initial package of members' benefits.

ARTHUR FROMMER, INC.
380 MADISON AVE., NEW YORK, N.Y. 10017 Date_____

Friends:
Please send me (postpaid) the books checked below:

$10-A-DAY GUIDES
(In-depth guides to low-cost tourist accommodations and facilities.)

- ☐ Europe on $10 a Day $4.95
- ☐ England on $15 a Day $4.50
- ☐ Greece on $10 a Day $3.95
- ☐ Hawaii on $15 & $20 a Day $4.50
- ☐ India (plus Sri Lanka and Nepal) on $5 & $10 a Day $3.95
- ☐ Ireland on $10 a Day $4.50
- ☐ Israel on $10 & $15 a Day $3.95
- ☐ Mexico and Guatemala on $10 a Day $4.95
- ☐ New Zealand on $10 a Day $3.95
- ☐ New York on $15 a Day $3.95
- ☐ Scandinavia on $15 & $20 a Day $4.50
- ☐ South America on $10 & $15 a Day $4.50
- ☐ Spain and Morocco (plus the Canary Is.) on $10 & $15 a Day ...$4.50
- ☐ Turkey on $5 & $10 a Day $3.95
- ☐ Washington, D.C. on $10 & $15 a Day $3.95

DOLLAR-WISE GUIDES
(Guides to tourist accommodations and facilities from budget to deluxe, with emphasis on the medium-priced.)

- ☐ England.............$4.50
- ☐ France.............$4.50
- ☐ Germany $3.95
- ☐ Italy $4.50
- ☐ Portugal..............$3.95
- ☐ California.............$4.50

ARTHUR FROMMER'S GUIDES
(Pocket-size guides to tourist accommodations and facilities in all price ranges.)

- ☐ Athens $1.95
- ☐ Boston $1.95
- ☐ Honolulu $1.95
- ☐ Ireland/Dublin/Shannon..$1.95
- ☐ Las Vegas $1.95
- ☐ Lisbon/Madrid/Costa del Sol $1.95
- ☐ London $1.95
- ☐ Los Angeles $1.95
- ☐ New York $1.95
- ☐ Paris $1.95
- ☐ Rome $1.95
- ☐ San Francisco $1.95
- ☐ Washington, D.C. $1.95

By the Council on International Educational Exchange

- ☐ Whole World Handbook ..$2.95 (A student guide to work, study and travel worldwide.)
- ☐ Where to Stay USA .....$2.95 (A guide to accommodations in all 50 states costing from 50¢ to $10 per night.)

Enclosed is my check or money order for $_____

NAME _____

ADDRESS _____

CITY _____ STATE_____ ZIP_____